Noam Chomsky

Noam Chomsky addressing a crowd at the University of Victoria, 1989.

Noam Chomsky

A Life of Dissent

Robert F. Barsky

The MIT Press
Cambridge, Massachusetts
London, England

This book was set in Sabon by Asco Trade Typesetting Ltd., Hong Kong.

Printed and bound in the United States of America.

Library of Congress Cataloging-in-Publication Data

Barsky, Robert F.
  Noam Chomsky : a life of dissent / Robert F. Barsky.
    p.   cm.
  Includes bibliographical references and index.
  ISBN 0-262-02418-7 (hc : alk. paper)
    1. Chomsky, Noam. 2. Linguists—United States—Biography. I. Title.
P85.C47B37   1997
410′.92—dc20   96-29013
[B]   CIP

Photographs: Cover (1989), frontispiece (1984), and illustrations 18, 24, 25 (1989), © Elaine Brière; illustration 1 (1992), © Donna Coveney, is used by permission of Donna Coveney; illustrations 2, 3, 4, 6, 7, 11, 12, 13, 14, 15, 16, 19, 20, 21, 22, 23, 26, © Necessary Illusions, are used by permission of Mark Achbar and Jeremy Allaire; illustrations 5, 8, 9, 10 (1995), © Robert F. Barsky; illustration 17 (1995), © Sydney Barsky; illustration 27 (1990), © Derek Roger, is used by permission of Derek Roger.

Published in Canada by ECW PRESS.

To Sam Abramovitch and Noam Chomsky, and the "good society" that they have described to me

Contents

Illustrations

Acknowledgments

I would like to thank Noam Chomsky, as well as some of the people most intimately familiar with his milieu, notably Sam Abramovitch, Norman Epstein, Edward S. Herman, Seymour Melman, and Carlos P. Otero. Their willingness to share their insights and experiences is further testament to their unfailing commitment to the "good society." Marc Angenot, Robert Freiden, Denise Helly, Martin Kreiswirth, Yzabelle Martineau, Michel Meyer, and George Szanto have contributed to broadening the scope and the value of this book. Lisa Travis and Robert Lecker provided me with the long-awaited opportunity to discuss the ideas it contains. Mark Achbar, Jeremy Allaire, Elaine Brière, Jim Kelman, and Derek Rodger generously assisted me with the difficult task of assembling the photographs. Benjamin and Tristan offer constant inspiration. The Social Sciences and Humanities Research Council of Canada funded two years of research and writing in the form of a postdoctoral fellowship, for which I am very grateful. Amy Pierce of MIT Press and Mary Williams of ECW PRESS undertook a careful and thoughtful edit of the manuscript.

I

The Milieu That Formed Chomsky

We've always tried to keep personal and other lives quite separate. We're actually "very private" people (and quite conventional). Not on the party circuit, keep pretty much to ourselves—which is kind of odd for me to say, since I spend a huge amount of my time speaking to thousands of people. But that's the way we prefer it.

—Noam Chomsky, letter to the author, 25 July 1995[1]

Introduction

The task of writing a biography of Noam Chomsky gives new meaning to the word *daunting*. Chomsky is one of this century's most important figures, and has been described as one who will be for future generations what Galileo, Descartes, Newton, Mozart, or Picasso have been for ours. He is the most cited living person—four thousand citations of his work are listed in the *Arts and Humanities Citation Index* for the years 1980 through 1992—and eighth on a shortlist, which includes the likes of Marx and Freud, of the most cited figures of all time.[2] Chomsky is also a vital point of reference in the sciences; from 1974 to 1992 he was cited 1,619 times, according to the *Science Citation Index*. Among the innumerable honors he has been awarded is the 1988 Kyoto Prize, described as the Japanese equivalent of the Nobel Prize, for his contribution to basic sciences.

Chomsky has published over seventy books and over a thousand articles in a range of fields including linguistics, philosophy, politics, cognitive sciences, and psychology. He was made associate professor at the Massachusetts Institute of Technology at the age of twenty-nine and full professor at thirty-two; he was given an endowed chair at thirty-seven, and became institute professor, an honor reserved for the most distinguished faculty, at forty-seven. An enormous array of awards and honors have been bestowed upon him for his work in a variety of disciplines and fields including those, such as linguistics and cognitive sciences, that he himself revolutionized. A multitude of articles and books have been devoted to his work, and recently an eight-volume collection containing over a hundred such articles has been published by Routledge as part of its Critical Assessments Series.

Figure 1
Chomsky, one of the world's most well-known activists and intellectuals, at the Massachusetts Institute of Technology, 1992.

An activist who is looked to by masses of left-leaning individuals and groups as one of the truly inspirational figures of this century, Chomsky has maintained a radical stance for more than fifty years, and it has embroiled him in controversy. It has led people to idolize him, debate about him, arrest him, utter slanderous comments about him, and censor his work.

The work of the Chomsky biographer is in no way simplified by the fact that Chomsky himself deplores the biographical genre, for both political and personal reasons. On the one hand, I think that Chomsky is right to condemn personality cults; on the other, I believe that much can be learned by looking at Chomsky's life and work in the context of the milieus from which they have emerged and to which they have contributed. For that reason, this book, although an exploration of Chomsky's life and work, is also a portrait of his milieus. My premise is that Chomsky's ideas, and in particular his political ideas, cannot be fully understood without some knowledge of the organizations, movements, groups, and individuals with whom he has had contact, either through study or discussion. I will look at Chomsky's incredible body of work and explore its relationship to the work of others in various fields and milieus.

For Chomsky, the work he has produced *is* his life. In response to comments I made about the 1992 film *Manufacturing Consent: Noam Chomsky and the Media*,[3] Chomsky remarked that he had not, and most probably would not, go to see it:

[F]irst, I hate watching or hearing myself. I can only think about how I should have said things better. Second, I'm not happy with the personalized framework. Things happen in the world because of the efforts of dedicated and courageous people whose names no one has heard, and who disappear from history. I can give talks and write because of their organizing efforts, to which I'm able to contribute in my own ways. Not having seen the film, I don't know whether this is brought out. I'm concerned that it may not be. (18 Feb. 1993)

Whenever possible, I have recalled in this book "the efforts of dedicated and courageous people," the people who have contributed to the ways in which Chomsky perceives the world and construes his own work, and to that degree "the personalized framework," if not eliminated (this would make for something other than a biography), is at least mitigated.

It could be argued that because there is already a huge amount of published work on Chomsky, there is no room for a biography. But while his linguistic work has been reasonably well covered (despite the weaknesses of many historical studies), there is only a relatively small quantity of commentary available on Chomsky's political background and his contribution to the field of political theory. This may be due, in part, to the prevailing belief that his work in this domain in some ways speaks for itself. Chomsky seldom mentions concurrent or competing schools of political theory or philosophy; when he does, he'll often just make passing reference to a text in order to establish his own point. Some may be misled by this and fail to realize that Chomsky has been profoundly inspired by various sources in his political thinking. The ways in which his approach to this particular area of thought differs from the approach he takes to others can be the substance of an intriguing and politically valuable discussion. Therefore, while I do look at Chomsky's contribution to linguistics and philosophy, my main focus is the political milieus that provide a context for understanding his approach to societal relations and the structures that regulate them.

The point of entry for my long-standing correspondence with Noam Chomsky and for my growing interest in his politics is Sam Abramovitch, who has introduced me to the ideas of left libertarianism and to the people and organizations that have struggled to promote them. Abramovitch is a former director of Hashomer Hatzair (in Montreal), a left-wing Jewish organization whose relation to Chomsky will be detailed in the following pages, as well as a close friend of people associated with a number of groups and individuals that have influenced Chomsky, directly or indirectly. This book is therefore filled with names of organizations, publications, and individual thinkers that have not been adequately discussed in relation to Chomsky's political work: the organizations include the left wing of Avukah, the Council Communists, Freie Arbeiter Stimme, Hashomer Hatzair, the Independent Labor Party, the Institute for Workers' Control, the League for Arab-Jewish Rapprochement, the Leninist League, the Marlenites, and Resist; among the journals I mention are *International Council Correspondence, Living Marxism, Avukah Student Action, Modern Occasions, New Politics, Politics,* and *The Spokesman*; and some of the individuals I look at are Chomsky contemporaries Yehoshua Bar-Hillel, Ken Coates, David Dellinger, Peggy Duff, Mitchell Goodman, Zellig Harris, Edward S. Herman, Jim Kelman, Denise

Levertov, Robert Lowell, Norman Mailer, Paul Mattick, Jerry Rubin, and Howard Zinn, to name but a few. While the work of another set of Chomsky contemporaries—Sam Abramovitch, Norman Epstein (whom Chomsky met fifteen years ago for the first time), Karl Korsch, Christopher Lasch, Dwight Macdonald (with whom Chomsky had contact in the 1960s), Seymour Melman (with whom Chomsky had casual contact early on, and who became a close friend), Karl Polanyi, and Arthur Rosenberg—had no direct impact upon Chomsky's endeavors, it does provide some important insight into his thinking, and is therefore explored here.

Reading through these lists raises the issue of the relationship between Chomsky and Judaism. Chomsky's father, William, was a Hebrew scholar and teacher who wrote a definitive study of the history of the Hebrew language. Furthermore, Chomsky was influenced by a strain of left-leaning Jewish intellectuals and has maintained contact with several influential Jewish thinkers. In short, Chomsky grew up in an intensely Jewish-Hebraic household, he was involved with the kibbutz movement, and he has always been interested in the actions of the Jewish state; nevertheless, it would be misleading to view his work solely from these perspectives, for reasons that will be discussed further on. So only when questions of his Jewish heritage illuminate his approach or overlap with biographical issues have I mentioned them.

As his massive body of publications attests, Chomsky's restless intellect has led him to embrace many fields, including social activism, history, the history of ideas, linguistics, philosophy, politics, cognitive sciences, and psychology. Due to the complexity of each of these domains, it would be inappropriate to take a solely chronological approach to the writing of his biography. Chomsky has pursued a range of distinct interests simultaneously, and has been drawn into controversy and intellectual debate on several fronts over the years. These interests are most clearly understood when looked at thematically. I have therefore divided this book into sections that deal individually with a series of subjects that are intimately connected to Chomsky's growth and impact. For the most part, I've written about each separately and chronologically, but when the sections are read together, they should combine to provide an overall sense of Chomsky's vast reach as a thinker and activist.

Discrete chapters can, then, be read as individual and autonomous wholes that reflect vital aspects of a complex personality. Chapter 1 covers Chomsky's youth and the milieu with which he came into contact through his reading, his studies, and his affiliations; chapter 2 describes his work as a university undergraduate and, more particularly, his relationship with Zellig Harris; chapter 3 explores the foundation and the impact of his Cartesian and rational approach to linguistic and political thinking; chapter 4 emphasizes his university career, achievements, and projects, and summarizes his thoughts concerning the role of the intellectual in contemporary society and the relationship of the individual to the institution; chapter 5 addresses his role as dissenting voice within the American political scene by considering the various struggles with which he has been involved and some of the new modes of thought, notably postmodernism, that have taken root around him. The conclusion looks at the relations between Chomsky's current work and the contemporary sociopolitical scene to which it speaks. Chomsky's intellectual and political endeavors do, of course, tend to overlap and intersect, and a casual pattern of these contact points gradually emerges as this biography unfolds. It also becomes apparent that Chomsky has consistently applied a characteristic rigor, sense of responsibility, and compassion to his pursuit of these diverse interests: this is the common element that unites them all.

1

Family, Hebrew School, Grade School

I was very active in all sorts of left Zionist (what would now be called "anti-Zionist") mostly Hebrew-speaking "groups," but the groups scarcely merited the name, and I was pretty much a loner even in them. Later, I was part of a lot of movement activities (like Resist), and took part in tons of things, but usually in my own way. I've often been close to radical Christians, for example, and have found much of what they did inspiring all right (even stayed in the Jesuit house when I visited Managua). But it would be absurd to say I was part of such communities.

—Noam Chomsky, letter to the author, 8 Aug. 1994

The Chomsky Household

Avram Noam Chomsky was born 7 December 1928 to Dr. William (Zev) Chomsky and Elsie Simonofsky, in Philadelphia, Pennsylvania. Dr. Chomsky had fled from his native Russia to the United States in 1913 in order to avoid being drafted into the Czarist army. Upon arrival, he worked in sweatshops in Baltimore, Maryland. He then managed to work his way through the Johns Hopkins University supporting himself by teaching in Baltimore Hebrew elementary schools. After moving to Philadelphia, he and his wife began teaching at the religious school of the Mikveh Israel congregation. Eventually, Dr. Chomsky was to become principal of this school.

Dr. Chomsky continued to pursue his research in the field of medieval Hebrew language and went on to become, according to a 22 July 1977 *New York Times* obituary, "one of the world's foremost Hebrew grammarians." He was the author of a seminal study called *Hebrew, the Eternal Language* (1957), as well as numerous other works, including

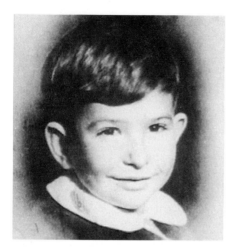

Figure 2
The young Chomsky.

Hebrew, the Story of a Living Language (1947; which was the basis of *Hebrew, the Eternal Language*), *How to Teach Hebrew in the Elementary Grades* (1946), and *Teaching and Learning* (1959). He also edited and annotated a study of thirteenth-century Hebrew grammar called *David Kimhi's Hebrew Grammar (Mikhlol)* (1952), a book that his son Noam read in an early form when he was about twelve years old. This kind of text, permeated with scholarly commentary and discussion, remains, even today, something that Chomsky enjoys enormously: "My idea of the ideal text is still the Talmud," he says. "I love the idea of parallel texts, with long, discursive footnotes and marginal commentary, texts commenting on texts" (qtd. in Parini).

At Mikveh Israel, students and professors associated with Gratz College practiced their teaching skills. In 1924, already teaching and acting as principal of Mikveh Israel, Dr. Chomsky was also appointed to the faculty of Gratz College, the oldest teacher's training college in the United States. Eight years later, he was made faculty president of Gratz, a position that he held for forty-five years. Beginning in 1955, Dr. Chomsky began to teach, as well, at Dropsie College, a graduate school of Jewish and Semitic studies. He retired from Gratz in 1969, and from Dropsie in 1977, the year of his death.

The impact that Chomsky's father had upon him seems clear in retrospect. Carlos Otero notes that "shortly before his death William Chomsky described the major objective of his life as 'the education of individuals who are well integrated, free and independent in their thinking, concerned about improving and enhancing the world, and eager to participate in making life more meaningful and worthwhile for all.' It is hard to improve on this as a description of Noam Chomsky as an individual" ("Chomsky and the Libertarian Tradition" 5). William Chomsky was, furthermore, described by friends of the family as a very warm, gentle, and engaging individual. Bea Tucker, who worked as his secretary for a period of five years in the 1930s, recalls that he was a warm individual, considerate and generous with students and staff. When a teaching position opened up at Mikveh Israel in the mid-1930s, Tucker asked Dr. Chomsky if she could apply, hoping that this would be her opportunity to embark on a new career. He hired her, and she went on to teach David Eli Chomsky, Noam's younger brother and only sibling, as well as Carol Schatz, who would eventually become Noam's wife.

Chomsky's mother, Elsie, was equally important to his development as a thinker, a teacher, and an activist. Her political sensitivity motivated him, from a very young age, to look far beyond his immediate social context and into the realm of political action and involvement. She also taught Hebrew at Mikveh Israel, and so by the time her son was ready to enter the teaching profession himself, it had become, for him, a very familiar domain. According to Otero, "The influence of his father on him is easier to trace than that of his mother, née Elsie Simonofsky, who was more left oriented than her husband and appears to have made an impression on her son 'in the area of general concern about social issues' and politics, 'one major part of [Chomsky's] intellectual life' " ("Chomsky and the Libertarian Tradition" 4). One can only imagine the dinner-table conversation in such a household. As Otero goes on to tell us, Chomsky simply reports: "During childhood, there was always plenty of discussion in [our] home about really interesting and important issues" (16n10). Among those issues was a form of Zionism, at the time considered mainstream, that had been inspired by the West European Enlightenment. The Chomskys, Otero says, were particularly influenced by Asher Ginsburg

Figure 3
Noam Chomsky, age 8, and his younger brother David, age 3, in 1936.

(1856–1927), a Hebrew stylist and writer who acted as a spokesman for the advocates of this Zionist movement, who went by the pen name Ahad Haam, "one of the people." Ginsburg's Zionism is today considered by many to be anti-Zionist.

Elsie is described as having been rather more reserved than William. Bea Tucker describes her as "cool," "distant," and "incredibly brilliant." She, like her husband, had a towering intellect, and was greatly in demand as a speaker on scholarly and communal subjects. People such as Tucker, who knew the Chomsky family well, considered each of its members to be gifted, and from very early on, there was a general expectation that Noam and David would follow in the illustrious footsteps of their parents. In hindsight, Noam Chomsky does, indeed, seem to combine the qualities of both his parents. He is warm and accessible, despite his formidable stature. He is also reserved, quiet, and even somewhat shy. He is most certainly comfortable speaking to large audiences, but there is no question that his world is, for the most part, one of solitary study, writing, and research.

From a very early age, Noam and David were immersed in the scholarship, culture, and traditions of Judaism and the Hebrew language through the work of both of their parents. David was also an exceptional child, and also active in family discussions. And, of course, Noam and David spent lots of time together. They enjoyed playing "basketball (of a sort) with some kind of rubber ball we found and a makeshift bushel basket with the bottom knocked out that I managed to tack on to the house wall next to a driveway" (16 Nov. 1995).

Those who knew both David and Noam as children agree that although the two were close, David did keep a somewhat lower profile than his older brother and possessed an easier temperament. Even as a young child, Noam was very competitive, trying, according to Bea Tucker, to "outdo his parents." She recalls an incident that occurred while she was visiting the Chomskys during a vacation they took in 1935. Noam was just seven years old. When William and Elsie left the room, Tucker found herself alone with him. To make conversation, she pointed to *Compton's Encyclopaedia* and asked Noam if he had looked through any of the volumes. "I've only read half of them," was Noam's reply. In short, Noam was, in the words of Bea Tucker, the "brain," while David was the "nice guy." David had the easygoing character of his father, while Noam was more aloof, like his mother. David went on to study medicine, and still lives and works in Philadelphia.

Noam and David were deeply marked by a remarkable home life. The entire Chomsky family was actively involved in Jewish cultural activities and Jewish issues, particularly the revival of the Hebrew language and Zionism. Chomsky told interviewer Eleanor Wachtel, "I would read Hebrew literature with my father from childhood—nineteenth and twentieth century Hebrew literature, and of course older sources. I spent my time in Hebrew school, later became a Hebrew teacher, and out of all of this my political interests converged to an interest in Zionism" (65). Carol Doris Schatz recollects that in Hebrew school Noam would take the lead in discussions. Carol and Noam remained close, and were eventually married; they have stayed together to this day. Bea Tucker remembers Carol Schatz as a very bright and warm girl. Carol's father was a medical doctor, and her family, like the Chomskys, was highly regarded in the community. Chomsky says that he "met" Carol "when I was about five and she was about three, when my parents went to visit her parents at a summer cottage near Philadelphia. Probably occasionally after that. I doubt if we spoke a serious word until she was maybe fourteen or so. Her older sister was a classmate of mine in Hebrew school, and her still older brother was the leader of the synagogue choir, and in that capacity, taught the kids there to chant their Bar-Mitzvah portions (me too)" (13 Feb. 1996).

It is certainly not surprising that, "as a boy of 9, in 1938, [Noam] used to sit in the front row of the Hebrew class at Mikveh Israel . . . paying little attention to the teacher [who happened, on occasion, to be his mother]. He was not being disrespectful; he happened to have covered the ground long before, at home, with his parents" (Otero, "Third Emancipatory Phase" 22). Said Itzhak Sankowsky, one of his Hebrew teachers, "it was expected from his family background that he should know more Hebrew than anybody else. Superficially, you couldn't tell there was something unusual there. You had to bring it out with a debate or a bit of knowledge. Then you knew" (qtd. in Yergin 41).

The Extended Family

Politically, Noam's parents were "normal Roosevelt Democrats," although many members of the next level of family—cousins and aunts and uncles—were part of a Jewish working class with ties to various strains of communism. Chomsky remarks that "several were seamstresses, but these were the days of union building. They were in the ILGWU, which was then finally getting people out of sweatshops (when they had work, that is; they were usually unemployed). Others were involved in everything from ordinary labo[r] to petty commerce to school teaching (for those who managed to work their way through school themselves)" (13 Feb. 1996). Many were involved in the radical political movements that thrived during the Depression. Chomsky explains: "Some were in the Communist Party, some militantly anti-Communist Party (from the left), some Roosevelt Democrats, and everything else from left-liberal to anti-Bolshevik left (whether the Communist Party fits in that spectrum is not obvious, in my opinion)" (31 Mar. 1995). That such diversity of political affiliation should exist within a single family was not unusual among Russian emigrés of the time, and Noam and David undoubtedly benefited from being exposed to a wide range of opinion. Within the extended Chomsky-Simonofsky family, issues were not resolved according to a narrow, status quo set of principles, which meant that Noam and David were given freer rein in their own choices. Their environment as a whole—parents, relatives, school, community—encouraged the brothers to engage in careful observation and analysis; no single approach to an issue was deemed adequate.

Chomsky was further marked by the socioeconomic situation of the period. He came of age in Quaker Philadelphia during the Depression; he told Wachtel that his early childhood memories included "seeing people coming to the door and trying to sell rags or apples," and " travelling in a trolley car past a textile factory where women were on strike, and watching riot police beat the strikers" (64). And the neighborhood in which the Chomsky family lived was inhabited mainly by Germans and Irish Catholics, who were, for the most part, anti-Semitic and pro-Nazi. Not all children raised under such circumstances develop a social conscience, but it is fair to say that Chomsky, who was immersed in an alien cultural tradition within a community of immigrants, had many occasions to stare hypocrisy and violence in the face and wonder about their sources.

Elementary School: Exploration and Creation

Chomsky began his formal education at a remarkably young age. Just prior to his second birthday, he was sent to a Deweyite experimental institution in Philadelphia called the Oak Lane Country Day School, where he remained until the age of twelve. This school was run by Temple University. John Dewey's progressive thinking about education is similar to that of the philosopher Karl Wilhelm von Humboldt, who was an important early precursor to Chomsky in both linguistic and political work. For Dewey, as for von Humboldt, "education . . . must provide the opportunities for self-fulfillment; it can at best provide a rich and challenging environment for the individual to explore, in his own way" (Chomsky, *Chomsky Reader* 149). Chomsky continues to support this position because he feels that individuals develop best when given the opportunity to create freely and to explore rather than follow rigid pedagogical principles.

At Oak Lane he was able, with other children of various backgrounds and possessing different levels of talent, to expand his creative faculties without being intimidated by a competitive evaluation system. Chomsky recalls that students pursued their interests either individually or in groups, and that each member of the class was encouraged to think of himself or herself as a very successful student. Since the standard of comparison at Oak Lane was creativity rather than grades, no activity was ever considered more important than another, and the notion of "healthy competition," often promoted elsewhere as a sign of rigor, was derided. "[A]t least as a child, that was the sense that one had—that, if competing at all, you were competing with yourself. What can *I* do? But no sense of strain about it and certainly no sense of relative ranking. Very different from what I notice with my own children, who as far back as the second grade knew who was 'smart' and who was 'dumb,' and who was high-tracked, and who was low-tracked. This was a big issue" (*Chomsky Reader* 5).

At this point, it is already possible to recognize certain truisms that tend to recur in Chomsky's lectures, discussions, and publications. What was and is important to him about the family is its diversity, not its single-mindedness, and what marked him as a child were his memories of free and unstructured exploration rather than imposed curricula. Inspired by his parents and by his own experience in school, Chomsky tries, in his own teaching, to act as a stimulator, to coax the latent enthusiasm and potential of each student into the light of day. The problem of teaching, he feels, is not that students lack motivation, but rather that their motivation is crushed by the oppressive pedagogic structures that exist at all levels of the education system. This concern hasn't changed over the years; as Chomsky has achieved international recognition it has continued to inform both his political and his linguistic writings.

One of the many activities Chomsky participated in at Oak Lane was writing for the school newspaper. Shortly after his tenth birthday, he published his first article, an editorial on the fall of Barcelona during the Spanish Civil War. This event he describes as "a big issue in my life at the time" (31 Mar. 1995). He found himself preoccupied with the fall of Barcelona and the eventual crushing of the anarchosyndicalist movements and the Marxist Partido Obrero de Unificación Marxista (POUM) group that had flourished in Spain since the spontaneous uprisings following the Franco insurrection of July 1936. It may seem incredible that a ten-year-old child could be so enthralled by a distant conflict and the complex issues upon which it hinged, but if we bear in mind the nature of Chomsky's family life and the kinds of interests he was encouraged to pursue, we may begin to understand how a child such as Noam could be capable of making the sort of important connections found in the Barcelona editorial. In fact, Chomsky often remarks that "even a ten year old could understand such a notion"; and he does not mean to imply that the adult is stupider than the child, but, rather, that the adult has been indoctrinated by the mainstream media and education system. This makes many adults impervious to what Chomsky considers obvious truths and makes politically realizable goals, such as the establishment of libertarian social movements, seem unattainable. In evaluating how Chomsky's home life, his education, and the events of the period led him down particular paths, it is helpful to look more closely at the Spanish Civil War and at the reasons he may have been so drawn to investigate and speak out about that conflict.

First Steps toward Libertarianism

At a conference held in Barcelona on 25 November 1992, called Creation and Culture, Chomsky began his address by telling the audience that it was a "particular pleasure" to speak in Barcelona because he had once written an article (by that time almost fifty-four years earlier) about the fall of Barcelona. In his words, "the events of the preceding years had an enormous impact upon my personal understanding of the world, and on my political and moral consciousness, and have left an impact upon my own thinking and understanding and feeling about things that's been of long duration" ("Creation"). The repercussions of the Spanish Civil War are indeed present in many of the political articles that Chomsky went on to write, because to him they demonstrated that people can, in the absence of a "revolutionary vanguard," rise up against systems of oppression and participate in spontaneous, loosely organized movements, the roots of which lie "in deeply felt needs and ideals of dispossessed masses" (*Chomsky Reader* 86).

This is an apt description of anarchosyndicalist ideals, as these ideals emphasize the inclusion of all individuals in projects that concern the generally ignored masses rather than the ruling elite. In a 1968 work called "Objectivity and Liberal Scholarship," Chomsky describes the Spanish conflict as a "predominantly anarchist revolution," which was "largely spontaneous, involving masses of urban and rural laborers in a radical transformation of social and economic conditions that persisted, with remarkable success, until it was crushed by force" (*Chomsky Reader* 86). The use of the word *spontaneity* in the context of this kind of revolutionary activity does need some qualification, because it falsely implies that change can be effected without effort on the part of those who are fighting against oppressive structures.

Of spontaneous revolutionary action in Germany and Italy after World War I and in Spain in 1936, for example, Chomsky declares:

The anarchosyndicalists, at least, took very seriously Bakunin's remark that the workers' organizations must create "not only the ideas but also the acts of the future itself" in the prerevolutionary period. The accomplishments of the popular revolution in Spain, in particular, were based on the patient work of many years of organization and education, one component of a long tradition of commitment and militancy.... And workers' organizations existed with the structure, the experience, and the understanding to undertake the task of social reconstruction when, with Franco's coup, the turmoil of early 1936 exploded into social revolution. (qtd. in Otero, "Introduction" 38)

This kind of political action is underwritten by a belief that only when people address issues of widespread concern together can their efforts be meaningful. So, by the age of ten, Chomsky was already convinced that such action, exemplified by the Spanish uprising, was not the aberration or failure it was portrayed to be, but rather evidence that anarchist movements could be successful and brought on from below. When they do succeed in this way, to judge by certain important examples, they can fulfil the fundamental needs of the working class and the majority of the population. This belief has permeated Chomsky's subsequent actions and work; it fuels his conviction that efforts in this direction are worth pursuing in spite of the apparent utopianism of such a project.

One might ask why, given the historical circumstances, the young Chomsky was not passionate about Leninism, a movement that seemed to many at this time to be a possible panacea, a positive alternative to the status quo. After all, the horrors of Leninism were, for the most part, uncovered later on, and a great number of people had been seduced by it. Chomsky describes his early interest in anarchism as a kind of "lucky accident": "I was just a little too young to have ever faced the temptation of being a committed Leninist, so I never had any faith to renounce, or any feeling of guilt or betrayal. I was always on the side of the losers— the Spanish anarchists, for example" (*Chomsky Reader* 13). A fortunate accident, as we shall see.

Informal Education

Despite the merits of Oak Lane Country Day School, no single educational institution could ever be considered the principal source of Chomsky's education. From a tender age, he was an avid reader, delving into many fields. He eagerly worked his way through Austen, Dickens, Dostoevsky, Eliot, Hardy, Hugo, Tolstoy, Turgenev, Twain, and Zola (this list displays the young Chomsky's taste for realism in literature; each of these writers attempted to describe *all* elements and strata of the societies in which their works are set), as well as the Bible (in Hebrew), and works of the nineteenth-century Hebrew renaissance and Yiddish-Hebrew writers of the late nineteenth and early twentieth centuries such as Mendele Mocher Sfarim.

At the age of twelve, Chomsky read a draft of his father's book on David Kimhi (1160–1236), a Hebrew grammarian working in the golden age of Jewish cultural creativity. Robert Sklar remembers a conversation he had with Chomsky concerning the impact his father's book had upon him. Chomsky said that he had come to the field of linguistics informed by the classical philology that he had learned from his father, and from his own readings, rather than by the prevailing structuralist position. In a sense, he became interested in the study of language without benefit of a theoretical background; but he was equipped with a feeling for, and an interest in, historical processes, which led him to seek explanations rather than formulate descriptions: "In fact, giving explanations was regarded as some kind of infantile mysticism. Really the only innovation I think I introduced into the field basically was to try to give descriptive explanations—to try to give a theory of the synchronic structure of the language which would actually explain the distribution of phenomena. In my early work, at least, this was very self-consciously modeled on the kinds of explanations that people gave in historical linguistics that I knew about ever since I was a kid" (qtd. in Sklar 32).

A passage from *David Kimhi's Hebrew Grammar* gives us some interesting insight into two lessons that were to mark Chomsky's thought: first, the young Chomsky learned the value of a grammarian's work; and second, he apprehended the ways in which useful knowledge is forgotten or played down in later periods. " 'The knowledge of Hebrew grammar'," he has written, " 'became a vital need at that time. Grammatical accuracy served as a criterion for the recognition of the merits of literary and religious compositions, and grammatical knowledge constituted the measure of Jewish learning and scholarship. Interest in Hebrew grammar was, therefore, not confined to professional grammarians, but gained vogue among statesmen, poets and philosophers' " (*Language and Politics* 79). The value of forgotten learning and the importance of language studies became key issues in Chomsky's later work, particularly in books such as *Cartesian Linguistics*.

To what extent Chomsky was inspired to follow this path by his father is impossible to know, just as it is impossible to measure the impact that realist literature had upon him in his youth. But it is clear that his parents, especially his father, nurtured in him an interest in the workings of language, and that his parents, especially his mother, fostered in him a commitment to confront social issues. It is also apparent that as a child Chomsky was immersed in Jewish and Hebraic culture. This does not mean that he was a product of Talmud-inspired questioning, as many Jews have suggested, but rather that the atmosphere of the Chomsky home was infused with concern for Jewish and Hebraic issues: " I grew up [with] an intense Jewish and Hebraic background, but not one where the Talmud played any special role (except for Agadah—the legends and stories). Yes, I studied some Talmud, and it was kind of fun, but frankly I never took it very seriously; at least, consciously. What was going on below, I can't know, of course" (31 Mar. 1995).

Figure 4
Chomsky with his parents outside the Mikveh Israel School, Philadelphia, which
also housed Gratz College, 1940. Noam and his brother David attended Mikveh
Israel, where both of his parents taught.

Central High School

At the age of twelve, Chomsky moved from the Oak Lane Country Day
School to Central High School, also in Philadelphia. There, Chomsky
became aware for the first time that he was a good student because he
began to receive high grades. He was shocked to discover the emphasis
that was placed upon this form of academic success. The curriculum, the
hierarchies, and the system of values that prevailed at Central High, a
generally well-regarded academic public school, literally compelled him to
block his memories of the time he spent there, whereas his recollections of
the freedom and creativity that he had experienced at Oak Lane lingered
on: "If I think back about my experience, there's a dark spot there. That's
what schooling generally is, I suppose. It's a period of regimentation and
control, part of which involves direct indoctrination, providing a system
of false beliefs." This "indoctrination" functions, presumably, by undermining natural impulses inherent in us all. When unfettered, these impulses

prompt us to explore in new and unexpected ways. Also, playing off systems of "prestige and value," this process of indoctrination reinforces an individual student's desire to beat other students, a dynamic that Chomsky sees at work in most educational institutions. The pedagogical practices of Central High were, for Chomsky, "the manner and style of preventing and blocking independent and creative thinking and imposing hierarchies and competitiveness and the need to excel, not in the sense of doing as well as you can, but doing better than the next person" (*Chomsky Reader* 6).

The shock Chomsky felt upon entering the world of high school was translated into the contention that society generally educates its constituents with the aim of meeting or furthering the needs of the ruling class. Although he is convinced that all schools could be run like the Deweyite Oak Lane, he does not think "that any society based on authoritarian hierarchic institutions would tolerate such a school system for very long.... [I]t might be tolerated for the elite, because they would have to learn how to think and create and so on, but not for the mass of the population" (*Chomsky Reader* 6).

Chomsky was, nevertheless, active at Central High. He belonged to a number of clubs and was well liked by his peers, but his interests were not those of the majority of students. He recalls, for example, that when he was in high school, he was "all excited, passionate, about the high school football team" (qtd. in Haley and Lunsford 7). But at some point during his high-school years, he had a revelation about the all-important high-school sporting events, and about those who became involved in them: "I remember very well in high school suddenly asking myself this kind of funny question: Why am I cheering for my high school football team? I don't know any of those people. They don't know me. I don't care about them. I hate the high school. Why am I cheering for the high school football team? Well that is the kind of thing you just do, you are trained to do. It is ingrained. And it carries over to jingoism and subordination and so on" ("Creation"). The notion of cheering for the right team is one that generally unnerves Chomsky, and even at this early point in his life he was not afraid of going it alone. Another example. The Americans dropped atomic bombs on Hiroshima and then on Nagasaki when Chomsky, a teenager, was attending summer camp. He did not respond to the call of patriotism and celebrate the actions that would mark the end of

World War II. He could not identify with the jubilant reactions of those around him, and was unable to find anyone with whom he could share his thoughts, although there were, of course, groups and individuals holding similar views. Even today, historians continue to laud the American initiative, justifying it by suggesting that one massive slaughter of civilians may have averted another. This kind of reasoning, which demands that one support the winning side no matter what measures it decides are necessary, is derided and condemned by Chomsky.

A "Literary Political Salon"

It is evident that Chomsky's passion for libertarian anarchism and political debate could not be accommodated by the school system. So, curious and free spirited, he began, at the age of thirteen, to travel alone by train to New York City. There he visited relatives and haunted the secondhand bookstores on Fourth Avenue. In the course of these visits he picked up lots of books, which he devoured at home in Philadelphia. But he also spent many of his precious New York hours with an uncle (his mother's sister's husband) who ran a newsstand on Seventy-Second Street. He was a very bright, though little-educated man with a varied background. He taught Chomsky about Freud, and indeed, attracted by his grasp of Freud's theories, people came to him for analysis. He had also been exposed to "Marxist sectarian politics—Stalinist, Trotskyite, non-Leninist sects of one sort or another"—things about which Chomsky himself was just beginning to learn (*Chomsky Reader* 11). A hunchback, Chomsky's uncle benefited from a program for people with physical disabilities. He was offered employment selling newspapers; however, given the unfavorable location of the stand, he did very little business. Instead, the stand became a lively "literary political salon" for Jewish professional and intellectual emigrés. Says Chomsky, "The Jewish working-class culture in New York was very unusual. It was highly intellectual, very poor; a lot of people had no jobs at all and others lived in slums and so on. But it was a rich and lively intellectual culture: Freud, Marx, the Budapest String Quartet, literature, and so forth. That was, I think, the most influential intellectual culture during my early teens" (*Chomsky Reader* 11). Chomsky's uncle eventually went on to become a successful lay psychiatrist, but he made his most indelible mark upon his young nephew during this period of informal contact in New York.

Deeply influenced by what he was reading and by the discussions he was having with a host of new acquaintances, Chomsky was moving more and more in the direction of anarchism and away from Marxism. Otero notes that since a number of his relatives were on the fringes of the Communist Party, the young Chomsky did develop interests related to Marxism, "but by the time he was twelve or thirteen he had already 'worked out of that phase'" ("Chomsky and the Libertarian Tradition" 4). So, during his visits to New York, Chomsky also frequented the office of *Freie Arbeiter Stimme*, an anarchist journal with notable contributors, such as Rudolf Rocker.

Chomsky was by then reading everything that he could find by Rocker, although "there wasn't a lot, in those days, but I dug up what I could" (8 Aug. 1994). Rocker was an important figure for many of the thinkers in Chomsky's early milieu. "[F]rom the moment of his arrival in the United States ... [Rocker] became a force within the Jewish anarchist movement in America, lecturing from coast to coast ... and producing a series of books that made a permanent contribution to anarchist philosophy and history" (Avrich, *Anarchist Portraits* 295). Chomsky has said that it was a 1938 Rocker text that first set him thinking about the relationship between anarchism and classical liberalism, which set the stage for many of the ideas that he would explore later (13 Dec. 1994). And Moishe Shtarkman, who was also writing for *Freie Arbeiter Stimme*, maintained that the left-libertarian movement that Rocker was promoting and that appeared so fresh and vital, actually had its roots in ancient Jewish history:

These were not ideas that young Jews had absorbed in London and New York. They were a revival of the old Jewish Messianic faith. The Libertarian movement used a new terminology for ancient Jewish ideas, which were near to the hearts of these young Jews. If such veterans of Jewish Anarchism as Zolotarov and Katz afterwards became spokesmen of the radical Zionist movement and of Poale Zionism, it was no contradiction to their Anarchist activity. (qtd. in Rocker, *London* 33)

Chomsky was reading other anarchist material by, for example, Diego Abad de Santillán, who, a few months before the onset of the Spanish Civil War (in March of 1936), wrote a book that was partially translated and republished as *After the Revolution*. During this period Chomsky also read works by left Marxists (non-Bolshevik Marxists), including Karl Liebknecht, Rosa Luxemburg, and Karl Korsch. Korsch's work was an important source of inspiration for some of the more theoretically oriented Marxist thinkers who, in turn, exerted various degrees of influence upon Chomsky. In fact, Chomsky claims that Korsch was a Spanish-anarchosyndicalist-movement sympathizer, suggesting that a broad camp of left-thinking individuals found much that was worthwhile in the Spanish anarchist actions: "Marxism also covers a pretty broad spectrum and there is a point at which some varieties of anarchism and some varieties of Marxism come very close together, as for example, people like Karl Korsch, who was very sympathetic to the Spanish anarchist movement, though he himself was sort of an orthodox Marxist" (*Language and Politics* 168).

These orthodox Marxists were generally less important to Chomsky because of the extreme level of their commitment to Marxism and because he felt their analyses were overly complex. This is a point of contention for others who, though in pursuit of goals similar to Chomsky's, nonetheless believe that the mechanisms and strategies of capitalism must be subjected to the kind of deeply philosophical and complex reflection that characterizes some Marxist analysis—for example, the works of Frankfurt School theorists. Chomsky comments: "The intellectuals around the Marxist tradition (Lukács, Frankfurt School, etc.) I read a bit but wasn't much interested in, frankly. I don't find that kind of work very illuminating, to tell the truth. The ideas that seem useful also seem pretty simple, and I don't understand what all the verbiage is for" (8 Aug. 1994). His early attraction to anarchism and resistance to the Marxist tradition was eventually translated into a strong interest in local activist work and a rejection of overly complexified studies class analysis, even though he did discover some crucial overlaps between the two.

Orwell and the Anarchist Position

Unlike the many members of the left who captivated him as a young man —such as Dwight Macdonald, George Orwell, and Bertrand Russell— Chomsky himself did not come to left-libertarian or anarchist thinking as a result of his disillusionment with liberal thought. He quite literally started there. At a tender age, he had begun his search for information on contemporary left-libertarian movements, and did not abandon it. Among those figures he was drawn to, George Orwell is especially fascinating, both because of the impact that he had on a broad spectrum of society and the numerous contacts and acquaintances he had in the libertarian left. Chomsky refers to Orwell frequently in his political writings, and when one reads Orwell's works, the reasons for his attraction to someone interested in the Spanish Civil War from an anarchist perspective become clear.

When Chomsky was in his teens he read Orwell's *Animal Farm*, "which struck me as amusing but pretty obvious"; but in his later teens he read *Homage to Catalonia*, "and thought it outstanding (though he overdid the POUM role I felt, not surprisingly given where he was); it confirmed beliefs I already had about the Spanish Civil War" (31 Mar. 1995). *Homage to Catalonia*, Orwell's description of the Spanish conflict, which he wrote after completing a stint as an active member of the POUM militia, is still a book to which people (including Chomsky) who are interested in successful socialist or anarchist movements refer, because it gives an accurate and moving description of a working libertarian society. The "beliefs" that it "confirmed" for the teenaged Chomsky were related to his growing conviction that libertarian societies could function and meet the needs of the individual and the collective.

There were three groups active on the scene in Barcelona during the 1930s: the Partido Obrero de Unificación Marxista, or POUM; the socialist PSUC (Partido Socialista Unificado de Catalunya), which was dominated by Stalinists; and the anarchist CNT-FAI (Confederación Nacional de Trabajadores-Federación Anarquista Iberica), which honored Rudolf Rocker as "their teacher" on the occasion of his eightieth birthday (Rocker, *London* 32). Orwell joined the POUM militia at the end of 1936 as a means of entering Spain to write newspaper articles. His description, in *Homage to Catalonia*, of the POUM line sets up an oversimplified but provocative relationship between bourgeois democracy, fascism, and capitalism:

Bourgeois "democracy" is only another name for capitalism, and so is Fascism; to fight against Fascism on behalf of "democracy" is to fight against one form of capitalism on behalf of a second which is liable to turn into the first at any moment. The only real alternative to Fascism is workers' control. If you set up any less goal than this, you will either hand the victory to Franco, or, at best, let in Fascism by the back door.... The war and the revolution are inseparable. (60–61)

Orwell maintains that revolution is the only way to remove from power the oppressive business-based ruling class of the type that has dominated the West since World War II. This concept is a difficult one to grasp for those of us who have been programmed, in large measure by the mainstream press, to think that battles must involve two opposing forces—one good and one evil. World War II is often portrayed this way: the Allied side is taken to represent freedom and democracy, while fascism and Nazism are considered synonymous with totalitarian oppression. Chomsky knew early on that there were other ways to conceive of contemporary political structures. He tended to lean towards the left-libertarian interpretation of events, and concluded that neither side deserved the support of those interested in a "good society." How "good" is the society that drops atomic bombs on Japanese civilians, or reduces German towns to rubble? Isn't there an alternative?

This subject is still hotly debated, even among members of the libertarian left. Norman Epstein, who has been active in leftist movements for many years and who is otherwise generally sympathetic to Chomsky's position, here dissents by taking exception to Orwell. He emphasizes that "fascism is *not* simply another name for capitalism. It is a form, and a particularly brutal one, which capitalism takes under certain historical circumstances (including today in many third world countries under the sponsorship of U.S. capital) which is different from bourgeois democracy. Someone like Chomsky is allowed to function under bourgeois democracy but not under fascism" (20 Apr. 1995). But we must recognize the similarities between a fascist agenda and that of the so-called democratic West if we are to understand where Chomsky is coming from in his political works, and to do so we have to engage with the anarchist position that he had begun to develop in his youth.

The most important point, perhaps, is that the anarchism of the type that reigned, in various degrees, in Barcelona in the 1930s, was not an anarchism of chaos, of random acts; it was not purely individualistic or hedonistic in character. When Chomsky considered the anarchist position as an alternative to the status quo, he may well have appealed to Orwell's description, in *Homage to Catalonia*, of Barcelona in 1936. He refers to this passage on a number of occasions in his later works. Orwell begins by describing his arrival in the city, noting the physical changes that had been effected by the anarchists and the workers. Most of the buildings had been seized by the workers, churches had been gutted or demolished, there were no private motorcars or taxis, shops and cafés had been collectivized, and symbols of the revolution abounded. But it was the effect that this collectivization had upon the people that was most striking.

Waiters and shop-walkers looked you in the face and treated you as an equal. Servile and even ceremonial forms of speech had temporarily disappeared. Nobody said "Señor" or "Don" or even "Usted"; everyone called everyone else "Comrade" and "Thou," and said "Salud!" instead of "Buenos dias." ... And it was the aspect of the crowds that was the queerest thing of all. In outward appearance it was a town in which the wealthy classes had practically ceased to exist. Except for a small number of women and foreigners there were no "well-dressed" people at all. Practically everyone wore rough working-class clothes, or blue overalls or some variant of the militia uniform. All this was queer and moving. There was much in it that I didn't understand, in some ways I did not even like it, but I recognized it immediately as a state of affairs worth fighting for. (4–5)

But how does one achieve such a society? How did the young Chomsky explain to himself the great distance between his own world and the one about which he read in books such as *Homage to Catalonia*? And why didn't he look to the Bolshevists rather than the anarchists?

The work of anarchist thinker Rudolf Rocker was a vital source of information and inspiration for him as he struggled to analyse these complex issues. Chomsky read Rocker's work, including his book on the Spanish Civil War called *The Tragedy of Spain*, as a teenager. Rocker's argument was that the Bolshevist rulers justified totalitarian practices by claiming to defend proletarian interests against counterrevolutionary actions. They were preparing society for socialism in accord with the teaching of Lenin. But Rocker's claim, which is in line with Chomsky's thinking, is that dictatorship and tyranny, even when couched in apparently libertarian ideology and objectives, can never lead to liberation. Says Rocker: "What the Russian autocrats and their supporters fear most is that the success of libertarian Socialism in Spain might prove to their blind followers that the much vaunted 'necessity of dictatorship' is nothing but one vast fraud which in Russia has led to the despotism of Stalin and is to serve today in Spain to help the counter-revolution to a victory over the revolution of the workers and the peasants" (35). The importance of the Spanish revolution is clear, for it served as a concrete example of how powers such as the Soviet Union and the United States, despite their apparent differences, did converge in their mutual fear of liberation movements. In this sense, apparent aberrations such as the Stalinist-Fascist pact that was forged during World War II, or the physical and verbal attacks made against the Spanish anarchists by both the Soviets and the Americans, make sense. The misrepresentation of events persists even today in standard historical texts.

Chomsky was fortunate to have made this connection early on, for it spared him from experiencing the disillusionment that ultimately afflicted many of his contemporaries. This sense of betrayal or surprise was very real for many members of Chomsky's generation. His friend Seymour Melman, for example, described in a personal interview the important role that the Spanish Civil War played in revealing to him the Stalinist-Fascist relationship and the so-called Communist hand:

We didn't know the full role of the Communists until 1939 when this famous Russian general defected and wrote articles in the *Saturday Evening Post*. Therein he described in detail how Stalin was using his secret police to wage a war against the Anarchists. He described Stalin's war within the war. He also described how the Stalinists stole the gold reserve of the Spanish Republic. He layed out a detailed analysis and prediction of the Nazi-Soviet pact.

Notice the time lag between the events of 1936 and the realization that the Soviets were "wag[ing] a war against the Anarchists." Even more remarkable, of course, is that the generally accepted view, subsequently perpetrated by the Western press, was that the Spanish Civil War was a colossal failure, and had achieved no concrete results. It was branded as a failure of socialist, anarchist, or Marxist principles, depending upon who was doing the branding.

Orwell had noted, in *Homage to Catalonia*, the obvious schism between the events as they occurred and as they were reported, and pointed to the way in which media types and intellectuals tended to dismiss anti-status-quo movements, such as socialism, by distorting the principles that supported them or the movements that grew from them: "I am well aware that it is now the fashion to deny that Socialism has anything to do with equality. In every country of the world a huge tribe of party-hacks and sleek little professors are busy 'proving' that socialism means no more than a planned state-capitalism with the grab-motive left intact. But fortunately there also exists a vision of Socialism quite different from this." This is the crux of the matter; other visions did exist, and Chomsky had access to them as a young man. But it did take a certain amount of effort to uncover them, unless one was fortunate enough to have participated directly in events of the time, as Orwell was. "[I]t was here that those few months in the POUM militia were valuable to me. For the Spanish militias, while they lasted, were a sort of microcosm of a classless society. In that community where no one was on the make, where there was a shortage of everything but no privilege and no boot-licking, one got, perhaps, a crude forecast of what the opening stages of Socialism might be like. And, after all, instead of disillusioning me it deeply attracted me" (104–06).

Detective Chomsky

So, against a backdrop of Hitler's ascent to power, the Spanish Civil War, and World War II—which were described in antirevolutionary ways in the mainstream press—the teenaged Chomsky was reading about, discussing, and evaluating other ways of conceiving societal relations. But while Orwell was traveling from Wigan Pier to Paris to Barcelona in order to witness events and evaluate possible alternatives firsthand, Chomsky was doing his own exploration through his reading. This required a strong commitment, particularly on the part of a teenager, who would have been tempted, presumably, by more immediate pleasures. Take, for example, Chomsky's interest in the CNT, the Spanish anarchist group:

I was most interested in the CNT, and the anarchists generally, from the early 1940s when I really began to follow these things beyond the press. Even to say that I was interested in the CNT is a bit misleading. I was influenced early on by the anarchist critique of the CNT leadership. What I really found inspiring was the original "collectivization" documents, then available only in French (possibly Spanish), and what I could pick up about Berneri and others. And also commentary like Rocker, Korsch in *Living Marxism*, and a few others. (31 Mar. 1995)

What motivated his interest? A powerful curiosity, exposure to divergent opinions, and an unorthodox education have all been given as answers to this question. He was clearly struck by the obvious contradictions between his own readings and mainstream press reports. The measurement of the distance between the realities presented by these two sources, and the evaluation of why such a gap exists, remained a passion for Chomsky. He persistently sought out marginalized left-libertarian perspectives on current and historical events, and gradually became aware that the monolithic world view that is propped up before us by the mainstream media is suspiciously consistent, and that it is used to establish the status quo.

This insight fueled his youthful investigations, and ultimately formed the foundations of much of his later work on propaganda, the media, and the ways that groups such as the Spanish anarchists are discredited in Western society. In "Language in the Service of Propaganda," one of his many later articles that draws upon George Orwell's writings and the reception of his work, he describes the "interesting and revealing" publishing history of *Homage to Catalonia*:

It appeared in 1937 but was not published in the United States. It was published in England, and it sold a couple hundred copies. The reason that the book was suppressed was because it was critical of communists. That was a period when pro-communist intellectuals had a great deal of power in the intellectual establishment.... It did appear about 10 years later, and it appeared as a Cold War tract because it was anti-Russian and fashions had changed. That was a really important book. I think there were things wrong with it, but it was a book of real great significance and importance. It's probably the least known of Orwell's major political books. (*Chronicles* 21)

The issue of ruling-class or corporate control of public access to information is a divisive one for many of Chomsky's critics. Some are convinced that works are, for the most part, printed and distributed according to capitalist profit motives. For example, another Orwell novel, *Keep the Aspidistra Flying*, was not distributed in the United States until many years after its publication in 1936 because it was deeply rooted in English life, and therefore considered by distributors to be of little interest to American readers. Yet other critics endorse Chomsky's belief that a type of elite control does exist: Chomsky himself has had his own work suppressed by publishers, and some media outlets have refused to print his letters and interviews with him.

Figure 5
Chomsky in his office at MIT. The poster is of Bertrand Russell.

Chomsky and Bertrand Russell

One of the few adornments in Chomsky's office at the Massachusetts Institute of Technology is a large poster of Bertrand Russell. As a young man, Chomsky discovered the British mathematician, logician, and philosopher who came to realize (quite a bit later in life than Chomsky) that the ruling classes own the means of production and are therefore driven to legitimize their power. Russell was an inspiration to Chomsky. First, he was an important influence upon Chomsky's thinking about philosophy and logic; second, he had a similarly profound commitment to the cause of popular liberation; third, he was closely affiliated with the university world as a scholar, while simultaneously acting on behalf of the oppressed lower classes; and fourth, he upheld his views even if it meant jeopardizing his reputation, or even his freedom.

Chomsky recently compared Russell to Albert Einstein on the question of social conscience:

Compare Russell and Einstein, two leading figures, roughly the same generation. They agreed on the grave dangers facing humanity, but chose different ways to respond. Einstein responded by living a very comfortable life in Princeton and dedicating himself to research that he loved, taking a few moments for an occasional oracular statement. Russell responded by leading demonstrations and getting himself dragged off by the cops, writing extensively on the problems of the day, organizing war crimes trials, etc. The result? Russell was and is reviled and condemned, Einstein is admired as a saint. Should that surprise us? Not at all. (31 Mar. 1995)

This comparison points to the deep sympathy Chomsky had, from very early on, for those who involved themselves in activist work and concrete political action such as marching, signing petitions, and promoting small- and large-scale libertarian movements. In remarking on Einstein, he also hints that the pursuit of personal comfort and gain, although not in itself contemptible, can nonetheless stem from a pernicious wish to separate oneself from the rabble—the very people who are oppressed or enslaved by the system. But Chomsky is quick to state that marching is not in itself a virtuous activity, just as theorizing about social problems is not necessarily ivory towerish; what matters is which particular issue is being promoted by these activities. Russell was on the right track, and this is perhaps one reason why, in Chomsky's opinion, he was vilified "when he took the path of political activism once again in the late '50s, and to the end of his life." That he received such treatment "was pretty shocking." Chomsky remarks, "Of course, it was never a bed of roses before, including a jail sentence during World War I, [being] kicked out of his Cambridge College (Trinity) for lack of sufficient patriotism, barred from teaching at City College in New York as a freethinker and other crimes, and on, and on, through most of his life. It even infects professional philosophy. He's known mostly for his work early in the century, when he was still a nice gentlemanly type" (25 July 1995).

The necessity of such personal sacrifice seems inevitable to Chomsky. But it must finally be accepted as secondary to the larger work that remains to be done, work that, while never losing sight of the ultimate goal of a "good society," has to begin with local action: "there are all sorts of people struggling very hard to make the world—if not 'good,' then a little better. And they desperately need help" (18 May 1995). Carlos Otero, Chomsky's good friend, sees in this kind of attitude what is a clearly anarchosyndicalist position.

A committed anarchosyndicalist is not satisfied with being a good arm-chair revolutionary—one who has made every effort to understand the contemporary world in the light of what is best in the libertarian socialist tradition, drawing from the achievements of the past lessons that will enrich the culture of liberation. Anarchosyndicalists are prepared to take their stand with those who wish not only to understand the world, but also to change it. They are perfectly aware of the power of non-violent resistance and direct action.... They are also more than willing to participate anonymously in the spontaneous actions of popular forces that are capable of creating new social forms in the course of the struggle for complete liberation, fully conscious that social creation enhances and promotes the very intellectual creation that inspired it. ("Introduction" 38)

Chomsky's early life, indeed his whole life, was and has been literally consumed by a desire for understanding and a penchant for political commitment. The important events, passions, and alliances in his early life were almost all linked to intellectual pursuits. Chomsky recalls: "I had, from childhood, been deeply involved intellectually in radical and dissident politics, but intellectually. At that point, I was feeling so uneasy with the usual petition-signing and the like that I couldn't stand it any longer, and decided to plunge in. I hated the decision. I'm really a hermit by nature, and would much prefer to be alone working than to be in public" (qtd. in Falk 596n1). This description of the deeply involved intellectual hermit applies as much to Chomsky the present-day activist and professor as it does to the child and teenager of the 1930s and 1940s.

The Circle Broadens

In his later teens, Chomsky's circle of influences broadened to include a number of compelling figures. Among them were Dwight and Nancy Macdonald, publishers, from 1944 to 1949, of the New York magazine *Politics*. Norman Epstein claims that *Politics* "had an enormous influence" on him and "most of my friends and, I daresay, also on Chomsky" (4 Feb. 1995). Chomsky did, in fact, read *Politics* in his late teens and found that "in some respects [it] answered to and developed" his interest in "anarchism, American involvement in the war and so forth" (qtd. in Whitfield 113). The chief contributors to the magazine were, with the exception of Paul Goodman, all immigrants: Andrea Caffi (Italian-Russian), Nicola Chiaromonte (Italian), Lewis Coser (German), Peter Gutman

(Czech), Victor Serge (Belgian-Russian), Niccola Tucci (Italian), and George Woodcock (English, and eventually Canadian).

In 1946, the magazine dropped its Marxist orientation "to whore after the strange gods of anarchism and pacifism," as Dwight Macdonald put it (*Memoirs* 27); and it managed to maintain its respectable but money-losing list of five thousand subscribers. Macdonald, who was also a libertarian critic, pamphleteer, and author, notes:

While I was editing *Politics* I often felt isolated, comparing my few thousand readers with the millions and millions of nonreaders—such is the power of the modern obsession with quantity, also of Marxism with its sentimentalization of "the masses." But ... I have run across so many nostalgic old readers in so many unexpected quarters that I have the impression I'm better known for *Politics* than for my articles in *The New Yorker*, whose circulation is roughly seven times greater. This is curious but should not be surprising. A "little magazine" is often more intensively read (and circulated) than the big commercial magazines, being a more individual expression and so appealing with special force to other individuals of like minds. (27)

Chomsky could perhaps be described as one of these "nostalgic old readers," for almost twenty years after its final issue he mentioned the magazine in a piece called "The Responsibility of Intellectuals" (1966), in which he discussed a series of articles published in *Politics* that deal with this subject.

These articles, although written so many years earlier, had "lost none of their power or persuasiveness" for him, particularly one by Macdonald himself concerning the question of war guilt. In this piece, Macdonald tries to assess the extent to which the German or Japanese people were responsible for the atrocities committed by their governments, and then goes on to ask to what extent the American or British people were responsible for Allied atrocities such as the bombing of civilian targets, the atomic destruction of Hiroshima and Nagasaki, and other war crimes. Chomsky writes: "To an undergraduate in 1945–46—to anyone whose political and moral consciousness had been formed by the horrors of the 1930s, by the war in Ethiopia, the Russian purge, the 'China incident,' the Spanish Civil War, the Nazi atrocities, the Western reaction to these events and, in part, complicity in them—these questions had particular significance and poignancy" (*American Power* 324). In his book about Macdonald, Stephen Whitfield points out "the resemblances between

Macdonald's and Chomsky's criticism," and claims that "Chomsky sought to uphold the *Politics* tradition 'that the policies of governments should be judged by their effects and not by the reasons advanced to justify them'" (114, 115).

There was a certain cohesion to Chomsky's ever-widening milieu at this time; many of those individuals whose work had commanded his attention were bound together in a web of interrelations. Prime examples are Macdonald and George Orwell. In a letter to Philip Rahv, written on 9 December 1943, Orwell mentions that "Dwight Macdonald has written telling me he is starting another review [*Politics*] and asking me to contribute. I don't know to what extent he will be in competition with PR [*Partisan Review*]" (*Collected Essays* 3: 53). Then, in his "As I Please" column for the *Tribune*, Orwell declared: "One cannot buy magazines from abroad nowadays, but I recommend anyone who has a friend in New York to try and cadge a copy of *Politics*, the new monthly magazine, edited by the Marxist literary critic, Dwight Macdonald. I don't agree with the policy of this paper, which is anti-war (not from a pacifist angle), but I admire its combination of highbrow political analysis with intelligent literary criticism" (*Collected Essays* 1: 172). Orwell eventually contributed a number of articles to *Politics*, and Chomsky, as we have seen, admired the work that was published there.

Paul Mattick and Karl Korsch, who often combined their efforts for various causes, were also discovered by Chomsky during the late 1940s, as he entered his twenties. Chomsky knew Mattick personally, and declared him to be "too orthodox a Marxist for my taste"; nevertheless, it is essential that we understand what theorists such as Mattick and Korsch were saying about the events surrounding Chomsky's youth if we are to comprehend Chomsky's developing attitudes and beliefs (8 Aug. 1994). Mattick (1904–80) immigrated to the United States from Germany in 1926. He emerged from the Council Communist movement in Germany, and he eventually edited two journals, *Living Marxism* (with the collaboration of Korsch) and *New Essays*, that were important sources for the young Chomsky; another journal that Chomsky read in his late teens, *International Council Correspondence*, also benefited from his input. Sam Abramovitch, a source of much information about the period, remembers both Mattick and Korsch very well, and recalls that *Living Marxism*

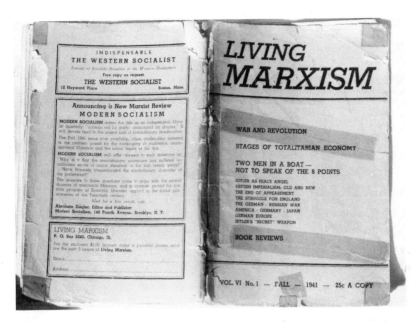

Figure 6
A copy of *Living Marxism*, dated 1941.

and *New Essays* "dealt with political issues, and the contributors were Marxists ... of the non-Bolshevik variety. Some of the people from the Frankfurt School, when they were in the United States, also had contact with this group" (12 Feb. 1991).

Mattick wrote a number of important texts concerning Marxism from a non-Bolshevik perspective, including a book called *Anti-Bolshevik Communism*, which described Marxist alternatives to the totalitarian Bolshevist rule, such as Council Communism (Gorter, Luxemburg, Liebknecht, Pannekoek), the German labor movement (Otto Rühle), Revolutionary Marxism (Korsch), and so forth. The journals Mattick was involved with and others like them were vibrant with urgent political debate; their contributors were driven by an unflagging desire to conceive an alternative social order. They refused to glorify popular figures or compose apologies for contemporary political structures. In them, authors' names are not highlighted to ensure academic promotion (often only initials are used); there are no inflated bibliographies; there is a spirit of sobriety and a sense that strict attention is being paid to the facts at hand.

A perusal of a single issue of *Living Marxism* provides insight into what Chomsky was reading in his teens; it is even possible to trace, in this magazine, some of the theoretical foundations for opinions that he would later come to hold. The fall 1941 issue featured "War and Revolution," by Karl Korsch; "Stages of Totalitarian Economy," by H. Bruggers; and a long article called "Two Men in a Boat—Not to Speak of the 8 Points" (beginning with an examination of the Churchill-Roosevelt Conference of 1941, and moving into long discussions of "Hitler as Peace Angel," "British Imperialism," "The End of Appeasement," "The Struggle for England," "The German-Russian War," "America-Germany-Japan," "German Europe," and "Hitler's 'Secret weapon'"), by Mattick. *Living Marxism* routinely took contemporary issues (fascism, imperialism, war, Bolshevism) and reflected upon them within their historical, social, and philosophical contexts. So, even in 1941, in the midst of the war with Germany, Korsch was writing about the *real* issues at stake in this conflict: "The struggle for the new order of society does not take place on the battlefields of the capitalist war. The decisive action of the workers begins where the capitalist war ends" ("War and Revolution" 14).

Bruggers, foreshadowing much of what Chomsky would later say about monopoly-capitalist practices, describes the dominant economic system as a "'corporate community' in which state and party officials share in property and managerial functions"; a "'Keynesian economy' in that the state is the greatest consumer and pyramid-building represents a considerable percentage of national output"; a "'war economy' in that problems of autarchy and of establishing new large-scale industries are resolved with the help of the state"; and "a capitalism based on 'conditioning measures' in so far as its development and expansion, as well as the forms and symptoms under which the abstract laws of capitalist economy are allowed to become manifest, are determined by state intervention and the monopolistic agreements of corporations." If we substitute "Cold War" for "war" in Bruggers's second description, we may see how valuable articles such as this one were. And, indeed, they continue to be relevant, despite the huge shifts that have occurred since 1941. Looking at Bruggers's definition of "managerial capitalism," the totalitarian nature of the corporation past and present—as described in our time by Chomsky—becomes clear as the basis for a merger of political and economic power is laid out: "the totalitarian system as we know it today may also be called 'managerial capitalism,' since the decisions dictated by technical and economic considerations are no longer hampered by the rights of ownership and title holders. Yet it should be emphasized—speaking of 'managers'—that the true technical directors have nowhere acquired the disposing power of technocrats; the real power rests mainly with economic and business managers" (23). Mattick's *Living Marxism* article sums up the issues at stake in World War II in a way that once again anticipates many of Chomsky's views of contemporary international politics. Here, for the word "war," we could substitute "any war in which First World powers play a part," or even "any invasion undertaken by large powers":

If all the other issues of this war are still clouded, it is perfectly clear that this war is a struggle between the great imperialist contestants for the biggest share of the yields of world production, and thus for the control over the greatest number of workers, the richest resources of raw material and the most important industries. Because so much of the world is already controlled by the small competitive power groups fighting for supreme rule, all controlled groups in all nations are drawn into the struggle. Since nobody dares to state the issues at stake, false arguments are invented to excite the population to murder. The powerlessness of the masses explains the power of current ideologies. (79)

Many other passages of Mattick's article bolster Chomsky's anti-Leninist, anti-Stalinist, anti-Bolshevik stance, and his more general belief that the revolution in Russia had simply led to the establishment of another autocracy, this one with lofty sentiments and totalitarian practices.

Other options to that autocracy did, of course, exist—options that clashed with what the Bolsheviks wanted. Granting Soviet workers direct participation in the new system, eliminating private property, and eradicating privilege based upon class are all positive steps that could have been taken towards a "good society." Unfortunately, the ruling classes in the Soviet Union were far more interested in maintaining their own power than in forming a union of Soviets according to the principles just described. The Soviet Union was, and still is, falsely referred to and condemned as a communist or Marxist state by historians, journalists, and political scientists. It was, in fact, a Bolshevik state led by ironfisted totalitarian leaders and supported by a powerful and omnipresent army committed to upholding interests and power structures that would never have been permitted to exist in a truly communist state.

Chomsky and Pannekoek

Nor did the Soviet regime conform in any way to the ideology of Council Communism, which had been of great interest to Chomsky, and which he went on to explore at length (for example, in "Industrial Self-Management" in his *Radical Priorities*). The movement was generated by Anton Pannekoek's International Council Communists in Amsterdam and Paul Mattick's Council Communist group, and it had as adherents Karl Korsch and Antonio Gramsci (who, like Lenin, supported the workers' councils in Turin after World War I). Lenin sensed the threat that Council Communism posed to the Bolshevik Party, and he wrote a pamphlet denouncing Pannekoek and Herman Gorter's position called *Left Wing Communism, an Infantile Disorder*. Abramovitch's description of workers councils emphasizes the distance that existed between Lenin's Bolshevist-directed version of organizing workers and that which was proposed by Mattick, Korsch, and Pannekoek. "The workers had to make the decisions in terms of the workplace, the people as a whole had to develop self-consciousness and a self-decision-making process, and not some sort of group, party, or what have you making decisions for the bulk of the population and lead[ing] them to the millennium" (12 Feb. 1991).

Pannekoek and Bertrand Russell were arguably the most important role models for Chomsky, and indeed their work most clearly resembles his own later efforts. An astronomer and professor of astronomy at the University of Amsterdam, Pannekoek was also interested in the theoretical relationship between science and Marxism. He was active in revolutionary movements in Holland and Germany from 1903 until his death in 1960, having come to the left through his early adherence to George Bernard Shaw's Fabian movement. Chomsky says that "Pannekoek is one of those whose work I found very interesting. I learned of it from Paul Mattick, who was circulating it in the United States" (31 Mar. 1995). Pannekoek played a major role in the Second International, in which theoreticians put forth "the assumption that the way to socialism lay through the building of a socialist party aiming at the capture of state power and nationalization of the economy." In the years before World War I, Pannekoek, together with Rosa Luxemburg, became involved "in the struggle to force the German socialist party to support mass direct action. During the war, he was among the first to attack the socialist parties of Europe for supporting the war and to call for class struggle against it" (J. B. and P. M. iii).

Like many members of the left with whom Chomsky sympathized, Pannekoek eventually broke with the Third International (he did so in 1920), and then, through his work with Council Communist groups in various countries, went on "to develop the theory of the self-organization of the working class (through the council structure) in opposition to all forms of social organization distinct from those of the class itself as a whole" (J. B. and P. M. iii). It was this later work that Chomsky found most interesting. He considered the Pannekoek pamphlet *Workers' Councils* to be "really excellent," although he added that another of his political books, *Lenin as Philosopher*, "I thought was very poorly reasoned, frankly, and the topic struck me as on par with 'Gauss as poet'" (31 Mar. 1995). *Workers' Councils* contains Pannekoek's critiques of social democrats and Bolsheviks, which were prompted by his experiences during World War I and "the failure of German and Russian revolutions to create free socialist societies" (J. B. and P. M. iii).

Although the pamphlet was written during the war years 1941 to 1942 when the Germans occupied Holland, it found a new audience in the late 1960s and early 1970s. This audience was made up of members of the student-based antiauthoritarian and libertarian New Left, who were trying to find out "how to organize [them]selves, how to find forms and means of action adequate to [their] desires, even to be clear about the content of [their] desires" (J. B. and P. M. ii). Chomsky's own remarks on *Workers' Councils* speak to the interests of these students:

The workers, [Pannekoek] wrote, "must be masters of the factories, masters of their own labour, to conduct it at their own will." Such "common ownership must not be confounded with public ownership," a system in which workers are commanded by state officials who direct production. Rather, they must themselves take over complete control of the means of production and all planning and distribution. Capitalism is a "transitional form," combining modern industrial technique with the archaic social principle of private ownership. Advanced industrial technology combined with common ownership "means a free collaborating humanity," the proper goal of the workers movement. [Pannekoek] also wrote that "the idea of their common ownership of the means of production is beginning to take hold of the minds of the workers." (*Radical Priorities* 263)

Chomsky emphasizes that Pannekoek's writing on the workers' councils was, in fact, almost unknown beyond a few small circles. He links Pannekoek to Orwell in the sense that each achieved a degree of fame based upon his worst work: that is, the work most easily assimilated into the ruling-class line. Orwell was renowned for *1984*, not *Homage to Catalonia*; Pannekoek became known for his contribution to the Second International, not for his post–World War I work on Council Communism, which for the left-libertarian cause was far more significant. Remarks Chomsky: "The peak of [Pannekoek's] influence was before World War I, when he was a major figure in the Second International. He got a different sort of fame when he was denounced as an ultra-leftist by Lenin. Virtually no one knew of him in subsequent years, to my knowledge, except through Mattick's efforts (and these reached a handful of people; I recall going to a talk of Mattick's in Boston, at which about 5 people were present, most of them personal friends" (31 Mar. 1995).

The Council Communists nevertheless kept alive an interest in the theory and practice of councils after the failure of the revolutions in Central Europe and the decline in importance of the soviets in the Soviet Union (Epstein says that it is important to differentiate between the two bodies: "Factory Councils are quite different from the Russian Soviets, which cut across factories and became municipal-type organizations of the working class" [20 Apr. 1995]). Both Pannekoek and Mattick ascribed a central role to the councils, which they identified as a spontaneous form of working-class organization. They were also strong critics of the Soviet Union, which had subordinated the councils to the dictates of the Bolshevik Party, thereby eliminating their power. The social revolution envisioned by Pannekoek would involve overturning systems of production present in both Bolshevik and capitalist societies so that workers would have complete power over their work and control over their destiny. Pannekoek writes:

The conquest of political power by the workers, the abolition of capitalism, the establishment of new Law, the appropriation of the enterprises, the reconstruction of society, the building of a new system of production are not different consecutive occurrences. They are contemporary, concurrent in a process of social events and transformations. Or, more precisely, they are identical. They are the different sides, indicated with different names, of one great social revolution: the organization of labour by working humanity. (*Workers' Councils* 108)

Sam Abramovitch describes, from a contemporary vantage point, how a Council Communist program might be set up.

People exchange the various commodities that they produce. Each factory is going to have its own committee, and they are going to get together, discuss, and decide that this year "We are going to produce ten thousand pairs of shoes and ten thousand automobiles, and we're going to put them into a pool and from the pool we're all going to get what we need." On a theoretical basis, that is very nice, and if it could work that way then it would be ideal; everybody contributes to social welfare in terms of the common good of the economy and you take whatever you need, and there is an abundance of all of the commodities, so you don't have to hoard or accumulate.

But this system requires, as well, a rather dramatic shift in thinking about commodities and their ownership. "You don't need four bicycles in your garage; in fact, you don't need any bicycles in your own garage. You don't have to hoard bread because it is always at the store; you just go and pick it up. You just go and exchange your work for the commodities you need." How would decisions about production and working conditions be made? "The people themselves, communally, would make the decision as to their working conditions, their hours, how they want to arrange the lighting and ventilation of the factory, and so forth." Some might argue that this is what was tried in China or the former Soviet Union; but such an assessment is far from the truth. "In Russia the attempt was [made] early on [with the creation of the soviets] but it was immediately put down by Lenin and the Bolshevik Party" (12 Feb. 1991).

Council Communism as a political alternative is rarely mentioned in the West (except in terms of very small-scale endeavors, such as the Israeli kibbutz), despite the support it has received from Chomsky and others. If it had been evoked when Marxism was under fire, the task of anti-Marxist or anticommunist propagandists would undoubtedly have been more challenging.

Chomsky and the Marlenites

In 1943, Chomsky was also busy developing a whole new domain of interest. He had discovered some sectarian leftist literature of a very strange nature: the writings of the so-called Marlenites. "I got involved with Marlenite literature, partly my own reading (at the downtown Philadelphia Public Library where I would hang out when I could, a pretty impressive collection in those days), partly through Rivkin. I recall being impressed that some of their crazy predictions about the war were coming true" (13 Feb. 1996). These people claimed that World War II was "phoney" because it had been instigated by both Western capitalists and state capitalists from the Soviet Union in order to crush the European proletariat (*Chomsky Reader* 14). (This is not exactly the *Living Marxism* perspective, but there are some parallels.) The Marlenite philosophy "fit pretty well into the kinds of things I was trying to put together from other sources, probably first my newsstand operator uncle, then anarchist offices and second-hand bookstores," says Chomsky. He was introduced to the writings of George Marlen by Ellis Rivkin, a student of Solomon Zeitlin at Dropsie College who went on to become a professor of history at Gratz College (the Hebrew college in Philadelphia where Chomsky's father taught). Although he had lost contact with Rivkin by the late 1940s, Chomsky recalls that he was an "influential figure (at least for me; maybe not for anyone else)." But their contact, which had been close during Chomsky's teenage years, had ceased by the late 1940s. "Very few people knew anything about Rivkin's politics," Chomsky maintains. "He was extremely secretive, and didn't publish in these areas (except by implication, if one understood what he was hinting at). He was very knowledgeable and smart, and we spent a lot of time talking about the Bolsheviks, their background, and what they were up to—something that never entered his writing or general conversation" (31 Mar. 1995). The Marlenite group was very small, "probably about 3 people" who were, as the name indicates, "still 'Leninist' in some sense, but highly critical of Bolshevism (including Trotsky), to the critical side of the Schachtmanites, with whom I didn't get along well because of their lingering reverence for Trotsky (which I didn't share)" (31 Mar. 1995).

While still in his youth, then, Chomsky became committed to anarchism, and inaugurated that precocious commitment with his editorial on the fall of Barcelona. By the time he had entered his late teens, he had read widely and had ingested a voluminous amount of information about the tradition he had inherited; he had developed affinities with a variety of thinkers, groups, and movements, had studied the ideas they generated,

Figure 7
Chomsky's graduation photo from Central High School in Philadelphia.

and had begun to identify his own course of action against the backdrop
of their example.

Chomsky continues to work within the tradition and the milieu he
embraced in the 1930s and 1940s. The long and detailed letters he writes
to virtually anybody interested enough to contact him (letter writing con-
sumes about twenty hours of his week [George ix], the close contact he
maintains with grass-roots organizations, and his adherence to a gruelling
conference schedule, are the outward signs of his deep sense of social and
academic responsibility. He is a highly productive worker who shuns the
perks of the ivory tower, perks that often seem to promote distance
between intellectuals and working people. Taking pride in the products of
his efforts, he tries, with each project, to improve his techniques for analysis and understanding.

Although Noam Chomsky had an extremely unusual childhood, his
college years, which got underway in 1945, were no less filled with ideas
and ideals. Into Chomsky's life now flowed a fresh stream of intellectuals
and activists, thinkers and movers.

2

Zellig Harris, Avukah, and Hashomer Hatzair

Things happen in the world because of the efforts of dedicated and courageous people whose names no one has heard, and who disappear from history.
—Noam Chomsky, letter to the author, 18 Dec. 1993

Undergraduate Years

At the age of sixteen, Chomsky began undergraduate studies at the University of Pennsylvania. It was 1945. He continued to live at home, paying for his education by teaching Hebrew school in the afternoons, on Sundays, and sometimes in the evenings. Hoping to build on the reading he had already done in the areas of philosophy, languages, and logic, he enrolled in a general program of study. He also resolved to study Arabic, and was the only undergraduate in the university to do so at the time. Although he plunged into his work with typical freshman enthusiasm, Chomsky soon became discouraged because he discovered that the institutional structure that he had so loathed in high school was largely replicated at Penn. There were some highlights: he was able to make contact with a few stimulating scholars. He met C. West Churchman in the philosophy department, and his Arabic teacher was Giorgio Levi Della Vida, "an antifascist exile from Italy who was a marvellous person as well as an outstanding scholar" (*Chomsky Reader* 7). It was not simply an interest in their academic work that drew Chomsky to certain people; he was also, and perhaps more powerfully, attracted by their general attitude. Della Vida, for example, excited him more politically than he did academically.

Dismayed by his undergraduate experience, Chomsky soon began to reflect on the possibility of dropping out of college, "to go to Palestine, perhaps to a kibbutz, to try to become involved in efforts at Arab-Jewish cooperation within a socialist framework" (*Chomsky Reader* 7). The decision was a crucial one at this stage in his life, and it also has a retrospective significance, given the lifelong difficulties he has had with the Zionist movement. Like numerous mainstream Zionist individuals and organizations, Chomsky opposed the idea that there should be a Jewish state in Palestine. The creation of such a state would necessitate carving up the territory and marginalizing, on the basis of religion, a significant portion of its poor and oppressed population, rather than uniting them on the basis of socialist principles. Opponents of the establishment of a Jewish state still raise the ire of the many contemporary Zionists who do not acknowledge the principles that underwrote mainstream Zionism earlier this century, and who, by extension, fail to recognize the problems created when a state is established according to religious precepts.

While Chomsky was doing his undergraduate work, various social movements were active in Palestine, but the one that interested him was the cooperative-labor movement. The approach its adherents took to organizing society, which was employed in numerous kibbutzim, bears important similarities to the Catalonian model as described by Orwell in *Homage to Catalonia*. So Chomsky's very early tendency to sympathize with cooperative libertarian impulses rather than Stalinist or Trotskyite visions— which were popular among contemporary Zionist youth groups, notably Hashomer Hatzair—once again prevailed.

As far as I recall, among the Zionist youth groups it was only Hashomer Hatzair that could seriously be described as involved in all of this, and in the U.S., at least, it was almost completely either Stalinist or Trotskyist. I met many activists from around the country at conferences, sometimes at the "Hachshara farms" (where young people would go to live in preparation for going to the kibbutzim), etc. I don't recall anyone in Hashomer Hatzair who was outside that framework. (13 Feb. 1996)

In 1947, at the age of nineteen, he began to date Carol Doris Schatz, whom he had first met when they were both young children. Today, almost fifty years later, they are still together. Also in 1947, Chomsky met Zellig Harris, a charismatic professor who shared many of his interests and who would have a profound influence upon his life. As a result of meeting Harris, Chomsky delayed his planned departure from university to work on one of the cooperative-labor kibbutzim and prolonged his studies at the University of Pennsylvania. This change of plans was to have important consequences.

Zellig Sabbetai Harris

Harris was born in 1909 in Balta, Russia; he left there with his parents in 1913. Completing his B.A., M.A., and Ph.D. (1934) at the University of Pennsylvania, he began to teach there in 1931. He eventually founded the first department of linguistics in the United States at that institution. In 1966, he was named to the prestigious position of Benjamin Franklin Professor of Linguistics.

Harris is known for his work in structural linguistics and is considered to be the father of discourse analysis. His work—which, by the time he died, included *Structural Linguistics* (1951), *Mathematical Structures of Language* (1968), *Papers in Structural and Transformational Linguistics* (1970), *Papers on Syntax* (1981), *A Grammar of English on Mathematical Principles* (1982), *Language and Information* (1988), and *The Form of Information in Science* (1989)—was described in the *Times Literary Supplement* as having a "fascinating consistency," and as being underwritten by a commitment "to study the forms of language in abstraction from their meanings" (Matthews, "Saying Something").

But the book for which Harris is best remembered is *Methods in Structural Linguistics* (1951), an attempt to organize descriptive linguistics into a single body of theory and practice. On the back cover of the Midway Reprints edition (1986), Norman McQuown makes the following remarks: "Harris's contribution [is] epoch-marking in a double sense: first in that it marks the culmination of a development of linguistic methodology *away* from a stage of intuitionism, frequently culture-bound; and second in that it marks the beginnings of a new period, in which the new methods will be applied ever more rigorously to ever widening areas in human culture." This book played a vital role in forging the Harris-Chomsky relationship, as Chomsky himself maintains in the introduction to his own great early work, *The Logical Structure of Linguistic Theory*:

My formal introduction to the field of linguistics was in 1947, when Zellig Harris gave me the proofs of his *Methods in Structural Linguistics* to read. I found it very intriguing and, after some stimulating discussions with Harris, decided to major in linguistics as an undergraduate at the University of Pennsylvania. I had some informal acquaintance with historical linguistics and medieval Hebrew grammar, based on my father's work in these fields, and at the same time was studying Arabic with Giorgio Levi Della Vida. (25)

While I do not want to suggest a parallel here, it is still notable that Marx and Engels contributed to the study of linguistics through their explorations of the nature and essence of language; Voloshinov and Bakhtin, as well as Lukács, also worked in the domain of linguistics from a Marxist perspective; and Gramsci had a background in linguistics. But it was not Harris's linguistics that first attracted Chomsky: he was tantalized by his professor's politics. Indeed, Chomsky commented that "in the late 1940s, Harris, like most structural linguists, had concluded that the field was essentially finished, that linguistics was finished. They had already done everything. They had solved all the problems. You maybe had to dot a couple of i's or something but essentially the field was over" (qtd. in Randy Allen Harris 31).

Harris was, according to Chomsky, "a really extraordinary person who had a great influence on many young people in those days." Although a linguistics professor, "he had a coherent understanding of this whole range of issues, which I lacked, and I was immensely attracted by it, and by him personally as well, also by others who I met through him." "[A] person of unusual brilliance and originality," Harris encouraged Chomsky to take graduate courses in philosophy with Nelson Goodman and Morton White, and mathematics with Nathan Fine. During this period Chomsky was considering dropping out: "I suppose Harris had in mind to influence me to return to college, though I don't recall talking about it particularly, and it all seemed to happen without much planning" (*Chomsky Reader* 7, 8).

Chomsky had also begun to read works suggested to him by Harris, such as those of the Sullivan-Horney-Rapoport school of psychoanalysis. The field of psychoanalysis was familiar to Chomsky because he had read Freud on the insistence of his uncle (the newsstand operator, who eventually became a psychoanalyst). His first encounter with Freud's works had occurred when he was an adolescent, and it had left Chomsky "much impressed," although "on re-reading years later I was appalled, frankly.

So I didn't re-do that when Harris talked about it (a lot), but did follow his particular interest" (31 Mar. 1995).

Harris introduced the young Chomsky to some well-known figures in the field of psychoanalysis: "He took me to visit Rapoport, one of the very few people in his circle I ever met (maybe Erikson was there too—it was at their clinic in Connecticut, I think)." A passionate interest in psychoanalysis had also led Harris to the Frankfurt School, notably to the work of Erich Fromm. This approach, which included studying on a very theoretical level the relationship between psyche and social movements, did not engage Chomsky, despite his bond with Harris: "I could never get much interested in any of this, or in most of the other things that were of interest to Harris and his circle apart from the left-Zionist (anti-state) things . . ." (31 Mar. 1995).

Drawn in by his professor's political work, his linguistic studies, and his unacademic approach, Chomsky began to realize that Harris had become his main reason for remaining in university. Harris encouraged the kind of unstructured, lively, and creative debate that had been a mainstay of Chomsky's early education and upon which he had thrived in the company of his uncle in New York. Course requirements, formal relationships, and scholarly hierarchies were rejected in favor of informal gatherings, broad-based discussions, and intellectual exchange. The University of Pennsylvania's linguistics department comprised, at that time, a very small group of graduate students who shared an enthusiasm not only for linguistics, but also for politics. They shunned the classroom, and met either at the nearby Horn and Hardart Restaurant or at Harris's apartment in Princeton or New York. The discussions could last for days, and Chomsky remembers them as being "intellectually exciting as well as personally very meaningful experiences" (*Chomsky Reader* 8).

Chomsky ultimately received an unconventional B.A. degree from the University of Pennsylvania, which reflected his interest in linguistics, philosophy, and logic. His B.A. honor's thesis, "Morphophonemics of Modern Hebrew," which set the stage for some of his later work and which is taken to be the first example of modern generative grammar, was completed in 1949 when he was just twenty years old.

That same year, while they were both still students, Chomsky married Carol Schatz, with whom he shared an array of interests, including Jewish culture and history, language studies, and philosophy. Carol was later to work in the area of linguistics herself. At the time of her marriage, she was also active in political issues, but in very different ways from Noam.

Graduate School

Inspired by people such as Harris, and experiencing an increasing intellectual fascination with the kind of work that he had undertaken for his B.A. thesis, Chomsky decided to enter graduate school at Penn. He began in the fall semester of 1949, and within a short period completed a master's thesis (his degree was granted in 1951), which was a revision of his B.A. thesis. The work underwent further editing in 1951, and was finally published in 1979 as *Morphophonemics of Modern Hebrew*.

His friendship with Harris was growing and it took on what could now be described as mythic proportions. Chomsky seemed to have been elected to follow up on, and expand, Harris's work, and Harris became for Chomsky a figure with whom, and ultimately against whom, he could measure his own achievement. Much has been written about this relationship, and much conjecture has been published as to the influence that each man had upon the other. But what was the real nature of the discussions that Chomsky had during this period with Harris and others? What effect did these exchanges have upon Chomsky's intellectual development?

Chomsky notes that Harris

thought of linguistics as a set of procedures for organizing texts, and was strongly opposed to the idea that there might be anything real to discover. He did think that the methods of linguistic analysis could be used for analysis of ideology, and most of my actual graduate courses were devoted to that; you can see some of the fruits in his articles on discourse analysis in *Language* in the early '50s, though he kind of downplayed the political side that was everyone's main interest. (13 Dec. 1994)

His attempts to make Harris's methods work constituted Chomsky's early linguistic research. Out of these endeavors came his first published article, which appeared in *The Journal of Symbolic Logic*. His undergraduate thesis also applied some of Harris's ideas, but he had by then totally abandoned all of his methods and adopted a "completely nonprocedural, holistic (in that the evaluation measure proposed was a measure applied to the whole system), and realist" approach (31 Mar. 1995):

Phrase structure rules can generate representations of syntactic structure quite successfully ... for quite a range of expressions, and were introduced for this purpose in the earliest work on generative grammar. It was at once apparent, however, that phrase structure rules ... are insufficient in themselves to account properly for the variety of sentence structures. The earliest approach to this problem, which has a number of subsequent and current variants, was to enrich the system of rules by introducing complex categories with features that can "percolate down" to the categories contained within them, expressing global dependencies not captured in a simple system of phrase structure rules.... I adopted this approach in an undergraduate thesis of 1949, modifying ideas of Zellig Harris from a somewhat different framework. (*Knowledge* 64)

So even at this early stage, Chomsky was producing highly original work, which diverged fundamentally from Harris's. In his B.A. thesis he was doing things that were, in his own words, "radically at odds with everything in structural linguistics ... which is why [it, and *Logical Structure of Linguistic Theory*] were published only 30 years later." The thesis was "as different from structural linguistics as anything could be," which was why "Harris never looked at it and no one in the field reacted to it." In fact, *Morphophonemics of Modern Hebrew* remains "the only text in existence, to my knowledge, that seeks to apply an evaluation measure in anything remotely like that detail" (31 Mar. 1995).

Beyond Contemporary Linguistics

One reason the fruits of Chomsky's research did not even seem to belong to the field of linguistics was that Chomsky was still reading widely and finding some unexpected insights in the realm of, for example, philosophy: "Recall that in those days, one wasn't supposed to read anything ... before the late Carnap, and that was read only to refute. There were exceptions for Frege and Russell, but limited ones. And there had been guys named Hume and Locke, but one didn't read them, just quoted falsehoods one had learned in graduate school. For Harris, none of this had any interest either, as far as I know" (13 Dec. 1994). Discussing linguistics and philosophy in Chomsky's work, Otero names German-born philosopher Rudolf Carnap as "the best known representative of the group of logical positivists"; he was to have "a direct and decisive influence on Chomsky's teachers," and was "the only non-American philosopher Chomsky read as a student" ("Chomsky and the Rationalist" 3). Carnap was deeply influenced by the work of Bertrand Russell, and made careful studies of Frege, Whitehead, and Wittgenstein, who were models for Chomsky, as well.

Just as his early readings in anarchism had led to revelations in the political domain, the readings Chomsky now undertook gave him a fresh perspective that his teacher Nelson Goodman considered to be "completely mad." When Goodman found out about Chomsky's work in the mid-1960s, he apparently ended their friendship, even though, as Chomsky says, they'd "been quite good friends until he learned about this, which he regarded somehow as a personal betrayal" (31 Mar. 1995). His thesis supervisor, Zellig Harris, considered this approach "a private hobby"; he "never paid the slightest attention to [it] and probably thought [it] was crazy" (13 Dec. 1994).

The one person who did pay attention to this early work was the Israeli logician Yehoshua Bar-Hillel, a colleague of Carnap's and a good friend of Chomsky's from 1951 onwards. Bar-Hillel was possibly the only one to have read *Morphophonemics of Modern Hebrew* closely at this time. He suggested changes that Chomsky integrated into the work. Writes Chomsky, "We had very different views on many things, even some controversy in print, but were always extremely close, even on politics." He further recalls that Bar-Hillel was "one of the first people in Israel to publicly speak up for the civil and human rights of Arabs and to oppose the creeping annexation after 1967." Interestingly, Bar-Hillel's work on this subject is rarely mentioned. Chomsky's explanation for this follows a by-now-familiar line: "He'd be well-known to activists in Israel (many of whom were his students, or influenced by him). But he was only a serious, intelligent, dedicated and honourable person with an important and influential role, not a 'public intellectual,' so he is unknown. These are again the kinds of facts that never make it [into] intellectual history" (31 Mar. 1995).

Another professor at the University of Pennsylvania who read Chomsky's B.A. thesis when Chomsky was still an undergraduate was Henry Hoenigswald, "a very good scholar of historical linguistics who also knew the Indic tradition, and was a committed Harrisian structuralist, also knowledgeable in European structuralism" (31 Mar. 1995). Hoenigs-wald—and Harris, as well—likely knew that there existed another example of generative grammar (albeit a less detailed one than Chomsky's 1948 thesis work, and limited to the phonological level) that had preceded Chomsky's by roughly eight years. It was called "Menomini Morpho-phonemics," and was published by American linguist Leonard Bloomfield in the Czech *Travaux du Cercle Linguistique de Prague* in 1939. It is re-markable, in Chomsky's view, that neither Hoenigswald nor Harris revealed the existence of this text to his student. "Menomini Morpho-phonemics" is an extraordinary text, completely inconsistent with Bloom-field's other writings about language and how research in the area should be done. This, Chomsky believes, was one of the reasons Bloomfield decided to publish it in Europe.

Hoenigswald and Harris were very close to Bloomfield, and certainly knew his work. But neither of them mentioned to their only undergraduate student that he was rediscovering, more or less, what Bloomfield had just done eight years before. It's not surprising in Harris's case, because he didn't know what I was doing. But Hoenigswald read it, and must have recognized the similarities, back to classical India. I learned nothing of this until the 1960s, when Morris Halle found out about Bloomfield's work. (31 Mar. 1995)

The Anxiety of Influence

A complex teacher-student relationship was under construction here—one that has provoked speculation, particularly among Harris's friends and followers. Harris's involvement in Chomsky's political and linguistic work, and the proximity between his own and Chomsky's approaches, has triggered debate about influence, authority, and power struggles. Similarly, speculation about the relationship between Chomsky and *his* students has sparked discussion and even controversy in more recent times. A number of commentators have talked about the proximity of Chomsky's linguistic theories to those of Harris. In "The Fall and Rise of Empiricism" (1976), Jerrold Katz and Thomas Bever write, "[C]ontrary to popular belief, transformations come into modern linguistics, not with Chomsky, but with Harris's rules relating sentence forms. These are genuine transformations, since they are structure-dependent mappings of phrase markers onto phrase markers. That this is so can be seen from the examples of transformations Harris gives" (292). Even the 1986 edition of the *New Encyclopedia Britannica* has something to say about this relationship: "Since [Zellig] Harris was Noam Chomsky's teacher, some linguists have questioned whether Chomsky's transformational grammar is as revolutionary as it has been taken to be, but the two scholars developed their ideas of transformation in different contexts and for different purposes. For Harris, a transformation relates surface structure sentence forms and is not a device to transform a deep structure into a surface structure, as it is in transformational grammar."

This kind of anxiety-of-influence inquiry, which often leads to psychoanalytic-style postulations and projections or else Foucauldian-style power analyses, excites the imaginations of some observers. In a recent gossipy history of linguistics since the 1940s called *The Linguistic Wars*, Randy Allen Harris maintains that there have been huge power struggles over the years between Chomsky and his own students and colleagues. Chomsky's opinion of this type of thinking in general, and of the R. A. Harris book in particular, is predictably denunciatory, to say the least: "There [are] a few people (neither students nor colleagues of mine, for the most part) who see themselves as having been involved in 'power struggles,' but that is part of their life, not mine—actually, their fantasy life. I was never involved" (14 Aug. 1995).

Any close teacher-student relationship is bound to involve an exchange of influence, and will often give rise to some bad feeling. But Chomsky believes that the field of linguistics is especially likely to set the stage for such interpersonal dynamics. As he sees it, the problem lies in the rift between linguistics as it is described by historians of linguistics such as R. A. Harris, Dell H. Hymes, or P. H. Matthews, and as it is actually practiced by linguists: "All of this has to do with the extremely sharp break that took place from the early '50s (and if you count my private hobby, from the late '40s)" (31 Mar. 1995). This break is not clearly demarcated in well-known histories of linguistics, such as those by P. H. Matthews or Dell H. Hymes. The general impression conveyed in these texts is that Chomsky was following up on, rather than radically questioning, previous work in the field.

Chomsky deplores the stance that many who are active in the area of linguistics research have adopted towards the origins and development of their discipline:

By the early '60s, linguistics was going off on a totally different course, and the people actively engaged in it aren't interested in history (I disagree with that attitude, but it's a fact, just as people active in research in chemistry don't tend to care much about the history of the subject, even if it's recent history). The result is that history is often written by outsiders most of whom have only the vaguest understanding of what was happening, or have special axes to grind. (31 Mar. 1995)

R. A. Harris doesn't give the impression that he has an "axe to grind," although in his historical chronicle he clearly takes sides against Chomsky on most issues. More striking, though, is his soap-opera style of fashioning a narrative: intrigues are developed, villains are created, and plots thicken. The work of R. A. Harris is an example of the so-called Foucauldian genre of history, an approach that emphasizes the power struggles among key players. One has the impression in reading this kind of work that these struggles are what drive researchers (including Chomsky) to pursue one or another avenue of research. This kind of work lends an air of intrigue to the field but, for Chomsky, contributes little to our understanding of it.

In the context of his studies, Chomsky continued to attempt "to make sense of Harris's *Methods* and procedural approaches to language altogether in the operationalist style of the day" (3 Apr. 1995), while still working on generative transformational grammar as a kind of hobby. He remained at Penn primarily because of Harris and the newfound stimulation of political and philosophical discussion. But he strongly believed that the things he really cared about, libertarian politics and a new vision of the entire field of language studies, were essentially personal interests (hobbies) that ultimately had to be pursued beyond the institution.

"Keeping to Politics": A Relationship Evolves

Chomsky claims that in the area of linguistics he and Harris "parted ways by about 1950 or so, definitively after I abandoned the *Methods* program a few years later." They continued to meet regularly, and "remained good friends, but kept to politics" (13 Dec. 1994). Despite this restriction, their common ground was still vast. "My picture of the world, as a teenager," Chomsky remarks, "was certainly shaped very strongly by [Harris's] influence, which in fact fit in very well to commitments I'd already developed elsewhere (anarchist and left anti-Bolshevik and anti-Marxist sources, particularly)" (13 Dec. 1994).

Yet the basis of Harris's beliefs, and their relationship to Chomsky's later work, has never before been elaborated. One way of doing this is to explore three related issues. The first is Zellig Harris's personality, which is mentioned by virtually all who knew him, and which has, of course, a direct bearing upon how he conceived of appropriate methods for exchanging views and carrying on relationships within society. The second concerns the history and the program of the group called Avukah, of which Harris was an important figure. Finally, the third involves the Zionist group Hashomer Hatzair, as well as its affiliated community in Israel called Kibbutz Artzi.

"A Very Powerful Personality"

Hilary Putnam, in his preface to *The Form of Information in Science*, recalls a graduate course that he took at Penn with Harris called Linguistic Analysis. There was only one other undergraduate in the class—Noam Chomsky; the course material was difficult and filled with technicalities; "but the powerful intellect and personality of Zellig Harris drew me like a lodestone, and, although I majored in Philosophy, I took every course there was to take in Linguistic Analysis from then until my graduation" (xi).

Now a professor at Harvard, Putnam has been a friend of Chomsky's since high school. He does not appear to have been part of the Harris circle, but his observations coincide with those made by many who knew Harris. Willie Segal, who now teaches at the University of Colorado, also knew Harris well, and speaks in reverential terms about his personality, adding, "No one person has had a greater influence on my personal development" (24 Apr. 1995).

Seymour Melman asserts that "Zellig was a very powerful personality [who] functioned for many people as a mentor, apart from his function as a teacher. He set a standard for honesty in personal dealings, and for a very unpretentious personal style that gave emphasis to, on the one hand, intellectual achievement, [and,] on the other, to the constructive activity that the kibbutz represented" (26 July 1994). Describing Harris's generosity, Melman remarks:

Harris was also very unassuming. To many people, that may have seemed to be almost reclusive. For example, he would rarely sign things. He was more interested in the intrinsic ideas, and in getting the cooperation of the whole group in thinking through political issues, and social issues broadly understood. It doesn't require a giant leap of imagination to see how many of these characteristics are mirrored in Noam Chomsky. Something else: he clearly stood for democratic dealings amongst people, and was never a friend of authoritarianism of any kind. (26 July 1994)

This evocation of Harris does resonate with that of Chomsky, and the sense that many who have been taught or influenced by him—such as Abramovitch, Epstein, Herman, Melman, and Otero—have of him. Harris's attitude towards the importance of the movement rather than individual achievement is reflected in Chomsky's attitude towards biographical studies. Harris's teaching style, so clearly charged with the spirit of left libertarianism, and his commitment to encouraging rather than stifling individual creativity, are echoed in Chomsky's approach to pedagogy, group relations, and appropriate political frameworks.

Whether Chomsky inherited this disposition from Harris, or whether Harris's values simply fit into his own is ultimately irrelevant. What matters is that an intriguing overlap exists. The power of Harris's personality remains vivid in Chomsky's recollection: "he was a much greater influence than is recognized, extending to all sorts of people. The first time I met Nathan Glazer [a member of Avukah], for example, after a few minutes I asked him whether he knew Harris. He said yes, he'd studied with him 25 years earlier. I didn't tell Glazer why I'd asked. The reason was that he was mimicking all sorts of idiosyncratic Harris gestures. Not the only case" (13 Dec. 1994).

Avukah

Avukah is the second context for this exploration of the link between Harris's nature and beliefs and the kind of thinker Chomsky was to become. It serves as a kind of critical connection both between Harris and

Chomsky and between Chomsky's present values and views and those held by others earlier in this century. Avukah was around before Harris came onto the scene, but he had an important impact on the Pennsylvania chapter, and many other chapters in North America, beginning in about 1933. Harris's singular leadership made the University of Pennsylvania Avukah particularly fascinating and somewhat unusual. Willie Segal, who was the president of the McGill University Avukah during this period, notes that "there is a developmental distinction to be made between Avukah and the Zellig Harris group, the latter evolving out of the former" (24 Apr. 1995).

Due to his magnetic personality and his appeal as an intellectual, Harris's contribution to Avukah led to a surge of activity at the Pennsylvania branch. Some remarkable people became involved, including Kurt Blumenfeld, a spokesperson for many German Jewish intellectuals, and a confidant of Hannah Arendt's. Arthur Rosenberg, the German historian, also joined forces with the group, as did Seymour Melman, who later produced extremely forward-looking work on the military-industrial complex and social responsibility as well as on worker self-management.

Documentation concerning Avukah and its activities has all but disappeared (except for that contained in the Jewish section of the New York Public Library, a gift from Seymour Melman), and even those who have chronicled American Zionism or libertarian movements have apparently forgotten its existence, so I have relied heavily upon firsthand accounts. In a letter concerning my biographical research, Chomsky said, "it would be interesting to dig up the history of Avukah, far more interesting than writing about me, in fact." I am, in a sense, following his suggestion, not simply because the subject has intrinsic interest, but because it bears in direct ways upon an understanding of Noam Chomsky.

Avukah's Goals

Avukah was based at 111 Fifth Avenue in New York City. According to a 1938 pamphlet entitled *Program for American Jews*, its founders felt that it would be attractive "to Jews interested in the survival of the Jewish people, to Zionists, to Jews not interested in the existence of a Jewish group, and to socialists." Specifically, the pamphlet was addressed to Jewish American students and broached the question of whether there are facts or problems that specifically apply to Jews. The group's goal, stated on the reverse side of the program itself, included determining "the relation of the Program to these interests and attitudes, and seeking to indicate to what extent it coincides or differs with them."

The premises the group accepted were that there existed at that time four million Jews in the United States who "constitute a group with special needs and special problems" (6); that Jews are confined to particular activities or, as in Nazi Germany, thrown "out of their jobs and into concentration camps" (7); that there is latent and blatant anti-Semitism in American society; and that *the whole Jewish environment, the society which young American Jews find around them, is not suited to their needs*" (8). Avukah believed that the existing support network—Jewish groups, Jewish publications, Jewish systems of education and political action—were inadequate in light of such threats. It identified for itself four objectives: first, the "eventual liberation from the difficulties arising out of [the Jews'] minority position" (11); second, the creation of "a new type of organization" (12); third, the provision of "such aid as [we] can to Jews in countries where anti-Semitism is strong" (13); and fourth, "the definitive construction of the new Jewish settlement in Palestine" (13).

The new settlement that Avukah described is an important manifestation of the kind of Zionist position promulgated by Harris and, of course, by Chomsky himself. In the view of Avukah, certain British, feudal Arab, and Italian interests were trying to exploit the situation in Palestine for their own ends. This was leading to significant conflict between the Arabs and the Jews: "these interests have obstructed the Arab masses from the liberation which Jewish immigration can bring them, but they have not been able to stop the immigration of Jews." According to Avukah, the Palestinian situation had to be "faced by the Jews and straightened out on the only possible basis of social equality. For the fundamental interests of Jewish and Arab people are the same." The *Program for American Jews* goes on to insist that:

the Jews who come do not displace the Arabs. On the contrary, they are necessarily leading the Arab peasants out of the feudal system which holds them as serfs. Such a change can not come without fighting, without the attempt of reactionary forces to thwart the liberation of peasants and to set them against the Jews. But the fall of feudalism in Palestine is unavoidable, and with it will come the basis for cooperation of the masses of Arabs and Jews. (16)

Norman Epstein remarks that this is an overly optimistic assessment of the effects of Jewish immigration to Palestine: "Avukah, despite its good intentions, contributed to Zionist mythology—for example, that Jewish immigration to Palestine would 'liberate' the 'Arab masses' and that 'the Jews who come do not displace the Arabs.' In fact, the Jews bought the land and 'liberated' them into unemployment, a result amplified by the policy of favouring employment of Jews over Arabs in Jewish enterprises" (20 Apr. 1995). Chomsky concurs that the Avukah position, which in the 1940s he would have agreed with, is overenthusiastic—"to put it mildly." Nevertheless, he continues, "I'm pretty sure I would have realized that by the time I started speaking out publicly on the matter in the '60s. In retrospect, I'm surprised at how much of the mythology I believed back in the '40s, including my failure to comprehend the racist elements in such matters as the 'Jewish labor' slogan" (18 May 1995). Since Chomsky was between twelve and twenty-two years old in the 1940s, it is perhaps not surprising that all of the perspectives on Zionist mythology were not then evident to him.

Avukah's Program

By the time Chomsky had become a student at the University of Pennsylvania, he had embarked on his own intellectual journey, but he remained attuned to his family's concerns—specifically, those related to Jewish cultural and political issues. He was finding a new level of autonomy during these years, but at the same time he was establishing links with people who shared his particular fascinations, Zellig Harris among them. But Harris came at some of these issues from a different angle, and this angle was, in a sense, reflected in Avukah's program.

Avukah's commitment was to "fight anti-Semitism," defend civil liberties, participate in "anti-fascist action," "liberalize and modernize the Jewish environment," and "organize for maximum assistance in the migration of Jews to Palestine." (It is interesting that this three-front approach was criticized as "inappropriate," however, in the summer 1942 issue of the Avukah student newspaper by none other than Bruria Kaufman, Einstein's brilliant young assistant, who eventually married Zellig Harris.) This program prompted Avukah members to initiate an array of activities. For example, they published *Avukah Student Action*, "a journal of progressive thought and action," throughout the early 1940s. The efforts of many young activists went into the periodical, including Nathan Glazer (managing editor), Arlene Engel, Jerry Kaplan, Lorraine Kruglov, Bernard Mandelbaum, Rachel Naimann, Jack Osipowitz, Milton Shapiro, Margolith Shelubsky, Hannah Weil, and Rosalind Schwartz. Avukah also produced pamphlets. In an unsigned article that appeared in the February 1942 *Avukah Student Action*, the author notes that "when frayed, censored envelopes arrive with requests for literature from England, South Africa and even a concentration camp in Canada [!], the work takes on zest."

Group members also engaged, later on, in research projects such as one described by Sam Abramovitch. Based upon the Marxist hypothesis that fewer and fewer people are required to feed the entire population, the project was an attempt to discover another way of organizing society's resources. Abramovitch recalls that "the study divided the activity of society into three parts, the first one being economic relations [of] output [ERO], which includes those activities necessary for people to eat, live, and what have you. The second is ERP, the economic relations of production, which includes the essential organizational functions related to production. The third one is economic relations of capitalism (ERC), which includes activities undertaken because we live in a peculiar society; in other words, transcendental activities." Defining tasks according to utility helped those involved in the project understand where the emphasis could be placed in the distribution of resources:

If war is not absolutely necessary, then armies and the military-industrial complex become a component of the ERC—the economic relations of capitalism. Insurance companies are ERC. If you build automobiles, then that is output. If you produce food, it is output. Things that are neutral were considered output—like restaurants, for example. Other things are there only because we live in this type of society. If society *could* change, then these things would no longer be necessary. If they are not necessary for people to survive, then they would change under a different system. (12 Feb. 1991)

In Seymour Melman's opinion, Avukah received support from Zionist leaders because it was the only Zionist student organization around; it was their only conduit into the university community. In 1939–40, Melman received an Avukah travel fellowship, which he used to attend the World Zionist Congress in Geneva and to visit the Kibbutz Artzi near Haifa. On the kibbutz, he met up with some of his friends (such as Sylvia Binder, who had been the secretary of Avukah in 1935), and became acquainted with Arabs, Poles (Poland had just been overrun by the Nazis), and Palestinians. Upon returning to the United States in the spring of 1940, Melman contributed to a special issue of the Avukah newspaper, *Avukah Student Action*, which focused on the condition of the Yishuv, the prestate Jewish settlement in Palestine, and on the Arab and British reactions to it. Melman remembers that

The American Zionists were taken aback by the stiff demonstrations that the Yishuv ran against the laws which prohibited land purchase. There were massive riots in all the big cities. The support to the Yishuv at the time from American Zionists was abridged, limited, constrained, by their unwillingness to be negatively critical [of] Roosevelt and Churchill. That was dogma. The leadership group in Avukah had a rather different view—that of critical support, not unconditional support. That marked us off from almost all the rest of the mainstream Zionist organizations. (26 July 1994)

The views of Avukah's leadership group both mirror and reinforce the opinions that Chomsky held on the same issues as an undergraduate and later on.

Avukah's Call to Action

Avukah diverged from the much larger B'nai B'rith Hillel Foundation in its socialist orientation and in its support for a binational state. Chomsky describes the positions of the two groups: Avukah proposed "a binational state that is not a Jewish state," while B'nai B'rith was in favor of "a Jewish state," period (18 May 1995). On 27 June 1942, Avukah rejected Abram Sachar's proposal that Avukah affiliate nationally with the B'nai B'rith Hillel Foundation in order to maintain its independence. In a summer 1942 article in *Avukah Student Action* called "Front II: Jewish Organizations Don't Meet Real Needs," Milton Shapiro claimed that B'nai B'rith, like the American Jewish Committee, represented the upper-class and upper-middle-class Jews who were fighting anti-Semitism "from behind cloaks" and failing to address the needs of the majority of Jews.

By this point, the early 1940s, Chomsky was still a high-school student and Avukah was growing into an important organization that had chapters on at least sixty North American university campuses. In 1943, Avukah published another pamphlet, this one probably written by Zellig Harris, called *An Approach to Action: Facing the Social Insecurities Affecting the Jewish Position.* It discusses the Jewish situation against the backdrop of World War II and the problems that "victory alone cannot solve." The author assumes that two million Jews had perished in Europe thus far, and that eight million more had been taken prisoner. Furthermore, in the United States there was discrimination against Jews and "a great social distance and frequent mutual suspicion between Jews and non-Jews, which makes the Jews, whether 'Jewish financier' or 'Jewish Communist,' ideal scapegoats onto which mass resentment may be deflected."

At the time the pamphlet was published, many feared that not only Europe but also the United States would become fascist. *An Approach to Action* sounded a warning: "the society in which we live becomes more authoritarian, more intolerant of minority differences, more regimented and militarized, with the freedom of individuals more limited." Its author declared that "the more democratic the society in which we live, the safer we are," because fascism is intrinsic to any society in which underprivilege, poverty, working-class discontent, and monopoly capitalism are permitted to thrive. The pamphlet is a call to social action, to resistance, to Jewish participation in all organizations committed to social libertarianism.

Despite its cautionary tone, however, *An Approach to Action* does not explicitly equate the fascism of Nazi Germany with that detected in the United States; such an equation would require huge qualifications. But Epstein does note that

both Avukah and the Council Communists (e.g. in *Living Marxism*) and, at times, Dwight MacDonald (in *Politics*) predicted fascism ahead in the U.S. proper (we're not talking about countries dominated by the U.S.), and they were all dead wrong. Fascism involves domestic militarism, dictatorship, negation of civil liberties, suppression of unions, suppression of all political opposition, and not simply "underprivilege, poverty, discontent of the working people, and the growth of monopoly," which has almost always been endemic to capitalism. As Chomsky has so well described, control of the American population by techniques involving the "manufacture of consent" has been more effective than outright repression. (20 Apr. 1995)

Believing that it was vital to establish in Palestine a viable and secure alternative society in case the struggle against fascism failed, Avukah encouraged Jews to buy land, settle, develop agriculture and industry, and maintain "an economically planned and progressive social structure and cooperative relations with a large part of the Arab population" in that country. This two-tiered approach—promoting social change in America and preparing Palestine for Jewish immigration—was compatible and desirable because both tiers addressed, to quote *An Approach to Action*, "the actual condition of the people and pose[d] the fundamental question[s]: How can we improve the situation of the people? How can we prevent it from becoming worse?"

Chomsky shared the growing desire among young North American Jews, awakened and fueled by the efforts of organizations such as Avukah, to settle in Israel. So did his girlfriend, Carol Schatz.

Chomsky and Arthur Rosenberg

Chomsky was never actually a member of Avukah. It no longer existed by the time he arrived at university: "I only knew it as a kind of 'aura' in the background" (18 May 1995). Nevertheless, its fundamental values were clearly in line with his own, and he learned of its activities from Harris and from the writings of Arthur Rosenberg, among others. Chomsky actually read Rosenberg on Harris's suggestion. Rosenberg, who died in 1943 during World War II, had been closely involved with Avukah.

Avukah ran a summer school for two weeks each year, which was held at the training farm for the Zionist group Hashomer Hatzair. The 1941 lectures were given by Shmuel Ben-Zvi, D. Mcdonald (*not* Dwight Macdonald), I. Mereminski, Alfred Kahn, Nathan Glazer, Adrien Schwartz, and Arthur Rosenberg. Melman recalls Rosenberg's summer-school talk and several others he gave at about the same time:

Arthur Rosenberg spoke about the case of the Hitler-Stalin pact, saying that this was not to be taken as an omen that all was lost. In fact, there were dynamics in both German and Russian society that gave a basis for continued internal politics and differences. This was not to be taken for a signal of a deep freeze and total victory of the most conservative part of the Nazi movement. A few days after the German invasion of Russia, he gave a set of remarkable lectures on the coming character of the war, pointing out that in opposing the Soviet army, the Nazis for the first time would be doing battle with another army that was trained and equipped for armoured warfare. That in fact turned out to be the case, despite the catastrophic failures of the Soviet government in the first days of the war. (20 July 1994)

Rosenberg served as a kind of intellectual leader, a touchstone for the Avukah movement. His influence as a historian and social thinker—upon Chomsky and others—has remained strong over the years.

There are, however, some key differences between Rosenberg's orientation and that adopted by Chomsky. Abramovitch says that "Rosenberg's approach is historical and Marxist without trying to be moral," while Chomsky's is anarchist (4 Apr. 1995). Even so, there would have been ample grounds for discussion between the two during this period and long afterwards. Rosenberg's position on World War II, for example, is one that upholds fundamental libertarian principles; it precluded him from taking sides during the war. This position, which is rarely represented in contemporary examinations of the war, is well described by Abramovitch, who held a similar one. He maintains that Rosenberg believed

Nazi society could not stabilize itself, and would have crises, even if they were to emerge victorious from the war. It isn't a "last chance" because the crisis of capitalism will persevere even with a Nazi victory.... [Rosenberg's] position was one whereby if you are against the status quo, then you have to be consistent in that respect. The support of a war against Germany would not help the conditions or the preparation for a change in the status quo or in people's attitudes against a status-quo position. (12 Feb. 1991)

Avukah Student Action honored Arthur Rosenberg in its April 1943 issue, two months after his death. Rosenberg's work (*The Birth of the German Republic, A History of Bolshevism, The History of the German Republic,* and *Democracy and Socialism*) is commended for its contribution to an understanding of "how the greatest political changes of modern times came about." This work is referred to regularly in Chomsky's later writings. Despite their differences, both men emphasize the empirical, describing the actual events that demonstrate the value of their theory.

The mechanism of social change proposed by Rosenberg is summarized in the *Avukah Student Action* article "Prof. Rosenberg's Works Analyze the Great Changes of Our Times: His Writings on Russian and German Revolutions Have Lessons for Today." Rosenberg is quoted in the article, putting this suggestion to the journal's readers: "first, the particular social class gives the people in that class, sooner or later, a particular political attitude which is aimed at improving their conditions of life." And, "second, the political attitudes of underprivileged classes lead them, sooner or later, to try to change the political-economic system to their own betterment. Such attempts are almost always made by force, that is, by revolution, because the over-privileged class, which is in control of the political power will not normally give up its power and privileged position of its own free will."

This vision of how social change comes about, which in retrospect seems so optimistic, is picked up in Chomsky's work, yet modified so that particular emphasis is placed upon the powerful forces utilized by Rosenberg's "privileged class" to protect its "power and privileged position." Chomsky and Rosenberg also intersect on the issue of the individual versus the collective: both believe that social processes constitute a far more powerful force than individual efforts. Furthermore, each man initiates his analysis of a given action or event by posing a single question: "Does it strengthen the power and the political understanding of the working class?"

There is an Avukah-Rosenberg-Harris connection, as well. The two prominent intellectuals were made faculty-advisory-committee members, charged with guiding and directing Avukah groups throughout North America—even one as far north as Montreal. Harris lectured during the Avukah summer-school session in 1942 as Rosenberg had done the previous year. He gave three lectures: one on "native fascism" and two on "how Jews should be political." An article in that summer's *Avukah Student Action* summarizes these lectures, and sheds light on another link between Harris's and Chomsky's political positions: their sense that the dangers of fascism were not limited to Europe. In his native-fascism discussion, Harris addressed the dangers of fascism in the United States and the misconception among Jews that "only Axis agents and fifth columnists are a menace to democracy." Referring to the role that leaders of the

Avukah Summer School:

Front I: Fascism a Real Danger; Jews Not Secure, Warns Dr. Harris

Pointing to the alarming condition that American Jews are not realistically aware of the danger of fascism in this country, Dr. Zellig S. Harris, of the Faculty Advisory Committee, highlighted the political discussions of the Avukah Summer School.

Leading two highly important sessions—on the dangers of native fascism in the United States and the specific political needs of Jews—Dr. Harris emphasized that there can be no victory for real democracy if fascism wins out on the home front.

A popular misconception among Jews, Dr. Harris said, is that only

Dr. Harris indicated that American fascism, which, if it comes, would differ only in form from the German example, would thrive primarily on the critical social and economic inequalities of our present society. These conditions make for permanent discontent and widespread insecurity, and furnish fertile soil for fascist demagogy.

Pre-Hitler Germany was sunk in deep economic de-

Zellig Harris

character, plus a hyp ism and a sadistic ra served as a cover-up pro-big-business role Nazis.

Legal Fascis

Dr. Harris pointed fascism also won ev through legal chan than by "militarist mentioning Mussolin on Rome" in a sleepi many South America so-called "democrat ments are actually be talitarian-fascist ruler

Figure 8
A rare photo of Zellig Harris.

press, industry, and government played in antiliberal and antilabor initiatives, Harris spoke of the "permanent center for the forces of fascism" and claimed that if fascism came to America it "would differ only in form from the German example [and] would thrive primarily on the critical social and economic inequalities of our present society." Fascism, according to Harris, thrives on insecurity and discontent, and is aided by the propaganda of big-business interests: "The fascist concoction of promises of a pseudo-socialist character, plus a hyper-nationalism and a sadistic racial doctrine served as a cover-up for the real pro-big-business role of the Nazis." The only defense is to launch social-betterment programs and to make a commitment to social progress, efforts that would both be attacked by powerful business interests: "In the fight against native fascism, Dr. Harris emphasized the need of following closely the moves of the native fascists—the Coughlinites and their allies in big business, the press and public institutions—since the fascist menace is permanent in our stage of society, regardless of the turns in the war."

In his second lecture, Harris described the failure of Jewish religious and cultural groups to address the fundamental issues facing Jews, concluding that "Jews need a political program pointing out the need to guarantee security in this country and indicating the steps to be taken. Jews also need Palestine, for Jews who need or wish to go to a center where they will not be a minority. For many American Jews Palestine is a potential second home."

Chomsky and Montreal

There are several lines, many of which may be traced through Avukah, that connect Chomsky and Harris to the city of Montreal. A significant number of Chomsky acquaintances and commentators were originally from Montreal, among them Sam Abramovitch, Norman Epstein, Meyer Mendelson, and Willie Segal. One of the presses that has published or reprinted many of Chomsky's political works, Black Rose (the others are South End, Pantheon, and Z Magazine), is located in Montreal. *Manufacturing Consent*, the National Film Board of Canada film about Chomsky, was produced in that city by two Montrealers, Mark Achbar and Peter Wintonick. There are quite a few Chomsky-trained linguists teaching at various Montreal universities and colleges, including McGill University.

In May 1942, an article entitled "McGill Rallies Students to Fight Anti-Semitism" appeared in *Avukah Student Action*. It described an anticonscription rally, held in Montreal on 24 March 1942, which turned into a riot against Jews. McGill Avukah members claimed that the melee was part of a "well coordinated plan of fascist groups in Québec," such as L'Ordre de Jacques Cartier and the Canadian Party and observed that the rally had been publicized in the violently anti-Semitic newspaper *Chez Nous*. The article also pointed a finger at certain individuals: Adrian Arcand (an anti-Semitic fascist), M. Raymond, M.P., and M. Bourassa (Quebec isolationist nationalists), and M. Bouchard. Rather than simply reporting on the activities of these profascists, the article asks, "Why has fascism grown in Quebec?" The answer recalls Harris's analysis of the social basis of fascism: "Because of the atrociously low standard of living in Quebec, the poor education system, the dire poverty, many thousands were swayed by these reactionary movements. The underpaid and op-

Figure 9
Issues of *Avukah Student Action*.

pressed French-Canadian workers in, for example, Dominion Textiles, took faith in organizations which promised to alleviate this condition." The approach taken in 1942 to address Quebec's problems is particularly interesting in light of contemporary discussions concerning the future of Quebec as a province of Canada. Class analysis, which would emphasize the fascistic aspects of corporate capitalism and nationalism, is as conspicuously absent from the debate today as it was then.

Zellig Harris and The People

A small, little-known group, "The People," also benefited from Harris's involvement. My knowledge of it comes solely from a single, unpublished, typed document—a kind of manifesto—sent to me by Norman Epstein. Harris may well be its author. The People, according to the first paragraph of the document,

> are in various measures disturbed by the suffering, inefficiency, dishonesty, inequality, lack of freedom, bourgeois and automaton character structures, etc., which occur in this culture; feel limited and insecure in the carrying out of their own work and career lines; believe that if anything can be done to improve things ... [it] is determinable only by careful empirical observation and scientific analysis. [Some would] be prepared to change their present occupations, e.g. to enter workers' occupations.

Group members (despite one or two exceptions) did not "intend to use their political interests in advancing their careers"; they vowed to "work cooperatively, without officers or orders"; and they often functioned in groups. Authors of their reports and publications were "rarely named." They "assume[d] nothing as being true *ex cathedra*, no person as repository of authority or truth." In the domain of economic and historical analysis, they claimed, "Marx fits the facts and is useful for prediction." The elements of this society that the group considered unsatisfactory would continue to exist "as long as there is a controlling class, wages and profits, and a lack of complete freedom in the utilization of the means of production." The People did not believe that reform is possible within the framework of the capitalist society, or that any bureaucratic structure, any attempt to manage or lead the people, "will in the long run aid in the development in the desired direction."

The document makes reference to historical-materialist works such as those of Erich Fromm (of the Frankfurt School) and Arthur Rosenberg, as well as works of American cultural anthropology, modern natural sciences, and mathematical logic. All of this points to a vital connection between Harris and The People, since Harris also combined his interest in Rosenberg's anti-Bolshevik Marxism with a commitment to Fromm's psychoanalytic-Marxist work.

The People had no dogma, Marxist or otherwise, and members pulled together as a "way of resisting the present social order, of helping spread the resistance to it." They did not consider themselves working-class leaders, although they did agree that revolution or "collapse" were the only means of ending present power relations. Finally, their route to social change lay in the

compiling of such information about the economy and culture and the control methods and development of the ruling class, and about the change of technology, social relations, working-class attitudes, etc., as would be useful to the political understanding and action of an increasingly restive working-class; the reduction of the methods of science to a form that will be graspable and usable by workers in the understanding and control of their social and natural environment; the development of the theory and prediction of social change; and the dissemination and elaboration of scientifically valid social-political discussion among those who may be expected to act, in terms of their position and times, in the direction of a free, egalitarian, classless society.

The tenets and values upheld by Chomsky in his work relate strongly to those set forth here either by Harris or his close associates in The People. Chomsky resists the suggestion that he was influenced by Frankfurt School members such as Adorno, Fromm, Horkheimer, Lowenthal, or Marcuse. But the importance of such figures to Zellig Harris, and by extension to groups such as Avukah, the Council for Arab-Jewish Cooperation, or The People, does imply that the Frankfurt School had an at least indirect effect on Chomsky's development.

Chomsky, Seymour Melman, and the Council for Arab-Jewish Cooperation

Chomsky made contact with Avukah through the knowledge and ideas of Zellig Harris, and, later on, through his friendship with former Avukah members such as Seymour Melman (who served as executive secretary). Melman is older than Chomsky (by about seven or eight years). The two became reacquainted in the 1960s, when Chomsky discovered Melman's work. They then established a close friendship. Chomsky now knows that Melman was compiling accomplishments well before this time. Both Harris and Melman were also associated with a group that grew out of the left wing of Avukah, known as the Council for Arab-Jewish Cooperation. Its main activity was publishing the *Bulletin of the Council on Jewish-Arab Cooperation*, 1944–1949. Its principal writers were Harris and his wife, Bruriah. The bulletin, which also had some Hebrew and Arabic issues, was respected by people like Hannah Arendt. Chomsky has expressed his respect for this organization and its publication on many occasions, notably in a passage from *Peace in the Middle East? Reflections on Justice and Nationhood* in which, citing a 1947 issue of the bulletin, he comments that the council focused on "the possibilities for independent political action by workers as a class, as contrasted to reliance on decisions of any of the big powers" (64). In a note Chomsky adds, "I should emphasize that my own point of view was heavily influenced by this group and a number of the people associated with it" (89), of whom Seymour Melman was the most important. When asked about Melman, Chomsky replies that he did "important work on workers self-management in the '50s, and was the only person, along with Lawrence B. Cohen, to have developed the major ideas that animated Harris and his circle in the late 1940s, when they were working intensively on all this, within the framework that Harris describes in his posthumous [unpublished political] manuscript" (31 Mar. 1995).

Melman trained in economics and industrial engineering and worked at Columbia University. In 1956, someone gave the university a grant to investigate the feasibility of developing an inspection procedure that would prevent the violation of a disarmament system; Melman ran the project. As a result, *Inspection for Disarmament* was published, with Melman as editor. He went on to become director of a wide-ranging series of studies and acquired a detailed understanding of the whole military complex, which he described in *Pentagon Capitalism: The Political Economy of War*.

Chomsky and the League for Arab-Jewish Rapprochement

There were other attempts to encourage Arab-Jewish cooperation with which Chomsky had great sympathy. For example, he remembers that he "read all the stuff" and had "great sympathies" for the work of the League for Arab-Jewish Rapprochement. This organization, which had been founded in Israel and was headed by an Israeli orange-grove farmer named Chaim Kalvarisky, upheld beliefs in Jewish-Arab working-class cooperation and anti-imperialism; its members, like Avukah's, were not in favor of the creation of a Jewish state. In the April 1942 edition of *Avukah Student Action*, Margolith Shelubsky explained that the league, which was founded in 1938, "comprises Arab and Jewish individuals and groups who see the need for working for rapprochement between the two peoples. Its activities are chiefly in the economic and social fields." Cited in her article was a report, written by Moshe Smilansky, that discussed the role foreign influences played in promoting the "Arab terror" of 1936–39:

The terror was never an outbreak of basic hatred towards Jews but rather an expression of temporary anger, inspired by foreign forces. Evidence of this can be found in the fact that when the terror stopped Jews and Arabs met once again as good friends and good neighbours. Even after the long period of terror, which many feared was permanent and deep rooted, Arabs literally fell into the arms of their Jewish neighbours and asked for peace. Even during the terror, there was evidence that basic friendship and trust existed. Arabs made use of Jewish medical and social services. The hostile relations stemmed from foreign influences. Today we witness Arab-Jewish rapprochement taking place naturally, almost spontaneously in many areas.

Regrettably, the league's project was not as rosy as one would gather from this report. Chomsky himself notes that "in retrospect, I'm afraid that most of this was wish-fulfillment, including the whole Avukah-League for Arab Rapprochement story, but I did believe it at the time" (31 Mar. 1995).

Chomsky and Hashomer Hatzair

Chomsky did have direct contact (through many of his friends) and even a loose affiliation with another group that was related to Avukah:

Hashomer Hatzair. Unlike Avukah, this group was still active when Chomsky arrived at the University of Pennsylvania. It still exists today. As a graduate student, Chomsky was sympathetic to the commitment Hashomer Hatzair had made to support socialist binationalism in Palestine and kibbutz values.

He has said that although he "was never a member of any group," he was "fairly close to ... Hashomer Hatzair, but couldn't join because it was split between Stalinists and Trotskyites and I very strongly disagreed with both of them on Marxism-Leninism" (31 Mar. 1995). The organization was founded in Lemberg, Poland, in 1917. According to Norman Epstein, "Hashomer Hatzair was a strong, well-organized Zionist-Socialist youth movement in Europe [and] North and South America which prepared young Jewish boys and girls for life on a kibbutz in Palestine (later, Israel), expedited their immigration and integration into a kibbutz ('making aliyah') and later became the main component of the Zionist left-wing political party in Israel—MAPAM (which is now part of the coalition known as Meretz)" (15 Dec. 1994).

Hashomer Hatzair's similarities to Avukah are obvious. The two groups also interacted; Avukah, for example, distributed pamphlets (such as *Youth Amidst Ruins*) for Hashomer Hatzair from its office in New York City. However, while Avukah was concentrated within American college campuses, Hashomer Hatzair had (and continues to enjoy) strong working-class ties and an international profile.

Zellig Harris, though not a member of Hashomer Hatzair, had contact with its members, as did Seymour Melman and Norman Epstein; Sam Abramovitch was the director of the Montreal-area branch. Members of the organization played important roles in the Warsaw Ghetto uprising against the Nazis in 1943, and former members went on to undertake important intellectual and political work.

There seem to have been differences between the branches of Hashomer Hatzair. Like Chomsky, Epstein recollects that "the membership of Hashomer Hatzair and subsequently MAPAM was various in its ideology, but the leadership for a long time was Leninist and even Stalinist (except when Stalin showed anti-Semitic tendencies or was explicitly anti-Zionist)" (15 Dec. 1994). He further remembers that "around 1942 there was a short-lived Left Jewish Youth Alliance in Montreal, consisting of

Avukah, the Outremont Cooperative Commonwealth Youth Move-ment (ie. CCF Youth), Hashomer Hatzair, and ex-members of Hashomer Hatzair" (20 Apr. 1995). Abramovitch, on the other hand, recalls no such political affiliation in the Montreal branch, suggesting that it upheld ostensibly Zionist socialist ideals, and citing its connection with the anti-Stalinist Second-and-a-Half International. This particular International is little known, although its members, according to Epstein, included a number of influential groups, such as "Hashomer Hatzair, the Austrian Socialists, the Independent Labour Party in Britain and, I believe, the Sozialistische Arbeiter Partei of Germany, which broke away from the Social Democratic Party around 1930" (20 Apr. 1995). Chomsky himself had no contact with the Montreal group: "I knew the people in Phila-delphia and New York mostly. Remember, in those days people of our income level rarely traveled anywhere. I didn't get to West Philadelphia until I went to Penn, and regarded Gettysburg as far West" (15 Dec. 1994).

Whatever ideological differences existed between the branches of Hashomer Hatzair, its various members and associates worked to in-crease working-class participation in the organization itself, to encourage emigration to its affiliated kibbutzim in Israel (notably Kibbutz Artzi), and to promulgate communist ideals for Israeli kibbutzim. Hashomer Hatzair was particularly active in Europe, where anti-Semitism was well entrenched and menacing.

Like Avukah—and indeed like Chomsky (from a Jewish perspective) and Edward Said (from a Palestinian perspective)—Hashomer Hatzair believed in Arab-Jewish cooperation, first in Palestine and then in Israel. An example of this kind of cooperation is given in a report issued by the League for Arab-Jewish Cooperation and relayed in an April 1942 *Avukah Student Action* article. According to the article, the Kibbutz Artzi, of the National Federation of Hashomer Hatzair,

recently started activity which is significant in establishing contact with neighbor-ing Arab villages. The Kibbutz Artzi has organized courses to train agents who will establish contact with Arab villages that are near Kibbutzim ... [and who will] seek to strengthen favorable attitudes to Zionism among Arabs. Some 300 are now taking courses which teach Arabic, Arab customs, and Arab community life. It is hoped that about one-seventh of the Arab village communities will be reached by workers trained in these courses.

Chomsky's "Anti-Zionism," Then and Now

Despite his loose, often indirect, connections to such Jewish organizations as Avukah and Hashomer Hatzair, Chomsky has, for many years, been branded an anti-Zionist by a large segment of American Jews. This has happened because he evaluates Israeli government actions according to the same criteria he uses to judge the actions of any government, and, moreover, because he does not support the idea that Israel should be a Jewish state. Reactionary Zionists confuse apology for Israeli state-sponsored terror and aggression against Palestinians or Arabs (or other out-groups) with Zionism, and, further, misconstrue Chomsky's position as anti-Zionist.

When Chomsky talks about a binational state, he is talking about the former Palestine, and thus refers back to pre-1948 plans to establish a socialist state in Palestine that would include equal participation of Arabs and Jews. If these plans, which were furthered by then-Zionist groups, had been realized, much of the violence that has occurred in the Middle East, and in Israel itself, might have been prevented. Just as a close look at the Spanish Civil War shows the power and the libertarian nature of anarchosyndicalism, an examination of Jewish labor movements in Israel shows the viability of efforts to establish a workers' socialist republic. Many so-called Zionists don't recognize this, and accordingly condemn Chomsky's work in this area.

In June of 1995, a press named after Avukah launched its first publication: *Partners in Hate: Noam Chomsky and the Holocaust Deniers*, by Werner Cohn, professor emeritus at the University of British Columbia. Norman Epstein explains how something such as this could occur: "In the later years of Avukah, the organization split into a Centre Right (e.g., Nat Glazer, Seymour Lipset) and a Left (e.g., Melman, Harris); apparently the [Centre] Right has now captured the name" (6 July 1995). The suggestion that there is any relationship between the now-defunct organization named Avukah and Avukah Press, is, according to Chomsky, "sheer fraud." He correctly notes that

Glazer-Lipset have not had the remotest connection with anything associated with Avukah or its ideals for half a century (in Lipset's case, ever, to my knowledge).

The name "Avukah" was dredged up in recognition of the fact that it would be more effective to pretend that the criticism is coming from the left than from where it really is, the ultra-right and extreme jingoist sector of pro-Israel fanaticism, with neo-Nazi connections via its support for Kahane. I presume that it was Glazer's idea to resurrect the name "Avukah." No one else in those circles would have heard of it. What they are hoping, of course, is that someone will catch the association (or if not, they'll bring it up themselves) [.] [They want] to insinuate that even the good leftie libertarian anti-Jewish state people are appalled by my awful doings—far more effective than to say that Kahanist ultrarightists are. (14 Aug. 1995)

A Place of His Own

In the meantime, Chomsky's unconventional graduate education continued. Due to the efforts made on his behalf by Nelson Goodman and others, Chomsky was, in 1951, named to the Society of Fellows at Harvard. One might imagine that despite the intellectual promise such a position must have held for him, a person with Chomsky's social background and views on education would have experienced feelings of revulsion at the thought of entering such an institution. Chomsky does, in fact, relate a humorous anecdote about this:

I grew up in a lower-middle class urban environment without any particular social graces, and when I went to Harvard as a graduate student in the early 1950s, in a special high-class research outfit that had all sorts of prestigious elite people, I discovered that a large part of the education was simply refinement, social graces, what kinds of clothes to wear, how to have polite conversation that isn't too serious, all the other things that an intellectual is supposed to do. I remember a couple of years later asking a distinguished English professor from Oxford, which was the model that this organization was attempting to imitate, how he thought that Harvard's imitation compared with Oxford's original. He thought for a while and he said that he thought it was the difference between genuine superficiality and phoney superficiality. We only had phoney superficiality, while they had genuine superficiality. This is a large part of what is called education. And it is teaching conformity to certain norms that keeps you from interfering with people in power and all sorts of other things. ("Creation")

Upon arriving in Cambridge, Chomsky discovered which intellectual trends ruled the day, and the disquiet this discovery filled him with would later contribute to his critiques of behaviorism. He was, however, also very happy to learn that at Harvard he would be able, for the first time in his life, to devote himself entirely to study and research. The stipend that accompanied his position meant that he no longer had to support himself with nonacademic jobs.

In the early 1950s, debate was raging over the breakthroughs that new technology was promising in the understanding of human behavior. Computers, electronics, acoustics, mathematical theories of communication and cybernetics were all in vogue, and researchers were busy exploiting them. Chomsky, a graduate student in his early twenties, was uneasy with this activity: "Some people, myself included, were rather concerned about these developments, in part for political reasons, at least as far as my motivations were concerned because this whole complex of ideas seemed linked to potentially quite dangerous political currents: manipulative, and connected with behaviorist concepts of human nature" (*Language and Politics* 44).

He had no way of confirming his suspicions about this type of research. Instead, he began to pursue what he thought of as hobbies; these were, specifically, concerted attempts to rethink the nature of human language in ways that would refute behaviorist currents. Two years later, it dawned on him that this work was far more promising than the research being conducted in the academy. "[O]nly about 1953 did I realize that the hobby was on the right track, and the whole structuralist approach, including everything I had thought was the real stuff, was beside the point—in fact, pretty worthless, to be honest" (13 Dec. 1994).

On the heels of this realization (which occurred while he was en route to Europe by boat and "desperately seasick"), the twenty-five-year-old Chomsky broke "almost entirely from the field as it existed" (3 Apr. 1995). It was a dramatic break, and one that he has never regretted. In some of his later work (*Syntactic Structures* and *Logical Structure of Linguistic Theory*), Chomsky even insists that linguists should abandon their hopeless quest for discovery procedures (that is, structural linguistics), "at least insofar," he has remarked in a letter, "as it [goes] beyond parts of phonology and ha[s] theoretical aspirations"; they should instead shoulder the "more modest task of finding evaluation procedures" (as he did for the first time in *Morphophonemics of Modern Hebrew*). "The methods they were proposing could not possibly lead to evaluation procedures, a concept unknown to structural linguistics and remote in conception from it, at a very fundamental level; it assumes a realist rather than operationalist stand, for one thing. The 'principles and parameters' approach did make it possible to reconstitute something like 'discovery procedures,' but now in a framework so radically different that comparison is meaningless" (31 Mar. 1995).

During this period, Chomsky not only deepened his commitment to linguistic studies but also continued to work in related fields. He was making contact with a great number of influential Cambridge-area teachers and students, including Yehoshua Bar-Hillel, Peter Elias, Anatol Holt, Eric Lenneberg, Israel Scheffler, W. V. O. Quine, and Roman Jakobson. Chomsky and Jakobson, one of the founders of the formalist approach to literary criticism, met at Harvard in 1951. Although they differed profoundly in approach (Chomsky says that Jakobson "hadn't the faintest interest or understanding of anything I was doing" [13 Dec. 1994], they became friends and remained so until Jakobson's death. Chomsky's closest friend was fellow student Morris Halle, at the time one of Jakobson's "main" students (and a researcher at the MIT electronics laboratory).

Quine is frequently mentioned in discussions of Chomsky's philosophical work, because Chomsky eventually renounced Quine's dispositions on the acquisition of knowledge of language:

[I]t took Chomsky several years to come to the realization that no inductive process ever proposed could lead from the kind of data that are available to the child to principles of the abstraction required in the theory of language, which can only mean that these principles are not determined by the data by anything resembling induction, a conclusion which is in sharp contrast with Quine's view that "the philosophy of inductive logic" is "in no way distinguishable from philosophy's main stem, the theory of knowledge," as he puts it in the opening lines of his *Philosophy of Logic*. (Otero, "Chomsky and the Rationalist" 4)

In the summer of 1954 Chomsky was asked to present material on grammaticality and degrees of grammaticality to the Linguistics Institute in Chicago; he was also invited to give a series of talks at Yale by Bernard Bloch, who had taken an interest in his (as yet unpublished) work. But although Chomsky's early linguistic work was fresh and promising, much of what he was doing remained relatively unknown within the academy. Chomsky was still an outsider to the field, and, despite these signals of recognition from Chicago and Yale, was most often limited to speaking at computer centers and psychology seminars. He did manage to publish a few reviews and articles, often outside the field of linguistics.

The Chomskys in Israel

In 1953, while Noam was still a member of Harvard's Society of Fellows, he and Carol decided to spend some time in Israel, a country in which both, for a long time, had thought of settling. In the end, however, they simply went and lived on a kibbutz for about six weeks. This experience was still an important one for the couple, because it allowed them to see what life could be like in a successful left-libertarian community where people engaged in manual labor and intellectual work. Noam was assessed as unskilled upon his arrival at the kibbutz, which was called Ha-Zorea, and so he became a supervised agricultural laborer. This was a very poor kibbutz. There was little food, lots of hard work, and, most importantly, what Noam described as an "ideological conformity." He became uneasy with "the exclusiveness and the racist institutional setting" (*Chomsky Reader 9*); he was even more disturbed that "these highly educated and perceptive left Buberites couldn't see it" (31 Mar. 1995).

The Israeli state had been established in 1947–48. Noam had been opposed to its creation as he feared the socialist institutions of the Yishuv and the potentially binational character of Palestine would be rejected in favor of the state system. While in Israel, he had withessed non-Jews being marginalized and "treated rather shabbily, with a good deal of contempt and fear" (*Chomsky Reader 9*), and his personal experience of this double standard justified his doubts about the virtues of a religious state.

The kibbutz where the Chomskys stayed had a Buberite orientation, and was populated by well-educated German Jews. The Chomskys' stay there coincided with the Slansky trials in Czechoslovakia and the last stages of the Stalin purges, which, strangely enough, found supporters even on this kibbutz. Although the ideological differences that Noam had with some fellow kibbutzniks were not what motivated him to leave, and although Carol had hoped to stay on, they both returned to Cambridge, and Noam received an extension from the society until 1955. Carol did go back for six months in 1955, and then returned to Cambridge with the intention of moving permanently to Israel with Noam; but "for one or another reason," Noam writes, "I'm not sure exactly why, it never happened" (31 Mar. 1995).

Dr. Noam Chomsky

On the strength of having submitted just one chapter of his thesis, Chomsky received his Ph.D. from the University of Pennsylvania in 1955. Except for the relationships he maintained with Goodman and Harris, Chomsky's ties to that university had been severed in 1951, and other than presenting this chapter he fulfilled no formal obligation for the degree. The period during which he had written his thesis, which delineated the basics of much of his later work, had been an intense but solitary one for him. In virtual isolation, he labored with "incredible intensity." "In looking back, I don't see how it was possible. In just a few months I wrote my book of close to 1,000 pages, and it had in it just about everything that I've done since, at least in a rough form" (*Language and Politics* 129).

This huge work was finally published (minus some of the technical material) in 1975 as *The Logical Structure of Linguistic Theory*. Its origins have, for a long time, been a source of confusion, although the history of the manuscript has been set out in the book's introduction: "During the fall semester of 1955 I revised several chapters of *The Logical Structure of Linguistic Theory*. At that time, two microfilms were made by Harvard Libraries, one of the 1955 version and one of the partially edited and revised January 1956 version. It is these two microfilms and the duplicated 1955 version that have been distributed over the years. I have not kept count, but there must be well over 1000 copies" (*Logical Structure* 3).

Chomsky did submit portions of the work to the Technology Press of MIT (which later became The MIT Press), but "it was rejected, with the not unreasonable observation that an unknown author taking a rather unconventional approach should submit articles based on this material to professional journals before planning to publish such a comprehensive and detailed manuscript as a book" (*Logical Structure* 3). The reason Chomsky had not tried to have sections of the work published in professional (that is, linguistic) journals "is that what I was actually doing had virtually no detectable relation to linguistics—at least, structural linguistics as practiced in the U.S. and Europe. That includes all of Harris's work" (31 Mar. 1995). The manuscript that was eventually published in 1975 contained portions of both the 1955 version and the 1956 version. In 1958, Chomsky was made a National Science Foundation fellow at the Institute for Advanced Study at Princeton University, during which time he revised six chapters of *Logical Structure*.

The strange history of this text is recounted by Frank Heny in his 1979 review of the book for the journal *Synthèse*. Heny points out that the book was written twenty years before its publication, and that it laid the foundations for an entirely new field of research: what has come to be known as transformational grammar. The manuscript of *Logical Structure* circulated within a small group of academics, and therefore remained "little more than a vague rumor. Yet the arguments for Chomsky's particular brand of transformational analysis, even in that confusing, degenerate and often grossly distorted form in which they were passed from hand to hand somehow won the day. The grammatical transformation very soon achieved undisputed dominance—at least in American linguistics" (308). So, by the mid-1950s, Noam Chomsky, a newly minted scholar, stood at the forefront of a nonexistent field. He was also unemployed.

Wherefore Zellig Harris?

During the tenure of his Harvard fellowship (1951–55) Chomsky spent much of his time in Cambridge, but still maintained his relationship with Zellig Harris, who continued to teach at the University of Pennsylvania. From the mid-1950s on, however, Chomsky had little contact with Harris, and from the mid-1960s none at all. Harris's linguistics project, as we have seen, became of marginal interest to Chomsky, who had by then taken off in a different direction. Linguistics, at that time, looked to Chomsky as though it were destined to reproduce the same exercise to the point of absurdity:

I remember as a student being intrigued [by linguistics]—the problems were fun and everything—but we were all wondering what we were going to do in ten years. Suppose you've done a phonemic analysis of every language. Suppose you've done an ic [immediate constituent] analysis of every language. It's fun to do. It's like a cross-word puzzle. It's challenging and hard. But it's going to be over in ten years. That's the way the field looked. It looked as if it were essentially over. (qtd. in R. A. Harris 83)

Zellig Harris, Chomsky recalls, "had this idea of trying to do something new by looking at the structure of discourse. He tried to use the features of linguistic analysis for discourse analysis" (qtd. in R. A. Harris 83). From this project discourse analysis was born. Chomsky was in search of transformations "to model the linguistic knowledge in a native speaker's head," while Harris was interested in "such practical purposes as machine translation and automated information retrieval" (R. A. Harris 84). Their linguistic interests were irrevocably diverging. Chomsky's last communications with Harris were in the early 1960s, "when [Harris] asked me to [approach] contacts at the [National Science Foundation] for a research contract for him, which I did. We then spent a couple of days together in Israel, in 1964. After that, there was no contact. No falling out, just a mutual understanding, better left unsaid" (23 June 1994).

Prior to his death in the early 1990s, Harris completed a political book, which he wanted to publish in England because he felt that the working classes there were more highly developed. It has just recently been accepted for publication, thanks to the efforts of Harris's wife, Bruria, and those of Seymour Melman, Norman Epstein, and others. Both Chomsky and Melman read the book in manuscript form, and Chomsky remarked that it contained "many interesting things." Melman assisted with the scholarly apparatus of the manuscript and sent it on to Chomsky, who contributed "a few missing references and the like" (18 Feb. 1993).

For those who know Chomsky and knew Harris, their relationship, despite its early demise, remains important for many reasons. The values, the intellectual rigor, and the concern for emancipatory movements that pervade the many works of both men testify to their tenacity and integrity as intellectuals and individuals. They inspired one another. Russell Jacoby does not mention Harris in his work *The Last Intellectuals: American Culture in the Age of Academe*, but what he says about Chomsky, Murray Bookchin, Paul Goodman, and Isaac Rosenfeld could be applied equally to Harris: "to the extent that they are anarchists, they distrust large institutions, the state, the university, and its functionaries. They are less vulnerable to the corruptions of title and salary because their resistance is moral, almost instinctual." Marxists charge that anarchists think ethically, not strategically. Jacoby, however, is convinced that this is one source of their power: "Marxist intellectuals can and do convince themselves to subordinate mind and ethics to a larger goal or distant cause that frequently slips out of sight. Anarchist intellectuals are less susceptible to this logic. To use the language of historical materialism, it is no accident that currently an anarchist, Noam Chomsky, is the most energetic critic of intellectuals apologizing for American foreign policy" (96–97).

Chomsky Arrives at MIT

In 1955, Chomsky's friend Roman Jakobson arranged for him to work as a researcher at the Massachusetts Institute of Technology. Chomsky, in his own words, "had no identifiable field or credentials in anything" (13 Dec. 1994), but MIT, "a scientific university which didn't care much about credentials," was willing to overlook his lack of certifiable "professional competence" (23 June 1994). Chomsky was made an assistant professor and assigned, ironically, to a machine translation project of the type he had often criticized. The project was directed by Victor Yngve and was being conducted at the MIT Research Laboratory of Electronics, which was subsidized by the U.S. military.

While he was being interviewed by laboratory director Jerome Wiesner for the position, Chomsky stated that the project had "no intellectual interest and was also pointless." Perhaps due to his candor, but also because Wiesner thought that his ideas were intriguing, Chomsky was hired as a full-time faculty member, which meant that he was required to spend half his time working in the research lab and the other half teaching—"pretty standard," he says, "for MIT faculty" (27 June 1995). He actually "never touched the translation project," and still speaks of it dismissively: "It may have [had] some utility; it could be on the par with building a bigger bulldozer, which is a useful thing. It's nice to have big bulldozers if you have to dig holes" (23 June 1994).

The immediate problem Chomsky faced was, as he puts it: "What was I going to do with my half-time teaching?" (27 June 1995). He started by giving "cram courses to graduate students offered by the Modern Languages Department as a service to help them fake their way through Ph.D. reading exams (now thankfully abandoned)" (31 Mar. 1995), even though he had never studied French and barely knew German. He was "also allowed to take over a course on language that had been in the undergraduate catalogue, and run it as I liked" (27 June 1995). Teaching this course was to be an extremely important experience for Chomsky; while doing so, he was able to elucidate some of his own ideas; it provided him with the opportunity to discuss with his students the idea of a generative grammar.

The institute was a comfortable place for the twenty-seven-year-old Chomsky: "I also began to teach undergraduate philosophy courses there, and later was able to help establish what became a very distinguished philosophy department. The Massachusetts Institute of Technology has always been a pretty free and open place, open to experimentation and without rigid requirements. It was just perfect for someone of my idiosyncratic interests and work" (27 June 1995).

This was a fruitful time for Chomsky. He writes that (machine translation project aside) "the Research laboratory of Electronics ... provided a most stimulating interdisciplinary environment for research of the sort that I wanted to pursue" (*Logical Structure* 2). Here, his *Aspects of the Theory of Syntax* was hatched. In the acknowledgments of that work, he describes the facility as "an interdepartmental laboratory in which faculty members and graduate students from numerous academic departments conduct research."

The funding for the research published in *Aspects* was provided by "the Joint Services Electronics Programs (U.S. Army, Navy and Air Force), the Electronics Systems Division of the U.S. Air Force, the National Science Foundation, the National Institutes of Health, and NASA." The link between these organizations and the university, the role of the intellectual, and the relationship between scientific and nonscientific research are all issues that have been raised with regard to Chomsky's own connection to MIT and to the university environment as a whole. They take on a greater urgency at a later stage in his academic career.

The Birth of Cognitive Science and the Publication of *Syntactic Structures*

The importance of Chomsky's work became evident quite soon after he was hired by MIT. In September of 1956, the twenty-seven-year-old

Chomsky delivered a paper entitled "Three Models for the Description of Language" as part of a three-day MIT symposium on information theory. According to Otero, the paper contained "the essential elements in [Chomsky's] innovative approach to language" ("Chomsky and the Cognitive Revolution" 14–15). Allen Newell and Herbert Simon presented work on problem solving with a "logic machine," and there were papers on signal detection and human information processing. This symposium—and these papers in particular—has been considered by some to mark the launch of the study of cognitive science.

At the suggestion of Morris Halle, Chomsky then showed some of his lecture notes for the undergraduate course on language he was teaching to Cornelis Van Schoonefeld, the editor of a series entitled Janua Linguarum, which was put out by Mouton, a Dutch press. Schoonefeld offered to publish the notes. They appeared in 1957 in the form of a monograph called *Syntactic Structures*. Like *Morphophonemics of Modern Hebrew* and *The Logical Structure of Linguistic Theory*, it radically opposes the entire Harris-Bloomfield tradition, though it does contain this frequently quoted remark: "During the entire period of this research I have had the benefit of very frequent and lengthy conversations with Zellig S. Harris. So many of his ideas and suggestions are incorporated into the text below and in the research on which it is based that I will make no attempt to indicate them by special reference" (6). It is apparent that Chomsky said this out of his great respect for Harris, but, as he explains, "on the understanding that every linguist who reads [the monograph] would understand, without my saying so explicitly, that I'm urging that the entire picture should be abandoned, from the ground up. I just didn't want to say that explicitly, for personal reasons. But it is explicit in the texts, and was obvious to professional linguists right away" (31 Mar. 1995).

Chomsky's work during this period, described in *Morphophonemics, Logical Structure*, and *Syntactic Structures*, was a rejection of the prevailing mandate of procedural linguistics (to seek an array of operations that can be employed to reduce a corpus to an organized form suited to a given analyst's goals). He was looking, instead, for ways to "find the truth about language and linguistic theory" (31 Mar. 1995)—that is, he sought a universal grammar. It was clear to others in the field that Chomsky was posing a very serious challenge. Otero claims that among linguists "the reaction in the early years ranged from indifference to hostility," depending upon the domain. There was "great hostility with regard to the work on phonology (where the efforts were concentrated when he appeared on the scene), either hostility or total incomprehension with regard to the general picture (which was well beyond their purview), and indifference for the most part with regard to the work on syntax, a field which until then had not received too much attention ..." ("Chomsky and the Challenges" 13–14).

Just as Orwell's *Homage to Catalonia* was, for a long time, not accepted for distribution in North America because it contradicted the accepted view of the Spanish Civil War, Chomsky's *Syntactic Structures* diverged so radically from the standard opinion that it was not even mentioned in current reviews of American linguistics. Chomsky recalls a solitary exception, perhaps by Harold Allen, "which did mention *Syntactic Structures*, but as Dutch, probably thinking that I was Dutch. It's also the reason why nothing could be published here, for years" (31 Mar. 1995).

The most important early review was by Robert Lees, who had asked to review the book before it was available, even in galleys. Lees was committed to the Harris model but nevertheless went to MIT in 1956 to work on the mechanical translation project. Encountering Chomsky there, he became convinced by his approach and went on to publish, in 1960, a book on transformational generative grammar entitled *The Grammar of English Nominalizations*, which was based on his dissertation. Lees's review was published in the influential journal *Language* in 1957; at that time, the journal was being edited by Bernard Bloch, who, "almost alone in the profession, was in favour of expression of a position that radically departed from the orthodoxy" (42).

"Chomsky's book on syntactic structures," Lees wrote, "is one of the first serious attempts on the part of a linguist to construct within the tradition of scientific theory-construction a comprehensive theory of language which may be understood in the same sense that a chemical, biological theory is ordinarily understood in those fields." Lees anticipated the dramatic shift that this book would generate, noting that,

it is not a mere reorganization of the data into a new kind of library catalogue, nor another speculative philosophy about the nature of Man and Language, but rather a rigorous explication of our intuitions about our language in terms of an overt axiom system, the theorems derivable from it, explicit results which may be compared with new data and other intuitions, all based plainly on an overt theory of the internal structure of languages; and it may well provide an opportunity for the application of explicit measures of simplicity to decide preference of one form over another form of grammar. (42)

Although, as Chomsky has remarked, Lees "did what he thought was important," he was later thrown out of his research position for insubordination. Chomsky explains:

What happened is that [Victor] Yngve's project was continually hiring very good linguists, but they all went the same way I did, at various rates. I'd made it clear even before I was appointed that I didn't think the project made any sense. Others (Lees, Matthews, Lukoff ...) had varying views about the matter, and did work on aspects of it. But gradually they all reached the same conclusion, and began to concentrate more and more on straight linguistics, then in a real ferment at MIT. Yngve wasn't happy about it: he was dedicated to machine translation. He's the one who fired Lees, in a pretty ugly way. (13 Feb. 1996)

Lees was finally admitted, thanks to the intervention of Chomsky and Halle, into the electrical-engineering department, where he eventually got a Ph.D. in linguistics, although he was regarded in the field as a kind of "traitor" (31 Mar. 1995).

Another review of *Syntactic Structures*, this one by John Lyons (who went on to write a very early study of Chomsky, in 1970), concludes with the statement: "Chomsky's whole discussion of the relations between syntax and semantics will stimulate the interest of linguists in these problems and that is all to the good. His treatment of the external criteria of adequacy and the internal properties of grammars of the kind considered in this book makes a definite contribution to the theory of their construction" (87).

In fact, Chomsky's own sense, then as now, was that the significance of *Syntactic Structures* was quite small, even "almost irrelevant." After all, the monograph was simply a collection of the notes that he had made for the undergraduate course he had been teaching. This course had been "geared to [the students'] interests"; Chomsky had, he maintains, been "trying to lead them from standard beliefs about Markov sources, information theory, automata, and the like, to an interest in language, which demonstrably could not fall within the range of the ideas then considered orthodox in 'hard science' (which had little relation to structuralism, except that both approaches were irrelevant to the issues, in different ways)."

What Chomsky considered to be the major contribution to linguistics was the last half of *Syntactic Structures*, which was taken directly from *Logical Structure*, "the only serious contribution of mine to the (then nonexistent) field at that period (in syntax-semantics, that is; the work on contemporary generative phonology traces from *Morphophonemics of Modern Hebrew* through the paper with Halle and [Fred] Lukoff and later work, including my unpublished 1959 paper at the Texas conference and Halle's 1959 dissertation, and on to *The Sound Pattern of English*, and beyond)" (31 Mar. 1995). But this, of course, was only the beginning.

"An Assault on the Bastions"

During that same year, 1957, the Chomskys had their first child. It was decided that Carol would stay home with the baby and Noam would support the family. They had delayed having children for some time (they had been married eight years) because of their lingering uncertainty as to whether they should live in the United States or in Israel; they had also been unsure whether Noam could find work in the academy.

He was, however, increasingly in demand as a lecturer and teacher. Throughout 1957, he commuted from Cambridge to Philadelphia, where he had been engaged by the University of Pennsylvania to teach. At the invitation of the Yiddishist and early sociolinguist Uriel Weinreich, he also became visiting professor at Columbia University in New York City. Then, at the age of twenty-nine, Chomsky was promoted to associate professor at MIT, and subsequently took up a one-year position as National Science Foundation fellow at Princeton's Institute for Advanced Study.

His work was causing significant upheaval within the field of linguistics. Two conferences—one to be held in 1958 and the other in 1959—known as the Texas Conferences on Problems of Linguistic Analysis in English, were being organized by Archibald Hill, the secretary of the Linguistic Society of America and one of the elder statesmen of the discipline. They were originally intended, Chomsky writes, "to give a fair hearing to a new and possibl[y] promising conception of language theory and its application to the analysis of English." Instead, he claims, they seem to

Figure 10
Chomsky at the Institute for Advanced Studies, Princeton University, 1959.

have been "organized with the specific purpose of nipping this heresy in the bud" (31 Mar. 1995).

The leading lights of American structuralism, referred to by Chomsky as "those known as 'hatchet men' in the profession," were all present, including Martin Joos, H. L. Smith, and Robert Stockwell—a rising young star. "They also invited Ralph Long, a traditional grammarian who was mostly the butt of adolescent humor. Their task was to mock Long and to destroy me" (31 Mar. 1995). They didn't succeed. The battle lines were ultimately drawn in a way they had not anticipated. Chomsky explains:

Long and I got along very well, and I was defending him throughout, in part for personal reasons—I didn't like what was going on—and in part because there are actually connections between generative and traditional grammar. This was pretty hard for them to take. I knew a lot of mathematics and logic, which meant I could follow their arguments, and they couldn't use the usual technical tricks to steamroller opposition. Also, it became pretty clear that they simply couldn't deal with the arguments and issues, and their whole stand (presented at the time with huge self-confidence and pride) collapsed on inspection. Stockwell understood it, and pretty much switched sides in the middle. (31 Mar. 1995)

The end result of all of this was that people in the field were eventually compelled to choose sides. Bernard Bloch was "intrigued, though he didn't believe a word" of it. W. V. O. Quine "lost interest" in him, Chomsky writes. Yehoshua Bar-Hillel and Morris Halle "did agree" with him, and "were supportive"; "ditto" Robert Lees, who then "completely abandoned the Bloomfieldian program"; Robert Stockwell responded in "more or less the same" way; and George Miller was "very supportive, after he abandoned the 'behavioral science' framework" (31 Mar. 1995).

The second conference, held in 1959, was "pretty much a replay" of the first. The rift within the profession that these conferences encapsulated was exacerbated yet again when the question of whether to publish the proceedings was raised. Hill finally agreed to publish the 1958 proceedings "after a lot of pressure" was brought to bear upon him, but the 1959 proceedings have, Chomsky points out, "never seen the light of day, including my first extensive paper on generative phonology of English, which was really an assault on the bastions—phonology." The basic material discussed in the 1959 conference did finally appear in the quarterly report of the Research Laboratory of Electronics at MIT, and was later worked into *The Sound Pattern of English*. But by then, recalls Chomsky, "Halle and I (with Fred Lukoff, another former Harris student who had found his way to MIT) had already published a paper on generative phonology of English, on stress (the major pride of American linguists), showing that the vast descriptive apparatus of which [mainstream linguists] were so proud was a pointless artifact, which could be explained in terms of some extremely simple generative rules" (31 Mar. 1995).

The type of linguistics that Chomsky had conceived during this period was concerned with issues so dramatically different from those that preoccupied his colleagues in most university linguistics departments that one might think he had invented an entirely new field. However, Chomsky was to take great pains demonstrating the links between his ideas and work undertaken hundreds of years earlier.

3

Humboldt and the Cartesian Tradition

Science is a bit like the joke about the drunk who is looking under a lamppost for a key that he has lost on the other side of the street, because that's where the light is. It has no other choice.
—Noam Chomsky, letter to the author, 14 June 1993

Fundamental Values and Theories

There is a remarkable consistency to Chomsky's political work. His fundamental values have remained virtually unchanged since childhood. He has supported and looked for ways to nourish the libertarian and creative character of the human being, and has sought the company of those who share his commitment to do so. Once one becomes familiar with the basic impulses that guide Chomsky—and, to a certain extent, the others who populate the broad milieu to which he has contributed and from which he has taken—it becomes possible to predict the approach that he will take to a particular issue, if not the substance of his response.

The same cannot, of course, be said of Chomsky's linguistic work. In this domain, Chomsky has distinguished himself by moving forward in his research on the basis of new data. Nevertheless, much of what has come to be considered Chomsky's major contribution to the field he produced quite early in his career: *Morphophonemics of Modern Hebrew*, his 1956 paper with Halle and Lukoff, his (unpublished) 1959 Texas-conference paper on contemporary generative phonology, and the linguistic parts of *The Logical Structure of Linguistic Theory*. Linguistic research has since been deemed a scientific area of study, and has been enriched by new insights into the nature of speech and language. But this innovation owes a great deal to Chomsky, who had the courage to reconceive the implications of what he had learned in the academy.

The details of Chomsky's early contribution to the field are complex, and have caused much confusion among historians (especially linguistic historians), particularly when it comes to the relationship between his early work and other work undertaken in the field. This confusion may be somewhat alleviated if we consider that except for "Systems of Syntactic Analysis," his 1953 article on procedural-constructional approaches that appeared in the *Journal of Symbolic Logic*, virtually all of Chomsky's work is a rejection of the Bloomfield-Harris school, particularly in terms of his emphasis on the generativity of human language and the tenet that any theory of grammar must account for the speaker's ability to understand sentences that he or she hears for the first time. This is not to suggest that there is in Chomsky's work an emphasis on the often-mentioned "distinction" between grammatical and ungrammatical sentences; in fact, as Chomsky points out, in *Logical Structure* and *Syntactic Structures* "there is no such bifurcation: there are just varying degrees of grammaticalness." Every expression "falls among them somewhere and there is no special two-way split" (27 June 1995). In the area of discovery procedures, another frequently discussed issue is that "a linguistic theory should not be identified with a manual of useful procedures, nor should it be expected to provide mechanical procedures for the discovery of grammars" (*Syntactic Structures* 55n6). The aim, instead, becomes to develop a grammar that is able to *generate* sentences, just as the speaker of a language is able to produce a virtually infinite number of sentences using the finite number of words and grammatical rules known to him or her.

Antibehaviorism

There is another difference between Chomsky and the Bloomfieldians who preceded him that ultimately proves to be of monumental importance: Bloomfield's model was based on behaviorism and its associated learning theory. Chomsky's rejection, political and intellectual, of such a notion became clear, and public, in the course of his "savage and exhilarating review" of B. F. Skinner's 1957 book *Verbal Behavior* (Goreing 15). This review appeared in 1959 in the journal *Language*, and it received a

Figure 11
Chomsky's condemnation of B. F. Skinner's brand of behaviorism helped popularize his own unconventional approach to language.

considerable amount of attention. The thirty-year-old Chomsky was taking on an established and well-entrenched figure, and, in so doing, was putting into question an entire school of psychological enquiry.

Skinner's work had been presented to specialists in the field ten years earlier in the context of the William James Lectures, and when Chomsky first arrived at Harvard in 1951 his ideas were in vogue. Six years later, the entire behaviorist program had gained significant currency at Harvard (where Skinner taught) and far beyond: Skinner had become the leading proponent of behaviorism by the early 1950s. He believed that human behavior, especially verbal behavior, can be explained and controlled by the same external processes (reinforcement, for example) as those employed to predict and control the behavior of animals.

This, in Chomsky's view, denies a fundamental characteristic of human behavior, creativity, which allows even very young children to comprehend a great variety of utterances when hearing them for the very first time.

Furthermore, Chomsky felt that the application to language processes of behaviorist-psychology terminology, such as "stimulus," "response," "habit," "conditioning," and "reinforcement," was so ambiguous and empirically vapid that it could be made to cover anything. What, for example, does paraphrasing "X wants Y" with "X is reinforced by Y" suggest? In Chomsky's view, "reinforced" can imply such a wide variety of responses that it is meaningless; the notion of reinforcement does not clarify or objectify descriptions of liking, wishing, wanting. John Lyons writes: "In the absence of any overt 'response,' the behaviorist takes refuge in an unobserved and unobservable 'disposition to respond'; and having accounted, in principle, for the association of words (as 'responses') with objects (as 'stimuli') and for the learning of a limited set of sentences in the same way, he either says nothing at all about the formation of new sentences or at this point appeals to some undefined notion of 'analogy' " (84–85).

In short, the examination of external conditions to explain verbal behavior "is simply dogma, with no scientific basis." Raphael Salkie summarizes Chomsky's viewpoint well:

> If we want to account for the fact that the language of English speakers has certain regularities in it, we must look at the external environment and at the internal structure of English speakers—that is, their knowledge of the language. If we want to look at how English speakers acquire knowledge of their language, we need to take into account their innate knowledge, genetically determined changes, and changes due to their experience. Insisting at the outset that one of these factors cannot be relevant is simply dogmatism, and has no place in science. (87)

The point of Chomsky's critique of Skinner was not, as many believed, to attack behaviorism, because this would import to the project a credibility that Chomsky denies. He writes: "It wasn't Skinner's crazy variety of behaviorism that interested me particularly, but the way it was being used in Quinean empiricism and 'naturalization of philosophy,' a gross error in my opinion. That was important, Skinner was not. The latter was bound to collapse shortly under the weight of repeated failures" (31 Mar. 1995).

Kenneth MacCorquodale published a counterattack called "On Chomsky's Review of Skinner's *Verbal Behavior*" in a 1970 issue of the *Journal of the Experimental Analysis of Behavior.* He fails, however, to address the issues raised by Chomsky relating to language and verbal behavior:

"The hypothesis of *Verbal Behavior* is simply that the facts of verbal behavior are in the domain of the facts from which the system has been
constructed. Skinner's stratagem is to find plausible referents in the speech
episode for the laws and terms in his explanatory system: stimulus, response, reinforcement, and motivation. The relevance of these laws and
their component variables for the verbal events is hypothesized only; it is
not dogmatically claimed" (185). Chomsky himself replied in the journal
Cognition that "MacCorquodale assumes that I was attempting to
disprove Skinner's theses, and he points out that I present no data to
disprove them. But my point, rather, was to demonstrate that when
Skinner's assertions are taken literally, they are wrong on the face of it . . .
or else quite vacuous" ("Psychology" 11).

An Early Leitmotif

This attack on behaviorist assumptions was the work of a confident and
competent young scholar. By the age of thirty, Chomsky had already
developed manifestly original views on numerous political, philosophical,
and linguistic concerns. But some of his challenges to contemporary
dogma had roots in long-forgotten texts. And just as his political work
was informed by the nineteenth- and twentieth-century radical libertarian
left, his work on language was eventually informed by studies that had
been undertaken as far back as the seventeenth century.

Chomsky was also developing a series of leitmotifs. He asserted, for
example, that the error of Skinner's ways was symptomatic of a larger
problem: determinism and behaviorism, as well as other intellectual ploys,
were being used on a much broader scale to control the masses and justify abhorrent acts. A representative Chomsky interview on this subject,
"Class Consciousness and the Ideology of Power" (1974), may be used to
gauge the force of his argument, and to illustrate the sarcastic humor of
his approach:

As far as the Skinner thing is concerned . . . I think it's a fraud, there's nothing
there. I mean, it is empty. It's an interesting fraud. See, I think that there are two
levels of discussion here. One is purely intellectual: What does it amount to? And
the answer is zero, zilch . . . I mean, there are *no* principles there that are non-
trivial, that even exist. . . . Now the other question is, why so much interest in it?
And here I think the answer is obvious. I mean, the methodology that they are

suggesting is known to every good prison guard, or police interrogator. But, they make it look benign and scientific, and so on; they give a kind of coating to it, and for that reason it's very valuable to them. I think both these things have to be pointed out. First you ask, is this science? No, it's fraud. And then you say, OK, then why the interest in it? Answer: because it tells any concentration camp guard that he can do what his instincts tell him to do, but pretend to be a scientist at the same time. So that makes it good, because science is good, or neutral, and so on. (*Language and Politics* 190)

Chomsky here reiterates his belief that there can be a strong relation between ruling-class interests and the promotion of particular theories. Skinner himself never offered a response to Chomsky's review, or to other remarks he has made, although in 1990 he did write a letter to the *Times Literary Supplement* in which he suggested that Chomsky did not address "the production of speech," and instead "was on the side of comprehension." He insisted that Chomsky's "contribution to an understanding of verbal behaviour was as 'negligible' then as it is now" ("Verbal Behaviour"). Chomsky's sense is that "there's no particular reason why he should have responded. We knew each other, and got along quite well, but virtually never discussed these issues" (13 Feb. 1996).

The Skinner-Chomsky debate emphasized Skinner's empiricist assumptions, "which restrict innate qualities of the mind to simple capacities of induction, comparison and so on" (Goreing 15). From Chomsky's perspective, these assumptions render Skinner's brand of behaviorism incapable of explaining even simple elements of human behavior, never mind the almost infinite variations of language. Chomsky's perspective is essentially a rationalist one; it encompasses ideas developed during the seventeenth century. As he extended linguistic frontiers, he was also reaching towards the realm of intellectual history.

The Founding of MIT's Graduate Program in Linguistics

At thirty-one, Chomsky seemed to be on the brink of a glittering career in the academy. As well, he and Carol were becoming deeply involved in domestic life; they were determined to provide a serene and comfortable environment for their young children. But the Skinner review in *Language* had been a first step towards the establishment of Chomsky as a controversial public figure, and the political views for which he would soon become infamous were rapidly taking shape, fueled by his voracious reading habit. Chomsky had managed to maintain his interest in Jewish cultural issues, as well; he was still close to his parents and brother, and during his frequent treks home to Philadelphia to see them, he was able to renew his involvement in these issues.

In the spring of 1959, Chomsky began working on a project involving generative phonology, applying to the English language theories that he had previously developed for analyzing Hebrew in *Morphophonemics of Modern Hebrew*. He also continued to explore the wider implications of his work, and was therefore becoming a point of reference for researchers in numerous fields, including philosophy, psychology, and, of course, linguistics. Chomsky's growing eminence was also the result of his having begun a graduate program in linguistics at MIT with like-minded colleagues, notably Morris Halle. The time was ripe for such a program. An evolution was occurring within the field of linguistics, and MIT was prepared to allow Chomsky and Halle to circumvent the usual red tape. As Chomsky recalls:

[W]e were able to develop our program at MIT because, in a sense, MIT was outside the American university system. There were no large departments of humanities or the related social sciences at MIT. Consequently, we could build up a linguistics department without coming up against problems of rivalry and academic bureaucracy. Here we were really part of the Research Laboratory of Electronics. That permitted us to develop a program very different from any other and quite independent. (*Language and Responsibility* 134)

The program immediately attracted a number of gifted scholars, including Robert Lees, who had by then completed his Ph.D. in electrical engineering at MIT; Jerry Fodor and Jerry Katz, graduates of the Ph.D. program at Princeton; and Paul Postal, who had completed his Ph.D. at Yale. All were eventually named to the MIT faculty—Lees and Postal in linguistics, Fodor and Katz in philosophy; Lees, of course, was hired to work on the mechanical translation project. There were also John Viertel, a personal friend of Chomsky's who was not, and never had been, a graduate student ("an interesting guy—an associate of Brecht's, among other things" [31 Mar. 1995]), and M. P. Schützenberger, a well-established mathematician and biologist who had often visited MIT ("where we became friends and to a certain extent colleagues, applying mathematical

ideas of his to formal languages in published work" [31 Mar. 1995]).
Fodor comments upon this era:

It's not much of a hyperbole to say that *all* of the people who were interested in
this kind of linguistics were at MIT. That's not quite true. There were others scattered around. But for a while, we were pretty nearly all there was. So communication was very lively, and I guess we shared a general picture of the methodology
for doing, not just linguistics, but behaviorial science research. We were all more
or less nativist, and all more or less mentalist. There was a lot of methodological
conversation that one didn't need to have. One could get right to the substantive
issues. So, from that point of view, it was extremely exciting. (qtd. in R. A. Harris
68)

At the age of thirty-three, Chomsky was made professor of foreign
languages and linguistics at MIT. He found himself emerging from the
shadows of what had initially been a personal hobby and entering the
newly revitalized and promising field of linguistic studies.

Chomsky's "Classic Period"

In his 1993 history of linguistics, P. H. Matthews characterizes the early-
to-mid-1960s as "Chomsky's classic period," a time of enormous productivity (see *Grammatical Theory*). In 1962, Chomsky gave a paper at
the Ninth International Congress of Linguists entitled "The Logical Basis
of Linguistic Theory," which outlined an approach to language known as
transformational generative grammar. The plenary speaker for this congress—who was, in a sense, supposed to represent American linguistics—
was to have been Zellig Harris, but Harris delayed deciding whether
to accept the invitation, and finally turned it down shortly before the
congress was scheduled to take place. Three of the congress organizers,
Morris Halle, Roman Jakobson, and William Locke (all MIT linguists),
convinced Chomsky to replace Harris. "Chomsky, never an avid conference goer, agreed, though his entire contact with the meeting was limited
to the drive into Cambridge the morning of his presentation, staying for a
late afternoon reception, and driving back that evening" (Anderson et al.
692).

Chomsky was suddenly thrust into the position of being "*de facto*
spokesperson for American linguistics" (Anderson et al. 692). He did not

disappoint; he gave a paper that introduced the topics covered in *Current Issues in Linguistic Theory* to an international audience and represented a clean break from structural linguistics of all varieties. This paper turned out to be "the initial germ of the research programme which was to lead to the principles-and-parameters modular theory, which in fact amounts to a discovery procedure, 'a scientific advance of the highest importance' that seemed to be 'hopelessly out of the question' at that time" (Otero, "Chomsky and the Challenges" 14). There was, however, a negative backlash to his presentation. Otero reports: "As often happens, some of the participants, including a variety of European professors, were apparently more concerned with defending what they took to be their territory than with any intellectual issues" ("Chomsky and the Challenges" 14).

In June of 1964, Chomsky delivered a series of lectures at the Linguistic Institute of the Linguistic Society of America (published in 1966 as *Topics in the Theory of Generative Grammar*). He also published *Aspects of the Theory of Syntax* (1965) and *Cartesian Linguistics: A Chapter in the History of Rationalist Thought* (1966). He gave another set of lectures to a general audience, in Berkeley, in January of 1967, which was expanded and published as *Language and Mind* in 1968 (an enlarged edition— several later essays were added—came out in 1972). And he completed *The Sound Pattern of English* with Halle in 1968. In Matthews's words, "few scholars can have published so much, of such value and on such varied topics, in such a short time" (*Grammatical Theory* 205).

But this "classic period" was also a time of mounting worldwide tensions; the Cuba Crisis erupted and was defused, bringing the world to the brink of nuclear war. That very year, the United States began a systematic bombardment of rural Vietnam. Chomsky was to become increasingly discontent in the wake of such upheaval, and the seeds of what was to be a lifelong commitment to active political resistance were sown. Chomsky offers a snapshot of his activities at this time: "Those were pretty hectic days. I was often giving many political talks a day all over the place, getting arrested, going to meetings about resistance and other things, teaching my classes, playing with my kids, etc. I even managed to plant a lot of trees and shrubs, somehow. Looking back, I can't imagine how it was possible" (13 Feb. 1996).

Cartesian Linguistics

The topics that were of interest to Chomsky during this period are interconnected in various ways. In *Cartesian Linguistics*, for example, Chomsky elaborates the relationship between empiricist and rationalist approaches. The book is part of the Studies in Language Series, which Chomsky and Halle edited for Harper and Row, and which was intended "to deepen our understanding of the nature of language and the mental processes and structures that underlie its use and acquisition" (*Cartesian Linguistics* ix).

Chomsky wrote the text while he was a fellow of the American Council of Learned Societies; he did so with the assistance of the National Institutes of Health at Harvard University, the Center for Cognitive Studies, and a grant from the Social Science Research Council. Prior to publication, he presented his findings in the context of the Christian Gauss Seminars in Criticism at Princeton at the invitation of R. P. Blackmur and on the suggestion of Edward Cone from the music department and Richard Rorty from philosophy. His presentation took the form of six weekly lectures, running from 25 February until 8 April 1964. Chomsky had been asked to link his interests in formal language and the analysis of syntax to literature; but since he did not consider himself to be "in a position to say anything significant relating to literature," he instead offered to address "the topic of structure of language and philosophy of mind, and, in particular, to try to develop some notions that were extensively discussed in the seventeenth through early nineteenth centuries, though rarely since" (Otero, "Chomsky and the Challenges" 15). Seminar participants made some useful comments in response to the lectures, as did several of Chomsky's friends and colleagues, such as William Bottiglia, Roman Jakobson, Louis Kampf, Jerry Katz, and John Viertel. According to Otero, "the audience included very sophisticated people and ... the lectures were well received" ("Chomsky and the Challenges" 16).

In a letter he wrote to Chomsky a few weeks after the seminars had ended, Cone wrote: "It's almost unheard of for a man to keep his entire audience through all six sessions. Your ideas are still resounding through the halls of the Philosophy Department here. Please come again!" (qtd. in Otero, "Chomsky and the Challenges" 15–16). The resulting text, which was substantially written up in a number of weeks, is an extremely original piece of research, and ranges beyond the field of linguistics; it stands as a contribution to the field of intellectual history, what is sometimes called the history of ideas. And it created a tremendous stir at the time—as it did later on.

The year after *Cartesian Linguistics* appeared, Hans Aarslef, regarded as a leading scholar in the field, published a major book "in which," Chomsky writes, "he described traditional universal grammar as solely 'Cartesian' in origin, completely ignoring the quite obvious Renaissance and earlier origins that are emphasized in *Cartesian Linguistics*" (31 Mar. 1995). He had not seen *Cartesian Linguistics* when he wrote his book, "though he knew I was working on it, and had lectured about the topics at Princeton—he was away" when Chomsky's lectures were given. But Aarslef did respond to Chomsky's book later, in a way that "shows something about the intellectual state of the field" (14 Aug. 1995). Chomsky recounts subsequent events: "a few years later ... [Aarslef] wrote savage denunciations of *Cartesian Linguistics* (in *Language*, and elsewhere), claiming that I had made this idiotic error, which he did make [himself] a year after *Cartesian Linguistics*, and which is explicitly and unambiguously rejected in *Cartesian Linguistics*" (31 Mar. 1995). As Chomsky writes, Aarslef identified the error as the failure of *Cartesian Linguistics* "to recognize the pre-Cartesian sources of Port Royal and later work, which was not only false (they were explicitly and carefully mentioned) but pretty audacious, since in his independent book a year after *Cartesian Linguistics* he had referred to all of this work as solely Cartesian, without any mention of the earlier sources" (14 Aug. 1995). Such "absurdity and falsification," in Chomsky's view, is only to be expected. "Furthermore, [Aarslef's] version has become accepted Truth. I've never bothered to respond, because ... my contempt for the intellectual world reaches such heights that I have no interest in pursuing them in their gutters, unless there are serious human interests involved, as [there often are] in the political realm ..." (31 Mar. 1995). Two other scholars (Ilse Andrews and Henry Bracken) picked up on Aarslef's "audacity," but their published remarks had no impact.

Chomsky's opening hypothesis in *Cartesian Linguistics* is that contemporary linguistics had lost touch with an earlier European tradition of linguistic studies, which he identified as Cartesian. The term "Cartesian" is not used here according to its generally accepted definition; Chomsky extends that definition to encompass, as he puts it, "a certain collection of ideas which were not expressed by Descartes, [were] rejected by followers of Descartes, and many first expressed by anti-Cartesians" (31 Mar. 1995). The work that Chomsky assigned to the Cartesian corpus, and the tradition of research that the Cartesians had upheld, was, in Chomsky's opinion, more pertinent than the research of contemporary scholars, and certainly more useful than that which was being produced in the field of the history of linguistics.

To provide a "preliminary and fragmentary sketch of some of the leading ideas of Cartesian linguistics with no explicit analysis of its relation to current work that seeks to clarify and develop these ideas" was Chomsky's goal. His "primary aim" was "simply to bring to the attention of those involved in the study of generative grammar and its implications some of the little-known work which has bearing on their concerns and problems and which often anticipates some of their specific conclusions" (*Cartesian Linguistics* 2).

Chomsky was reaching back to sources of knowledge that date from the Renaissance. Especially drawn to the seventeenth and eighteenth centuries, he embraced the works of, among others, René Descartes (1596–1650) and Wilhelm von Humboldt (1767–1835). To understand this impulse is to comprehend Chomsky's frequent claim that, despite his loathing of labels, he would be satisfied to be labeled a contributor to an anarchist (if properly defined) or an eighteenth-century rationalist tradition. In other words, in the same way that left-libertarian values run through much of Chomsky's political work from the 1940s on, rationalist ideas permeate much of his linguistic work from the late 1950s to the present.

An Emphasis on Human Creativity

Chomsky came to realize in the early 1960s that the emphasis he placed upon creativity was, in some ways, simply a renewal of a similar emphasis applied in earlier centuries, particularly in the works of Humboldt. He also recognized that the concept itself was based upon largely unarticulated presuppositions "dating back to the very beginnings of Western linguistic theory in the ancient world" (Lyons, *Chomsky* 37). Acknowledging that he found Humboldt's work compelling, if not illuminating, Chomsky remarks: "I read Humboldt for the first time around 1960 or so, I guess. Yes, I was surprised and delighted, but not really enlightened. That is, I didn't learn anything new, except about intellectual history, a topic that happens to interest me a lot" (13 Dec. 1994).

Chomsky also admits that a thread of rational thinking is woven through his work: "I didn't begin writing about intellectual history until the early '60s, not until *Current Issues in Linguistic Theory* [written in 1962, while he was a resident fellow at the Harvard Cognitive Studies Center], though you can see the beginnings in my review of Skinner (written in 1957)" (13 Dec. 1994). Intellectual history had hooked Chomsky and drawn him in; it was to have a lasting influence upon his work. He reflects:

> I haven't convinced anyone, but I think there is an important and detectable "thread" (to borrow your term) that runs from Cartesian rationalism through the romantic period (the more libertarian Rousseau, for example), parts of the enlightenment (some of Kant, etc.), pre-capitalist classical liberalism (notably Humboldt, but also Smith), and on to the partly spontaneous tradition of popular revolt against industrial capitalism and the forms it took in the left-libertarian movements, including the anti-Bolshevik parts of the Marxist tradition. I also disagree with lots of things along the way, and putting all of that material in a lump yields immense internal inconsistencies (even within the writing of a single person, say Humboldt or, notoriously, Rousseau, most of them pretty unsystematic). But I'm speaking here of a thread that can be extricated, and that may have only been dimly perceived (as is standard, even in one's own scientific work, when one thinks it over in retrospect). (8 Aug. 1994)

One way to trace the series of connections that Chomsky alludes to here is simply to look at the material he quotes in *Cartesian Linguistics*.

Here, in what amounts to a historical discussion, but which could still be understood as a continuation of his diatribe against Skinner's vision of behaviorism (particularly "the way it was being used in Quinean empiricism and 'naturalization of philosophy'" [31 Mar. 1995]), Chomsky also notes that Descartes, in the course of studying the limits of mechanical explanation, "arrived at the conclusion that man has unique abilities that cannot be accounted for on purely mechanistic grounds, although, to a very large extent, a mechanistic explanation can be provided for human bodily function and behavior" (3). The difference between man and animals, in Descartes's view, is most clearly exhibited in human language—specifically in the phenomenon previously referred to as creativity.

To illustrate his point, Descartes cites the machine's limited ability to speak in response to stimuli. Although he imagines that a machine could be set up to make particular responses to particular actions performed upon it, "it never happens that it arranges its speech in various ways, in order to reply appropriately to everything that may be said in its presence, as even the lowest type of man can do" (qtd. in Chomsky, *Cartesian Linguistics* 4). But, unlike a machine, a human being is "incited" or "inclined" to act in certain ways, and not compelled. It is due to this, Chomsky says, that "prediction of behavior may be possible within a certain range, and a theory of motivation might be within range, but all of these endeavors miss the central point. The person could have chosen to act otherwise, within the limits of physical capacity, even in ways that are harmful or suicidal" ("Creation"). So, he continues, even if theories elaborated to predict human behavior or motivation are deemed successful in their own terms, they "would not qualify as serious theories of behavior. Human action is coherent and appropriate, but uncaused, apparently.... These considerations lie at the heart of the dualist metaphysics of the Cartesians, which again accords rather well with our common-sense understanding" ("Creation").

Despite its accordance with "our common-sense understanding," however, much of what was postulated by Cartesian dualist metaphysics has subsequently been thrown into doubt. "[B]ut," Chomsky asserts, "it is important to recall that what collapsed was the Cartesian theory of matter; the theory of mind, such as it was, has undergone no fundamental critique" ("Creation").

Chomsky remarks on the notion Descartes put forward that we can train the smartest animals to perform various tasks and tricks, but no matter how high their level of competence they will never equal even the least skilled human in terms of linguistic ability. Descartes wrote: "[I]t is a very remarkable fact that there are none so depraved and stupid, without even excepting idiots, that they cannot arrange different words together, forming of them a statement by which they make known their thoughts; while, on the other hand, there is no animal, however perfect and fortunately circumstanced it may be, which can do the same" (*Cartesian Linguistics* 116–17). Nonhuman primates and other animal species do not all necessarily lack the physiological characteristics and general intelligence needed to use language creatively; they nonetheless lack this human-specific capacity because of the particular organization of their minds. This observation and others made by Cartesians were not addressed by the Bloomfieldian linguistic framework.

Chomsky and Humboldt

All of this is crucial to an understanding of Chomsky's position on human nature, human language, and even politics. And in order to comprehend his intellectual development, it is vital to relate his earlier work to his Cartesian historical studies. Chomsky traces the Cartesian viewpoint through the Enlightenment and the Romantic period, and stresses its value as a means of grasping creative discourse.

He ultimately dwells upon the work of Humboldt, who serves as another context for Chomsky's work on linguistics and his postulations on what constitutes appropriate societal makeup. Humboldt focuses on the creative aspects of human language from what could be construed as a Cartesian perspective in that he considers language to be a manifestation of thought and self-expression rather than simply a form of functional communication.

Perusing his writings, one may find that they yield a sense of his insight and range, as well as—by extension—the key to the relationship between Humboldt's work and that of Chomsky. For example, Humboldt claims that "language ... must be looked upon as being an immediate given in mankind.... Language could not be invented or come upon if its archetype were not already present in the human mind. For man to understand but a single word truly, not as a mere sensuous stimulus (such as an animal understands a command or the sound of the whip) but as an articulated sound designating a concept, all language, in all its connections, must already lie prepared within him. There are no single separate facts of language. Each of its elements announces itself as part of a whole" (*Humanist* 239–40).

It is rather startling to compare this kind of reflection with the behaviorist and structuralist approach that dominated the field during this time. Here is Humboldt on language acquisition: "Everyone when he learns a language, most notably children who create far more than they memorize, proceeds by darkly felt analogies which allow him to enter the language actively, as it were, instead of just receptively" (*Humanist* 243). On the relationship of language to the functions of the mind: "The mutual interdependence of thought and word illuminates clearly the truth that languages are not really means for representing already known truths but are rather instruments for discovering previously unrecognized ones" (*Humanist* 246). On general considerations of human development: "The production of language is an inner need of mankind, not merely an external vehicle for the maintenance of communication, but an indispensable one which lies in human nature, necessary for the development of its spiritual energies and for the growth of a Weltanschauung which man can attain only by bringing his thinking to clarity and definition by communal contact with the thinking of others" (*Humanist* 258). On the nature and attributes of language: "the whole of language lies within each human being, which only means that each of us contains a striving, regulated by a definitely modified capacity, which both stimulates and restricts, gradually to produce the entire language, as inner or outer demands dictate, and to understand it as it is produced by others" (*Humanist* 290–91); also: "A further proof that children do not mechanically learn their native language but undergo a development of linguistic capacity is afforded by the fact that all children, in the most different imaginable circumstances of life, learn to speak within a fairly narrow and definite time span, just as they develop all their main capacities at certain definite growth stages" (*Humanist* 292).

And finally, adopting a generative approach to linguistics, von Humboldt, in Chomsky's words, suggests that the lexicon is "based on certain organizing generative principles that produce the appropriate items on given occasions," and he develops "the notion of 'form of language' as a generative principle, fixed and unchanging, determining the scope and providing the means for the unbounded set of individual 'creative' acts that constitute normal language use," thereby making "an original and significant contribution to linguistic theory . . . that unfortunately remained unrecognized and unexploited until fairly recently" (*Cartesian Linguistics* 20, 22).

Discussing deep and surface structures in *Cartesian Linguistics*, Chomsky points out the value of a universal or philosophical theory for a study of transformational generative grammar. He does so with reference to both the grammar and the logic described in the Port-Royal *Grammaire générale et raisonnée*, which dates back to 1660:

Such a theory is concerned precisely with the rules that specify deep structures and relate them to surface structures and with rules of semantic and phonological interpretation that apply to deep and surface structures respectively. It is, in other words, in large measure an elaboration and formalization of notions that are implicit.... In many respects, it seems to me quite accurate, then, to regard the theory of transformational generative grammar, as it is developing in current work, as essentially a modern and more explicit version of the Port-Royal theory. (38–39)

This theory was formulated by a group that was associated with Port-Royal, a Parisian monastery. Daniel Yergin explains: "In 1660, influenced by Descartes, [the Port-Royal group] produced a 'philosophical grammar' that suggested a distinction between deep and surface structures, and argued for psychological rules which, like Chomsky's, would permit us to make infinite use of finite means" (53).

Chomsky elaborates the ways in which the rationalist theory of mind and the Cartesian approach to linguistics offer valuable support for studies of the acquisition and utilization of language as described by certain factions of the linguistic community (most of whom worked in building 20 at MIT). Such studies—of common forms of language, of general grammars, and of the conditions that prescribe the forms of human language—build on work undertaken by Cartesian linguists, and, in the process, acknowledge "the quite obvious fact that the speaker of a language knows a great deal that he has not learned" (Chomsky, *Language and Responsibility* 60). Making reference to the work of Herbert de Cherbury, and then to works by Descartes, the English Platonists, Leibniz, Kant, and the Romantics—notably Schlegel and Humboldt—Chomsky takes a fresh look at "the preconditions for language acquisition and at the perceptual function of abstract systems of internalized rules" in order to demonstrate the ways in which contemporary linguistic studies were "foreshadowed or even explicitly formulated in earlier and now largely forgotten studies" (*Language and Responsibility* 73).

Politics and the Cartesians

But no matter how valuable they were to Chomsky as he rediscovered the study of language, it is not solely through their power to illuminate contemporary linguistic concerns, theories of deep and surface structures, and questions concerning the acquisition and use of language (which Chomsky also discusses in *Cartesian Linguistics*) that the Cartesians enter Chomsky's realm of influences. There is a political connection as well. Plenty of political issues were commanding public attention at this time. The United States supported a military coup in Brazil in 1964, the same year it initiated bombing raids on Laos. The following year, a constitutionalist coup occurred in the Dominican Republic against the country's military dictatorship, and once again the United States sent in troops. A few months later, a pro-American general led a military coup in Indonesia, precipitating the slaughter of over half a million people.

As the work of the Cartesians (and of Humboldt, in particular) demonstrates, both social *and* political theory must be addressed in any worthwhile attempt to determine the best way to allow the creative impulses of man free rein. In other words, once we accept the Cartesian perspective on language, the next step is to support natural rights and to oppose authoritarianism. In the course of the Barcelona conference, Chomsky remarked:

the principles of people like von Humboldt and Adam Smith and others were that people should be free. They shouldn't be under the control of authoritarian institutions. They shouldn't be subjected to things like division of labor, which destroys them, and wage labor, which is a form of slavery. They should, rather, be free. Now, back in the eighteenth century the forms of centralized authority that people saw in front of their eyes were the feudal system, the Church and the absolutist State, and so on. They didn't see the industrial corporation because it wasn't around. ("Creation")

In a dramatic bid to link Cartesian ideals with anarchism, Chomsky then insists:

if you take their principles and you apply them to the modern period, I think you'd come pretty close to the revolutionary principles that animated Barcelona in the

1930s. And I think that is about as high a level as human beings have achieved in trying to achieve these principles, and I think that they were the right ones. Not to say that everything was done was right, but ... the idea of developing the kind of society that Orwell saw and described ... with popular control over all institutions, economic, political and so on ... is the right direction to move. This is not a new idea; in fact, its roots are as old as classical liberalism. ("Creation")

In light of these remarks, so-called radical political theory is a misnomer. Radical theory is, in Humboldt's sense, or in Chomsky's sense, a truism: human beings require liberty and a nurturing environment in which to express their humanity. On artists, for example, Humboldt writes that, when free of external control, "all peasants and craftsmen could be transformed into *artists*, i.e., people who love their craft for its own sake, who refine it with their self-guided energy and inventiveness, and who in so doing cultivate their own intellectual energies, ennoble their character, and increase their enjoyments" (*Humanist* 45). On freedom of thought: "Let no one believe ... that the many are so exhausted by activities dictated by the need for earning a living, that freedom of thought is useless to them, or even disturbing. Or that they can best be activated by the diffusion of principles handed down from on high, while their freedom to think and to investigate is restricted" (*Humanist* 33).

Humboldt's vision, shared, in various ways, by other Enlightenment thinkers, is another kind of leitmotif in Chomsky's work. It surfaces, for example, in his commentary on language and freedom. In a lecture he delivered to the University Freedom and the Human Sciences Symposium in January of 1970, Chomsky explored the language-freedom bond in relation to historical texts, notably works from the Enlightenment period. Citing Rousseau (especially his *Discourse on Inequality* [1755]), Kant, Descartes, Cordemoy, Linguet, and, of course, Humboldt, Chomsky describes how Enlightenment thinkers anticipated a society set up to encourage rather than stifle human potential. Humboldt is particularly important here, because he forges a link between characteristic human traits, an appropriate social setting, and the language that sets man apart from animals. He also "looks forward to a community of free association without coercion by the state or other authoritarian institutions, in which free men can create and inquire, and achieve the highest development of their powers"; "far ahead of his time, [Humboldt] presents an anarchist vision that is appropriate, perhaps, to the next stage of industrial society" (*Chomsky Reader* 152).

Chomsky, in fact, looks forward to

a day when these various strands will be brought together within the framework of libertarian socialism, a social form that barely exists today though its elements can be perceived: in the guarantee of individual rights that has achieved its highest form—though still tragically flawed—in the Western democracies; in the Israeli *kibbutzim*; in the experiments with workers councils in Yugoslavia; in the effort to awaken popular consciousness and create a new involvement in the social process which is a fundamental element in the Third World revolutions, coexisting uneasily with indefensible authoritarian practice. (*Chomsky Reader* 152)

This is where common sense meets intellectual history, anarchism meets creative output, pedagogical practice meets contemporary linguistic theory, and the kibbutz meets Enlightenment thinking. Humboldt and other Enlightenment thinkers don't *join* the intellectual milieu surrounding and influencing Chomsky, they were always already there, waiting to be reilluminated.

Cartesian Common Sense

An appeal to rationality and common sense—which he defined in his 1992 Barcelona talk as "things that are obvious to us if we pay a little attention to what we experience and what we do" ("Creation")—recurs regularly in Chomsky's work. Its source is in Cartesian thought. In explaining what he means by Cartesian common sense, Chomsky expands on the notion in a modern-day context:

[I]t does not require very far-reaching, specialized knowledge to perceive that the United States was invading South Vietnam. And, in fact, to take apart the system of illusions and deception which functions to prevent understanding of contemporary reality [is] not a task that requires extraordinary skill or understanding. It requires the kind of normal skepticism and willingness to apply one's analytical skills that almost all people have and that they can exercise. It just happens that they exercise them in analyzing what the New England Patriots ought to do next Sunday instead of questions that really matter for human life, their own included. (*Chomsky Reader* 35)

Chomsky employs this appeal to reason in probing two important issues: the relevance of the irrational and the role of the intellectual in society. To the irrational he consigns "fundamentalist religion; JFK conspiracy cults; realist theory in International Relations—Morgenthau, etc.; loony invocation of Stalin's genius or the 'free market' or 'Wilsonian idealism' and other forms of secular fanaticism, such as most of Marxology" (31 Mar. 1995). These "forms" are not only ignored by Chomsky (and those who comprise his milieu), but are also, on occasion, linked to reactionary movements, primarily because they promulgate a belief that understanding is for the initiated.

Rational thinking, of course, does not necessarily protect us against authoritarian politics, but, as Chomsky notes, "irrationality leaves open the door to anything, hence in particular to the worst forms of authoritarianism" (13 Dec. 1994). And viewpoints that deviate from one's own —whether they be judged irrational, reactionary, or even morally unacceptable—should clearly not, for that reason, be subject to controls. Chomsky suggests, instead, that we pay attention to right-wing ideologues: "if their arguments hold up to scrutiny [they] should be respected; I don't regard this as even a matter of dispute. I do that all the time, and often find arguments of 'the right' much more impressive than those of 'the left.' Why should this be surprising?" (15 Dec. 1992). Should we, nevertheless, play down certain kinds of knowledge or limit research in some areas? Chomsky is skeptical:

The idea that some kinds of knowledge should be "played down because of negative implications" is one that I find a bit frightening. Who makes the decision to "play down the truth?" Who determines the "implications"? Where does that power lie, and what are its sources or its justification? I see here the road to fascism and Stalinism, ideas that have great appeal to the intellectual class—including those who call themselves anti-Stalinist, anti-fascist, liberal, etc. [—and this is] something I've attempted to document. (15 Dec. 1992)

The second issue that prompts the appeal to reason—the role of the intellectual in society—is reflected in Chomsky's teaching, lecturing, and research habits. His approach to work, and indeed his very manner of living, derives from a rationalist perspective that emphasizes ideas and their advancement rather than honors and their procurement, or power and its accumulation. In 1971, one of his former classmates, Israel Shenker, wrote:

At the Massachusetts Institute of Technology, where he is the Ferrari P. Ward Professor of Modern Languages and Linguistics, Noam Chomsky could pass as an aging student. His office is unkempt and weary—torn green shades, dusty volumes, a chair in the final stages of disintegration—but he presides with blithe unconcern over such externals, and with intense devotion to what he considers essentials. ("Noam Chomsky" 105)

This, of course, is typical of the many testimonials to Chomsky's unconcern with appearances, his lack of interest in the star status that has been accorded to him, and his fierce determination to identify and concentrate upon what is most important on numerous fronts.

II

The Milieu Chomsky Helped to Create

I'm usually working on quite a number of different things at the same time, and I guess that during most of my adult life I've been spending quite a lot of time reading in areas where I'm not working at all. I seem to be able, without too much trouble, to work pretty intensively at my own scientific work at scattered intervals. Most of the reasonably defined problems have grown out of something accomplished or failed in an early stage.

—Noam Chomsky, "Creative Experience" (71)

4

The Intellectual, the University, and the State

[T]here is a middle ground which I would like to occupy, and I think people are going to have to find ways to occupy: namely, to try to keep up a serious commitment to the intellectual values and intellectual and scientific problems that really concern you and yet at the same time make a serious and one hopes useful contribution to the enormous extra-scientific questions. Commitment to work on the problems of racism, oppression, imperialism, and so on, is in the United States an absolute necessity. Now exactly how one can maintain that sort of schizophrenic existence I am not sure; it is very difficult. It's not only a matter of too much demand on one's time, but also a high degree of ongoing personal conflict about where your next outburst of energy should go. And unless people somehow resolve the problem I think the future is rather dim. If they do resolve it I think it might be rather hopeful.

—Noam Chomsky, *Language and Politics* (98–99)

"Soldier, Scholar, Horseman He ... "

The individuals and institutions that have in various ways shaped Chomsky's thinking and his approach to social and linguistic issues have been emphasized up to this point. It may seem odd that we now, at this relatively early stage in Chomsky's life and career, turn to those individuals and institutions that Chomsky has had a hand in forming.

The primary reason for doing this is that most of the basic philosophy and underlying tendencies that inform Chomsky's work were set in place by 1961, when he was just thirty-three years old. Second, it was at this juncture that Chomsky achieved the stature of established intellectual and became a tenured professor at MIT. Issues relating to the role of the academic, and to the relationship between the academy and the broader social context, now began to take on greater importance for him. Third,

Chomsky entered the public debate concerning American foreign policy during this period, and in so doing assumed the role of political observer—and "muckraker." His burgeoning involvement in the ongoing critique of domestic and foreign policy provoked a general interest in the relationship between his linguistic work and his political commentary. Although Chomsky himself was quick to dismiss the notion that such a link existed, there was much interesting discussion on the subject, which broadened to include an examination of the relationship between the natural sciences and the social sciences. The discussion also encompassed speculation about Chomsky's engagement at a scientific university, his attraction to Enlightenment thinking, and, ultimately the distinction he drew between the knowable (and therefore worth studying) and the obvious (and therefore worth commenting upon).

In short, Chomsky was now prepared to put his accumulated knowledge to work for scientific advancement in the field of linguistics and for social advancement in the realm of the community.

In Demand

Growing famous in the academy for his revolutionary work in the fields of linguistics and philosophy, Chomsky found himself the recipient of many invitations to speak and lecture. He continued to travel frequently. In 1966, he visited a number of institutions in California, first as the Linguistics Society of America Professor at the University of California in Los Angeles, and then as the Beckman Professor at the University of California, Berkeley. Awards and honorary degrees were bestowed upon him—notably an honorary D. Litt. from the University of London in 1967 and an honorary D.H.L. from the University of Chicago in 1967. It therefore comes as no surprise that Chomsky was increasingly immersed in debates about the role of the university in society.

An academic of Chomsky's stature could quite easily have benefited from the perks that are available to academic superstars. He chose, instead, to forgo them, because they seemed incompatible with the political and social concerns that had preoccupied him since his youth, and that remained centrally important to his existence. He was now speaking out against human-rights violations, the invasion of Vietnam, the oppressive actions of the ruling elite. And he was doing so in all kinds of forums, from classroom to lecture hall, from correspondence to personal discussion. He didn't mix politics into his linguistics courses, and indeed he notes that he has always been "superscrupulous at keeping my politics out of the classroom." But he did at this time begin to teach undergraduate courses in the humanities program with Louis Kampf: "For me it was just extra courses, outside my teaching responsibilities and department, on social and political issues of various kinds." These courses were, however, not in the mainstream of political sciences and not under the auspices of the political-science department at MIT. In fact, says Chomsky, "that department ran a course for a while, for graduate students, which was literally devoted to finding errors in things I had written (so I was informed by graduate students and young faculty)." One of his courses was called Intellectuals and Social Change, and he describes it as "partly history and 'sociology of intellectuals,' and about half about alternative lives in some way other than an academic career—all sorts of fascinating people. Another course was on politics and ideology ... the contents of which can be found in, for example, *American Power and the New Mandarins*" (13 Feb. 1996).

The student-protest movement was exploding in the United States, and within it Chomsky found allies and audiences. But this is not to say that universities were the focal point for political discussions. Chomsky says: "My first talks about the war were in churches (with maybe four people: the organizer, some drunk who walked in, the minister, and some guy who wanted to kill me) or someone's living room, where a few neighbors were gathered." There were talks at colleges, "but then usually in a classroom, and we would mix up a dozen topics in the hope that someone would come. You could get as many students out about Venezuela as about Vietnam in those days" (13 Feb. 1996). The student interest came later on.

The first big public event was in October of 1965, on the Boston Common (sort of a Hyde Park institution). I was to be a speaker, but the demonstration was attacked by raging crowds (many of them students, marching over from universities), and I was more than thankful that hundreds of cops were there—not very sympathetic, as you can guess, but the city didn't want people murdered on the common. The press, including the most liberal press, was extremely hostile; radio was hysterical. It's true that a couple of years later there were many—sometimes thousands—of people in lecture halls. But even then, most of the talks were elsewhere; open air demonstrations, churches, etc. (13 Feb. 1996)

While he admired "the challenge to the universities" that the students were so vehemently presenting, Chomsky thought their rebellions were "largely misguided," and he "criticized [them] as they were in progress at Berkeley (1966) and Columbia (1968) particularly. Same at MIT, later" (27 June 1995). He maintained that it was not sufficient merely to speak out against the ruling classes; drawing upon his knowledge of previous revolutionary activities, he gauged the actions and effects of the current uprisings. "It was rather complex because the students generally considered me a natural ally and were often surprised at my skepticism about how they were focusing their protests, and criticism of what they were doing—sympathetic in spirit, but quite critical. Led to considerable conflict, in fact" (27 June 1995).

The Responsible Intellectual

The tenacity with which Chomsky has upheld his position on the role of the academic institution and the conformity that it enforces is extraordinary. Many leftists, even radical ones, eventually revise their positions: witness the cliché of the sixties hippie-turned-stockbroker. Never one to sacrifice his viewpoints to peer recognition or material reward, Chomsky came out more and more strongly against the apparently willing collaboration of the intellectual community with the state.

He now turned to assembling the Beckman lectures—which trace historical developments concerning the study of language and mind with particular reference to rationalist philosophy—for publication (they appeared as *Language and Mind* in 1968). At the same time, he worked on a series of political articles. "Responsibility of Intellectuals," the first of these articles, which were published in the *New York Review of Books*, excited considerable interest. This article had appeared one year earlier in the Harvard student journal *Mosaic*, published by the Hillel Association, and had been brought to the attention of the NYRB's editor by Chomsky's friend Fred Crews. Through his contributions to the NYRB, Chomsky solidified his public persona and his power as a political renegade. These writings would, especially after the 1969 publication of his book *Ameri-*

can Power and the New Mandarins (which contained a number of them), facilitate his association with the vocal dissenters of America's New Left.

One characteristic of the articles, and, in fact, of all Chomsky's writings, is the clarity of the prose. There are very few obscure passages in his work; no matter how complex the philosophical issue in question, and no matter how much prior knowledge must be assumed on the part of the reader, Chomsky provides readable analyses accompanied by easy-to-grasp examples. From an early age, he had suspected that obscurity is generally self-serving or deliberately deceptive. In this sense, the clarity of his prose is, in itself, a consistent political position:

It's true that I don't appeal to philosophical texts, in [political analysis], because I don't find them terribly revealing. Sometimes they are suggestive, but usually I find that when I've cleared away the usually unnecessary rhetoric and complexity, what remains is pretty straightforward. I feel the same about the areas of philosophy where I have done a fair amount of writing and research (philosophy of mind, philosophy of language). (8 Aug. 1994)

This tendency to reject complex philosophical arguments raises questions, even from those otherwise sympathetic to Chomsky, concerning the degree to which issues of individual liberty are straightforward. There is no doubt that corporate agendas, military-backed regimes, and individual-interest-driven institutions can be analyzed and understood as such. But people's willingness to tolerate high levels of personal restriction or persecution, even in the face of possible alternatives, is arguably a phenomenon of considerable complexity. Some theoreticians —members of the Frankfurt or Birmingham schools—suggest that aesthetic media such as visual arts, theater, literature or music offer spaces within which alternative forms of expression can be contemplated or realized. Such issues are linked to the science-versus-nonscience distinction and its implications for useful social engagement.

"Deeper and Deeper"

Now frequently solicited to lend his support to radical causes, and often soliciting the support of others for the same purpose, Chomsky was acutely conscious of the price one had to pay for being a dissenting voice on the domestic scene. He knew what had happened to figures such as Rosa Luxemburg (murdered), Antonio Gramsci (jailed), Bertrand Russell (jailed, as well), Karl Korsch (marginalized), and Sacco and Vanzetti (executed). In short, by the early sixties Noam Chomsky was faced with a dilemma that was to have dramatic consequences. He was being forced to make a conscious decision about the kind of life he would lead. He had a family to consider, a private life, and related responsibilities. He had a flourishing university career, and could anticipate a future filled with rewards both symbolic and tangible. And he had the same number of working hours in a day as anybody else—far too few to sustain ongoing intellectual and polemical debates on a variety of fronts. But Chomsky was, and is, driven: his commitment to the ideal of the good society inspired him to work at a furious intensity. There was no turning back. He undertook to question the government policies that gave rise to the major issues of this period: the ongoing embargo of Cuba and the many terrorist acts directed against the Cubans by the Kennedy administration, the war in Indochina, the arms race, Soviet-American relations, the Soviet occupation of Czechoslovakia, Sino-American relations, American involvement in the Middle East, and the role of the intellectual in all of these.

Looking back on this volatile time, Chomsky has said:

I knew that I was just too intolerably self-indulgent merely to take a passive role in the struggles that were then going on. And I knew that signing petitions, sending money, and showing up now and then at a meeting was not enough. I thought it was critically necessary to take a more active role, and I was well aware of what that would mean. It is not a matter of putting a foot in the water, now and then, getting it wet and then leaving. You go in deeper and deeper. And I knew that I would be following a course that would confront privilege and authority. ("Noam Chomsky" 66)

It was not, then, just a matter of undermining his own status in the academy or giving up his free time. He would have to oppose a powerful ruling class whose interests were deeply entrenched and jealously defended.

Historically, it is a truism that people who uphold libertarian ideas will suffer for it. Chomsky was to spend long nights in custody and was threatened with lengthy jail terms; he even ended up on Richard Nixon's enemy list. It finally got to the point where Carol returned to university to study linguistics so that she would be prepared to support the family in the now-likely event that Noam would no longer be able to do so. How could this happen? Wasn't this America, land of free expression? Didn't

Figure 12
Chomsky giving an open-air political talk in the 1960s.

THE NEW YORK TIMES, WEDNESDAY, JUNE 27, 1973

ys White House Kept 'Enemy List' That

ACADEMICS
Avram Noam Chomsky,
Professor₁ of Modern Lan-
guages, MIT.
Daniel Ellsberg, Professor,
MIT.
George Drennen Fischer,
Member, Executive Commit-
tee, National Education Assn.
J. Kenneth Galbraith, Pro-
fessor of Economics. Har-.
dent Ford Foundation.

Figure 13
A number of academics were named to Nixon's "enemy" list, including Chomsky.

all citizens have the right to voice their opinions? And wouldn't Noam Chomsky, prodigy at MIT, that prestigious institution, be protected by virtue of his position in the academy? Judging by the experience of others in similar situations, the simple answer is "No." Says Chomsky:

> We confidently expected that I'd be in jail in a few years. In fact, that is just what would have happened except for two unexpected events: (1) the utter (and rather typical) incompetence of the intelligence services, which could not find the real organizers of resistance though it was transparent, and kept seeking hidden connections to North Korea, Cuba, or wherever we must have been getting our orders from, as well as mistaking people who agreed to appear at public events as "leaders" and "organizers"; and (2), the Tet Offensive, which convinced American business that the game wasn't worth the candle, and led to the dropping of prosecutions.... (31 Mar. 1995)

Carol's decision to work toward attaining a Ph.D. and, eventually, an academic career, was as difficult to make as Noam's decision to remain politically active. The couple worried about the effect it would have on their children to be raised by working parents; but, of course, both of Noam's parents had taught school throughout his childhood. Back at school, Carol resumed research in a domain to which she had been attracted years earlier: language acquisition. Now, after having had three children, her efforts were enriched by personal experience. She finally secured a position at Harvard's School of Education, and has gone on to enjoy a successful career. In 1969, she published *Linguistic Development in Children from 6 to 10*, which explores those aspects of grammar acquisition that are delayed to later childhood (most grammar is acquired before the age of five). She has also worked on the language ability of deaf-blind subjects in the Sensory Communication Group of MIT's Research Laboratory of Electronics and studied the invented spelling of children who began writing before learning how to read. Carol's major focus in the past fifteen years has been on educational technology, which she taught at the Graduate School of Education at Harvard until last year, and she has consistently done independent work as well.

Marching with the Armies of the Night

There are rewards for working for the common good, not least of which is the sense of personal satisfaction that comes from having a long-standing commitment to the struggle against exploitation and to a good society. Many seasoned activists date their initiation into the cause from the late 1960s, particularly from the spring of 1968; but Chomsky, and a small army of others, had made their commitment much earlier still.

In recognition of his friend's long experience with activism, Paul Lauter asked Chomsky (who had been trying to organize a national tax-resistance movement with Harold Tovish, a well-known sculptor) to team up with him and others to support draft resistance. It was 1966. This was one factor leading to the formation of Resist, which, Chomsky remembers, "very quickly became involved in other forms of resistance to illegitimate authority" (31 Mar. 1995). One of the activities in which Resist became involved was the March on the Pentagon.

The march is described by Norman Mailer in his book *The Armies of the Night: History as a Novel, The Novel as History*. According to Mailer, it all began in September of 1967, when he received a phone call from Mitchell Goodman, a novelist who was married to poet and fellow activist Denise Levertov. Goodman had led antiwar protests in the past, and was on this day calling to urge Mailer to participate in Resist. He said: "On Friday ... we're going to have a demonstration at the Department of Justice to honor students who are turning in their draft cards" (Mailer 9). A week later, Mailer was asked to write and sign a form letter in support of these students, and a week after that, he was invited to speak at a meeting; fellow speakers were to be Robert Lowell (the poet), Dwight Macdonald (Mailer claims that he was, "of all the younger American writers ... the one who had probably been influenced most by Macdonald" [25]), Ed de Grazia (the leading lawyer for the Mobilization's Legal Defense Committee), and Paul Goodman (who "had been the first to talk of the absurd and empty nature of work and education in America" [24]). The meeting took place on Thursday, the day before the demonstration to support draft resisters, and two days prior to a planned march on the Pentagon aimed at crippling some of its operations.

Chomsky was, of course, the right person to call upon to lend support to such activities. During the week leading up to the demonstration, Chomsky and others had put forth a "call to resist illegitimate authority," which was published in the 12 October 1967 edition of the *New York Review of Books*, and which was signed by thousands of people interested in participating. The stage was thus set for the 20 October March on the Pentagon, led by the likes of David Dellinger and Jerry Rubin, "serious men, devoted to hard detailed work" (Mailer 53). The leaflet promoting the march reads:

WE ARE PLANNING AN ACT OF DIRECT CREATIVE RESISTANCE TO THE WAR AND THE DRAFT IN WASHINGTON ON FRIDAY, OCTOBER 20. The locale of our action will be the Department of Justice. We will gather at the First United Congregational Church of Christ, 10th and G Streets, N.W., Washington ... at 1 P.M. We will appear at the Justice Department together with 30 or 40 young men brought by us to Washington to represent the 24 Resistance groups from all over the country. There we will present to the Attorney General the draft cards turned in locally by these groups on October 16.... We will, in a clear, simple ceremony, make concrete our affirmation of support for these young men who are the spearhead of direct resistance to the war and all of its machinery....

[Signed] Mitchell Goodman, Henry Braun, Denise Levertov, Noam Chomsky, William Sloane Coffin, Dwight Macdonald.

NOTE: Among the hundreds already committed to this action are Robert Lowell, Norman Mailer, Ashley Montagu, Arthur Waskow, and professors from most of the major colleges and universities in the East. (qtd. in Mailer 59–60)

The resistance-group representatives were to turn in the draft cards, and then Mitchell Goodman, Reverend William Sloane Coffin, Dr. Benjamin Spock, and seven others would give speeches; the marchers would next make their way to the Office of the Attorney in the Department of Justice Building, where they would inform the attorney general that they were planning to assist draft dodgers. All went according to plan, and 994 draft cards were turned over to the assistant attorney general.

The next day, the demonstrators congregated for the March on the Pentagon. On arriving at their destination, they were met by military police who squirted mace into the eyes of anyone who attempted to enter the building. Mailer was intent on either getting inside the Pentagon or being arrested. He was arrested. Chomsky, along with Dwight Macdonald, Robert Lowell, Dave Dellinger, Dagmar Wilson, Dr. and Mrs. Benjamin Spock, Sidney Lens, and Barbara Deming, had been turned away by the military police, so they instead committed acts of symbolic disobedience, including conducting a teach-in. Dellinger, Wilson, and Chomsky were arrested and hustled off to a police station. Chomsky remembers the scene: "the Pentagon was surrounded by troops, the marchers approached, and then all sorts of things happened, from young women putting flowers in rifles, to prayers, to the 'teach in,' and on, and on. Those were pretty chaotic days, and there was no direction at all to this thing, apart from following the route from Washington across the river that had been settled with the police, and a few large rallies where no one could hear the speakers." And what did this whole scene look like from the other side of the blockades? "Dan Ellsberg later told me," Chomsky recalls, "that he'd been standing next to McNamara up in the Pentagon somewhere, the two of them ridiculing the tactics of the protestors and talking about how they would have done it more efficiently. Hate to think how" (13 Feb. 1996).

Arrested, Questioned, and Charged

Most of the people who had been brought to that police station with Mailer were released. But after many hours of waiting in a cell, word finally came through to Mailer that he was to remain in prison for at least a night. He resigned himself to his fate, and chose a bunk. Mailer recounts these events in the third person, but they are based on his own experiences. He found himself

next to Noam Chomsky, a slim sharp-featured man with an ascetic expression, and an air of gentle but absolute moral integrity. Friends ... had wanted him [Mailer] to meet Chomsky at a party the summer before—he had been told that Chomsky, although barely thirty, was considered a genius at MIT for his new contributions to linguistics—but Mailer had arrived at the party too late. Now, as he bunked down next to Chomsky, Mailer looked for some way to open a discussion on linguistics—he had an amateur's interest in the subject, no, rather, he had a mad inventor's interest, with several wild theories in his pocket which he had never been able to exercise since he could not understand what he read in linguistics books.... [Mailer] cleared his throat now once or twice, turned over in bed, looked for a preparatory question, and recognized that he and Chomsky might share a cell for months, and be the best and most civilized of cellmates, before the mood would be proper to strike the first note of inquiry into what was obviously the tightly packed conceptual coils of Chomsky's intellections. Instead they chatted mildly of the day, the arrests (Chomsky had also been arrested with Dellinger), and of when they would get out. Chomsky—by all odds a dedicated teacher—seemed uneasy at the thought of missing class on Monday. (180)

One month later, Dr. Spock, along with Coffin, Marcus Raskin, Michael Ferber, and Mitchell Goodman, were all indicted by a grand jury. They were charged with advocating resistance to the draft law, a felony punishable by up to five years in prison. Chomsky, in *Radical Priorities*, doesn't fail to point out the absurdity of this case. "As becomes perfectly obvious when you look at the latest government list of co-conspirators, of whom I am one, this is a group of people who did exactly one thing in common: namely, they appeared at a press conference on October 2 to state independently their views against the war and in support of resistance, and then separated, many of them never to meet again" (193). It is, of course, ironic, given the events of the time, that this peaceful gathering intended to demonstrate resistance to authority and to inform the public about the reality of the war was considered a conspiracy. It is even more ironic that it was these specific individuals who were singled out for their participation. "But this is the government's concept of 'conspiracy,'" Chomsky remarks, "and it's quite possible, I don't know if it's likely, that a number of them will face several years in jail for their participation in the conspiracy of which this was the central event and in fact the only event that unites all conspirators" (*Radical Priorities* 193–94). Chomsky's own involvement with the indictment stemmed from his having signed a statement, along with 560 others (including Norman Mailer), "implicating themselves legally to aid and abet draft resisters" (*Radical Priorities* 286).

The trial of Spock and the others attracted national media attention and, according to Chomsky, the entire focus of the news reports was purposefully misdirected. "The idea that Spock and Coffin were involved in forming Resist was invented by the FBI, and lent a comical touch to the Spock-Coffin trial. In fact, Ben Spock and Bill Coffin were very decent and honest people, who were willing to appear at our press conferences and meetings to try to draw some press and a crowd. Neither of them had anything to do with Resist, apart from that" (31 Mar. 1995). The FBI had overestimated the role of Spock and Coffin, but they nonetheless put the two on trial. Chomsky maintains that they initiated the proceedings "by announcing publicly that I was next in line, and if the FBI had even a clue as to what was going on, I would have been a defendant, not a named co-conspirator, at that trial and Spock and Coffin would have been reading about it in the papers. But one can only speculate about what would have happened" (13 Feb. 1996).

Chomsky and the '68ers

From accounts of this particular October weekend in 1967 emerges a compelling portrait of Chomsky the activist. The hallowed events of 1968 were not of monumental consequence to people such as Chomsky, precisely because he, like many others, had been at the center of similar events the year before. Moreover, he had been fascinated by politics all his life, and politically active throughout the late 1950s and early 1960s. He had, in fact, great reservations about the form that the 1968 student uprisings ultimately took.

Chomsky (like others on the left, notably Theodor Adorno) questioned the objectives of the student activists. He even publicly criticized the Columbia University strike at a public forum in 1968:

There, and in meetings afterwards, I was very harshly criticized for that by student leaders and their adult supporters; and I paid virtually no attention to what was going on in Paris as you can see from what I wrote—rightly, I think. SDS [Students for a Democratic Society] had by then "self-destructed"; its leaders were running around saying that the war is a "liberal issue" and they have to get on with revolution. I kept my connections with serious activists and organizations, which were expanding rapidly, though they are beyond the view of most historians and those who bother to write memoirs, most of them (not [Mike] Albert, Dellinger, and others who are rarely mentioned). (31 Mar. 1995)

The events of the late 1960s are, however, fondly recalled by nostalgic leftists, and the mainstream historical record is filled with evocations of the period. Certainly, some of the advancements made at this time were of great significance, and it looked, for a brief moment, as though the student-worker links that had begun to form could advance the cause of radical social change. Students and workers had found a common cause, and had taken to the streets of Paris in the spring of 1968; students throughout Europe and America were becoming vocal in their disillusionment with the institutions that they claimed stifled the individual. Workers had been fighting for control over their own labor conditions throughout the century, but now, suddenly, it seemed possible that cohesion and mutual support could be achieved among a number of disenchanted groups. Ken Coates quotes one of the many posters that appeared in Paris during the uprising:

I participate
Thou participatest
He participates
We participate
You participate
They profit.
    (*Quality* 5)

Also in 1968, Bertrand Russell spoke at Nottingham University in England on the occasion of the Sixth National Conference on Workers' Control. He talked about the relationship between contemporary events and earlier socialist ideals:

I welcome the growing importance of the workers' control movement because its demands go to the heart of what I have always understood socialism to mean. The Prime Minister and his friends have developed a quite new definition of socialism, which includes the penalising of the poorest, capitulating to bankers, attacking the social services, banning the coloured and applauding naked imperialism. When a government makes opportunism the hallmark of its every action, it is the duty of all socialists to cry "halt" and to help create an alternative based on socialist principles. (qtd. in Coates, et al., 9–10)

The workers', peace, civil-rights, Black Power, and women's-liberation movements all looked forward to making important gains. In England, Ken Coates was writing incendiary pamphlets on workers' control and Raymond Williams was offering another take on social history. In Germany, colleagues and workers, members and associates of the Frankfurt School (Adorno, Fromm, Horkheimer, Lowenthal, and Marcuse, all of whom had spent time in the United States during or following World War II) were still publishing powerful Marx-inspired works on psychological, sociological, legal, and aesthetic issues. In France, Simone de Beauvoir was claiming for women a more dominant place in society. In the United States, Abbie Hoffman, Malcolm X, and Martin Luther King seemed to offer proof that change within particular disenfranchised sectors of society, and in society as a whole, was not only essential, but also possible (although Malcolm X and King tended more towards liberal reform than radical change). Activists recognized that there were common obstacles. In his 1973 pamphlet *The Quality of Life and Workers' Control* Coates states:

When Malcolm X and his friends began to preach "Black is beautiful," and the movement for Black Power started rolling, the first and key element in the upsurge of the black population was a new self-recognition. Black people had to recognize themselves, but they also had to learn to like what they recognized. In the same way, the movement for Women's Liberation has to begin with an attack on all the complex attitudes *held by women* which contribute to their subordination. And with working people, things are not fundamentally different. Whilst workers take for granted their right to political suffrage, they are prevented, by attitudes which pervade their whole upbringing, from conceiving industrial suffrage as natural or just. (10–11)

Noam Chomsky was one particularly articulate voice among many, a single note in a growing chorus. Carol Chomsky also became politically active at this time, but entirely on her own terms. Noam writes: "in the sixties, she took part in anti-war activities as she chose, and in her own way; not as part of my activities. Thus when she took the children to a demonstration in Concord of women and children in about 1966 or so (where they were attacked with tin cans, abuse, etc.), that was her initiative, not mine. Same with other things. We have both always felt, strongly, that one should not simply assume that X's wife is automatically interested in and participant in what X happens to be doing" (14 Aug. 1995).

Though he was courted by activists and students who valued his advice on finding appropriate venues and strategies for expressing their urgent concerns, Chomsky was not an American Che Guevara who would take up arms and lead his band towards self-government on horseback. And he was not a Mao or a Lenin who promised to show faithful followers the way to a workers' paradise—and to exact from the unfaithful the price of dissent. He was a scientist who had rational ideas that had made him famous in his field, and a social conscience that gave him the courage and the confidence to recognize that rationality could also be employed to a greater social end: encouraging people to think for, and believe in, themselves.

Public Intellectuals and Radicalism

The fact that Chomsky was immersed, primarily, in a scientific environment had a profound impact on his perception of the role of the intellectual, the way that institutions in this society function, and the value to society of science. His extremely well-developed, libertarian-inspired political sensibilities, and his awareness of individuals and groups far more radical than those of the late 1960s, was the source of his acute skepticism about the ability of many high-profile contemporary activists to contribute anything of lasting value. Chomsky therefore involved himself in popular struggles with activist communities, rather than with the endeavors of well-known figureheads of the left. "I knew Marcuse [who was the guru of the New Left and certainly the most politically active of the Frankfurt School members in the United States] and liked him," he writes, "but thought very little of his work. I liked Fromm's attitudes but thought his work was pretty superficial. Abbie Hoffman I knew a bit (I lent him some money, in fact, expecting that he'd probably use it to jump bail, as he did). King was an important figure, thanks primarily to the platforms created for him by SNCC [the Student Nonviolent Coordinating Committee] workers and other activists. Guevara was of no interest to me; this was mindless romanticism, in my view" (31 Mar. 1995).

It is interesting that the people Chomsky mentions here, although all important contemporary figures, vary tremendously in the approaches they took to the social unrest of the 1960s. It is also interesting that heading Chomsky's list are Herbert Marcuse and Erich Fromm. The two men were highly regarded intellectuals associated with prestigious universities, and they were political activists—much like Chomsky. (Fromm, incidentally, had been an inspiration to Zellig Harris.) But, unlike Chomsky, they directed their efforts towards conducting complex, and ultimately influential, analyses of revolution and history (Marcuse) and violence and psychology (Fromm), which Chomsky evidently considered to be of little real value.

Here, again, we see the peculiar strain of anti-obfuscation—or, better still, anti-intellectualization—that Chomsky deploys against those who speculate in what he considers to be unscientific ways about behavior. This trait gives many who are familiar with Chomsky's linguistics and his politics pause; they cannot come to grips with the vast distance between Chomsky the philosopher, linguist, and cognitive scientist, who formulates intellectual concepts of the most complex kind, and Chomsky the activist, who denigrates the activities of those who speculate from a non-scientific perspective about revolutions, the social psychology of the masses, and the underpinnings of violent behavior. Had Chomsky not refused the role of activist oracle, which he probably could have played successfully had he adopted a more appeasing political stance, he might have proceeded to engage in the kind of clement rabble-rousing to which Americans are accustomed. He did reject that option, and those on the left who chose to support status-quo positions suffered for it. There is no simple rationale for this dichotomy that Chomsky embodies, but somewhere in the ongoing debate about science versus nonscience, self-aggrandizement versus serious work, the knowable versus the unknowable, we may discover some answers.

Chomsky and Irving Howe

By contrasting Chomsky's views with those of Irving Howe we may reach a better understanding of the public intellectual. Chomsky knew Howe personally—they were next-door neighbors for a few years. Howe was the founder of the magazine *Dissent*, and functioned as a kind of guiding light in "left-ish" circles for decades. In the end, however, he may have done more harm than good to genuinely left-wing causes because he became an acceptable version of a left-winger. For example, although he criticized the Vietnam War, he did so in such narrow terms that, in the eyes of some, he eventually lent credibility to its instigators, and to those of other such atrocities. It was partly to avoid, at all costs, such a derailment that Chomsky opted to affiliate himself with the activist community rather than the Marxologists, the intellectual left, or the ivory-tower theoreticians of emancipation. Such a concern also prompted him to maintain consistent viewpoints and to choose his battles carefully.

Howe's role as a left-wing intellectual evolved from the 1930s to the 1970s. In Chomsky's view, it is not Howe's work for *Dissent* (which that journal first began to publish in the 1950s) that was significant. Chomsky was impressed by the even earlier work Howe submitted to the little-known journal *Commentary*, and the work that he had done for yet another journal called *Labor Action* (now virtually unknown) when he was still quite young. Says Chomsky: "[Howe] and Hal Draper particularly had quite interesting commentary on current affairs [in *Labor Action* during the 1940s] (though I didn't go along with the Leninist line, of course). I was never part of the *Dissent* circle, though I read it and occasionally would go to a meeting" (14 Aug. 1995). Journals such as *Dissent*, *The Nation*, *The New Left Review*, and newspapers such as *The Village Voice*, *The Manchester Guardian*, and *Libération* do serve a useful purpose on the left, but they often veer far too close to the status quo to be the organs of radical change. Chomsky remarks:

It's too strong to say that *Dissent* was of no interest to me, then or now. I've always read it, and sometimes find interesting things—much more so in the 1950s, before Howe's bitter resentment of the student movement and the New Left for failing to pay enough attention to him, and the post-1967 switch to unthinking Zionist commitments (largely as a weapon against the New Left, it seems), which changed the character of the journal quite sharply, as you can tell by reading it (try to find something about Israel or Zionism pre-1967, for example). (14 Aug. 1995)

The Example of Peggy Duff

The activist community Chomsky entered during this period was vast and loosely knit. Many have attempted to draw a portrait of this milieu— David Dellinger and Howard Zinn have each written about it. Here, however, with the aim of exemplifying what Chomsky considers to be useful activist work, I've chosen to focus on one important individual: Peggy Duff. Chomsky's own lists of key activists generally contain names that are rarely mentioned beyond certain small circles. Duff was for decades a serious activist who, despite her enormous output, has remained relatively obsure (especially in the United States).

One of the most influential figures in the British peace movement from the 1940s onward, and general secretary of the Campaign for Nuclear Disarmament (CND) from 1958 to 1967, Duff was deeply involved in the Israel-Palestine issue; moreover, according to Chomsky, she kept "the international opposition against the Vietnam War on some kind of serious and useful track, and she helped organize some of the most important aspects of it" (13 Feb. 1996). She was also the general secretary of the International Confederation for Disarmament and Peace (ICDP—a grouping of independent movements in Europe, North America, Asia, and Australasia); one of the leading figures in CND, and antinuclear work generally; the editor of two journals, *Vietnam International* and *Peace*

Press; a contributor to the *Peace Press* and the *Tribune*; editor of *War or Peace in the Middle East?* (to which Chomsky contributed); author of *Left, Left, Left*—in short, Duff was, in Chomsky's assessment, "one of the people who really changed modern history."

[S]he is a woman, an activist, a serious intellectual, a knowledgeable and informed writer—and therefore unknown outside the universe of others who are actually engaged in the problems of the world. She has disappeared from history. She's not a "public intellectual"; she was far too important in modern history for that. She spent no time posturing before other intellectuals or inhabiting the various cocoons of the literary intellectual culture. She belongs to the same category as the SNCC [Student Nonviolent Coordinating Committee] workers who carried out the civil rights movement in the U.S., or the dedicated Christian activists who were at the core of the solidarity movements of the '80s, or the unknown people who created the labor movements, or the other people who have mattered in history, and are therefore unknown and forgotten (if ever known in respectable—i.e., intellectually and morally corrupt—circles).... [Duff is] typical of people who make a difference in history. She's also typical of the people in my actual milieu, since childhood, except for her unusual international prominence.... (31 Mar. 1995)

True intellectuals, like Peggy Duff, are unattractive to the ruling elite because they reveal things that those in power would prefer to conceal. Unlike (say) Irving Howe, Duff was not relied upon by the popular media for commentary on current events; she is not mentioned in mainstream history books; and her work has been played down or ignored. The mainstream historical record of the late 1960s, like that of virtually any period, contains very few references to really important activist work. The prevalence of this kind of willful ignorance is another leitmotif for Chomsky.

If it weren't for Howard Zinn and a few others, few (apart from actual participants) would even know about the SNCC, the leading element in the civil rights movement. Similarly, the truth about the Black Panthers is not, and never will be, made known, I suppose. Resist was supporting elements of the Panthers from very early on, discriminating quite carefully between the serious organizers (like Fred Hampton) and the criminal elements and hustlers. (31 Mar. 1995)

Of course, resistance has a price—as Mailer, Spock, and Coffin, among so many others, learned during this era—and people such as Black Panther Fred Hampton ended up by paying with their lives. Chomsky writes: "I was one of the few white faces at Fred Hampton's funeral in Chicago in 1969, after he was murdered by the Chicago police and FBI" (31 Mar.

1995). That even a supreme sacrifice such as this can go virtually unnoticed beyond a limited community is appalling to Chomsky. He points out that "only actual participants … would know or understand any of this, and they don't write their reminiscences.… Without serious oral history, the truth will never be known" (31 Mar. 1995).

One of the existing organs for accurate recollections of history is the activist press. I mentioned earlier that Chomsky's political books are available through a number of presses, including Pantheon, Black Rose, Common Courage, South End, Columbia, and Verso, and that his articles have been published in dozens of different journals, notably Z Magazine. South End Press and Z Magazine merit special attention here in the context of a discussion of activist groups since they are collective enterprises that concentrate upon activist works. South End Press has published more books by Chomsky than any other publisher, and Z Magazine has published more of his political articles than all other outlets combined. This indicates Chomsky's determination to participate in collectives, here initiated by his former students at MIT.

These particular collectives were born from the Rosa Luxemburg student group at MIT, for which Noam Chomsky and Louis Kampf were faculty advisers (just as Rosenberg and Harris were faculty advisers for

Figure 14
Michael Albert and Lydia Sargent launched South End Press.

Avukah). Kampf and Chomsky had been teaching the previously described social-sciences courses at MIT, and some of the students studying
with them were leaders of the intellectual/political-activist ferment in and
around Cambridge. The most active of these students was Mike Albert,
who became student president and then went on to participate in the
launching of South End Press and *Z Magazine*. Other students, including
Steve Shalom and Peter Bohmer, also went on to participate in the collectives. "In fact," notes Chomsky, "it's a more cohesive and politically
active group than Avukah and what came out of it—which was interesting and important, but mainly a small group of intellectuals with narrow
concerns, very Jewish-Palestine centered—and has had far more of an
impact on the political scene, for 30 years now" (31 Mar. 1995).

Serendipity and Self-Justification

To the degree that Chomsky's activism was the product of his very conscious determination to be instrumental in the creation of a good society,
his scientific achievement was serendipitous. While, in retrospect, it may
seem as though he moved smoothly from one academic triumph to
another, Chomsky's ascent to the status of recognized figure within the
academy was, at times, haphazard: he got into linguistics "more or less by
accident"; he became a Harvard Fellow and was subsequently offered the
research position in the electronics lab at MIT thanks to the intervention of
friends; Morris Halle put him in contact with an editor who agreed to
publish the results of his "hobby" (*Syntactic Structures*); he was praised in
a long and detailed review, which attracted the attention of many key
people in the field. If we take into account his approach to institutions
(particularly places of higher learning), his renegade attitude towards
academia in general, and the broad number of fields that interested him
(logic, mathematics, philosophy, linguistics, languages, literature), it is
surprising that his career has been such a success.

The most frequently discussed aspect of Chomsky's career path is his
having chosen/been chosen by MIT, an institution that didn't even have
a linguistics department when Chomsky first arrived (or for that matter
a department of philosophy or even psychology), and that, moreover,
was the epicenter of research for the United States military. Some have

suggested that Chomsky's institutional affiliation has hampered his work because it has compelled him to defend its scientificity while forcing him into a direct collaboration with the military.

In 1969, the Pentagon and NASA were financing two MIT laboratories; one (now called Draper) was working on inertial guidance systems, while the other (Lincoln) was (to the best of Chomsky's recollection) "engaged in some things that involved ongoing counterinsurgency" (13 Feb. 1996). Chomsky maintains that it was impossible at that time for MIT and its researchers to sever ties with the military-industrial complex and continue to function. What he proposed then he stands by even today: universities with departments that work on bacterial warfare should do so openly, by developing departments of death. His intention was to inform the general population of what was going on so that individuals could make informed and unencumbered decisions about their actions. Such thinking was behind his response to the Pounds Committee, which was formed to defuse the tension that was mushrooming between the MIT administration and a group of students who were adamantly opposed to the military connection: "The students and I submitted a dissident report disagreeing with the majority. The way it broke down was that the right-wing faculty wanted to keep the labs, the liberal faculty wanted to break the relations (at least formally), and the radical students and I wanted to keep the labs on campus, on the principle that what is going to be going on anyway ought to be open and above board, so that people would know what is happening and act accordingly" (31 Mar. 1995).

Of course, there was resistance to the report from the majority of faculty members, "including all the liberal faculty, [who] were smart enough to understand just what that implied, and wanted what amounted to a formal administrative change, so that technically the labs weren't part of the Institute, hence the connections remained pretty much invisible, though not much changed" (31 Mar. 1995). In short, Chomsky's position on this issue is that no formal constraints should be put on research. So at this time he took what he calls "a pretty extreme position," and indeed "one that might be hard to defend had anyone ever criticized it," which he describes as follows:

Nothing should be done to impede people from teaching and doing their research even if at that very moment it was being used to massacre and destroy. That was not academic. At the time, the MIT political science department was doing just that (in my opinion), and the issue was very much alive as Kennedy-Johnson "action intellectuals" started returning to the universities after Nixon's election. In fact, as a spokesman for the Rosa Luxemburg collective, I went to see the President of MIT in 1969 to inform him that we intended to protest publicly if there turned out to be any truth to the rumours then circulating that Walt Rostow (who we regarded as a war criminal) was being denied a position at MIT on political grounds (claims that were hardly plausible, and turned out to be utterly false). (13 Feb. 1996)

So, according to Chomsky, no institution should legislate what people are permitted to work on. Instead, "people have a responsibility for the foreseeable consequences of their actions, and therefore have the responsibility of thinking about the research they undertake and what it might lead to under existing conditions" (13 Feb. 1996).

When berated for accepting a salary from an institution so intimately involved in the business of death and destruction, Chomsky pointed out that receiving financing from an institution only limits one's ability to speak out if that institution is totalitarian in nature. Interestingly, most of the criticism came from the left, prompting Chomsky to ask: "Did you ever hear anyone suggest that Marx shouldn't have worked in the British Museum, the very symbol of British Imperialism?" (31 Mar. 1995).

Chomsky has also defended his affiliation with MIT in the context of the hard-sciences-versus-social-sciences debate. Defining the parameters of that discussion, he writes:

[T]here is a noticeable general difference between the sciences and mathematics on the one hand, and the humanities and social sciences on the other. It's a first approximation, but one that is real. In the former, the factors of integrity tend to dominate more over the factors of ideology. It's not that scientists are more honest people. It's just that nature is a harsh taskmaster. You can lie or distort the story of the French Revolution as long as you like, and nothing will happen. Propose a false theory in chemistry, and it'll be refuted tomorrow. Fakery in scientific experiment is a very marginal phenomenon, contrary to what you read in the press, and is quickly discovered, for a very simple reason: people replicate, and it's their professional task to check results and the thinking that leads to them. (22 July 1992)

The natural or "hard" sciences are "driven by internal considerations, by what can be studied *next*, what is on the fringes of understanding" (14 June 1993). Advancement in science progresses in an incremental fashion, and while a given end may be morally reprehensible to some, the accidental discoveries made in the process of attaining that end may be of enormous benefit to many. For example, although a government might decide to give massive funding to a researcher who is working on a truth serum so that its agents can extract information from captured spies, that researcher will be obliged, in formulating the serum, to analyze how particular drugs affect the thinking process, and thus be of use to the population at large in a variety of crucial ways.

Such considerations lead Chomsky to compare Harvard and MIT—the institutions within which he has worked. He describes them as two of the most influential universities in the world. "Harvard is humanities based: it's the place where people are trained to rule the world," while "MIT is science-based: it's the place where people are trained to make the world work" (18 Feb. 1993). Although Chomsky's linguistic research clearly belongs to the domain of the hard sciences, it may be consigned to its softer edges as it is still far from having the depth of mathematics or physics according to his own definition. It is obvious, however, where his sympathies lie:

For political dissidents, MIT is a far more friendly place. Virtually all the faculty peace activism in Cambridge, for example, has come from MIT, with some drifters occasionally from Harvard. My own experience is typical. If I walk into the Harvard Faculty Club, you can feel the chill settle, literally. It's inconceivable that I could be asked to give a talk at the Kennedy School of Government (ADA-style liberalism, in large measure), unless it's organized by some group they can't control (like the foreign press, which runs regular programs), in which case they grit their teeth and bear it. In contrast, I've had a very friendly and supportive environment at MIT, no matter what I've been doing. (18 Feb. 1993)

This is a contentious point, for there are, of course, exceptions to the rule that Chomsky is at pains to illustrate. One such exception is the case of Elaine Bernard: although she is not a Harvard faculty member, she finds the atmosphere of that institution reasonably supportive. Bernard moved from Canada to the United States in 1989. She had been an activist for many years and had served as president of the British Columbia New Democratic Party. She is now the executive director of the Harvard Trade Union Program and a member of the *New Politics* editorial board. Another is the case of David Noble, a historian who taught for nine years at MIT and conducted research on how science and technology develop as products not only of accumulated knowledge and skills, but also of social power and conflict. Noble, like Chomsky, is, as well, an activist and social

critic who assists rank-and-file groups in several industries in their struggle with new technologies. He was the cofounder, with Ralph Nader, of
the National Coalition for Universities in the Public Interest. In 1984, he
was fired by MIT "for his ideas and his actions in support of those ideas."
He subsequently "brought a suit against MIT to obtain and make public
the documentary record of his political firing and on the basis of this
record the American Historical Association subsequently condemned MIT
for the firing" (Noble, *Progress* 165). Chomsky comments: "As for David
Noble, it's always hard to make judgments about such issues, but my own
is that it wasn't primarily his (quite outstanding) dissident work that led
to the tenure denial—in a department that considers itself rather to the
left-liberal side, I suppose" (27 June 1995).

The basis of Chomsky's reputation at MIT is his scientific research. He
is acclaimed within the university for being a valuable contributor to the
scientific fields within which he works—not for his actions and writings in
the political realm. This gives him a certain leverage and a freedom from
ideological control that he would not enjoy if he had become attached to a
humanities-based university.

Chomsky the "Muckraker"

At the beginning of the 1970s, Chomsky, now in his early forties, continued to lecture, receive honors, and hone his linguistic works. He published *Studies on Semantics in Generative Grammar* in 1972; he received
honorary D.H.L.'s from Loyola University in Chicago and Swarthmore
College in 1970, Bard College in 1971, Delhi University in 1972, and the
University of Massachusetts in 1973. He also debated Michel Foucault on
Dutch television in 1971, and criticized Richard Herrnstein's work (the
early version of *The Bell Curve*) in the journal *Cognition*. On the political
side, he was increasingly active, giving the Bertrand Russell Memorial
Lectures in Cambridge in 1971, which were published the same year as
Problems of Knowledge and Freedom. *At War with Asia* appeared in
1970, and *For Reasons of State* in 1973 (published in two volumes in
Britain, *For Reasons of State* and *The Backroom Boys*).

The focus of much of his political work during this period, aside from
the relationship between the intellectual and the state, was the Vietnam

Figure 15
Chomsky and Michel Foucault appear on Dutch television, 1971. The moderator
is Fons Elders.

War. (Given the support of the intellectual community and the so-called
doves for this conflict, at least at the outset, these two issues were strongly
related.) In tackling the enormous issues arising from the war, Chomsky
always worked from the assumption that the specific actions of a capitalist imperialist government are but symptoms of the larger problem: working classes and marginalized groups are being oppressed by an ever-
shrinking minority, so movements must be founded that encourage people
"to develop their own consciousness and initiative to free themselves"
(Abramovitch 3 Apr. 1995).

In some of his political writings from this period onward, when he
comments on specific interventions, Chomsky engages in a form of muckraking. (Not all of his political works fall into this category, however;
exceptions include his analyses of the role of the intellectual in society, his

studies of the history and ideology of the left, and some of his historical writings, including those concerned with Cartesian thought, the Spanish Civil War, World War II in the Pacific, and the Arab-Jewish relationship.) Muckraking is spreading the dung around in an attempt to make it more evident. The practice actually became a kind of movement with a history. In his autobiography, Lincoln Steffens recalls that he was once told by a professor of history: "You were the first of the muckrakers. If you will tell now how you happened to start muckraking not only will you contribute to our knowledge of an important chapter of American history; you may throw light upon the rise and the run of social movements" (357). In fact, Steffens refutes the "original muckraker" label, claiming that "the prophets of the Old Testament were ahead of me, and—to make a big jump in time—so were the writers, editors, and reporters (including myself) of the 1890s who were finding fault with 'things as they are' in the pre-muckraking period" (357).

Furthermore, Steffens claims that his contribution to history was but "a story, a confession of innocence" because "I did not intend to be a muckraker; I did not know that I was one till President Roosevelt picked the name out of Bunyan's *Pilgrim's Progress* and pinned it on us; and even then he said that he did not mean me" (357). Chomsky, as well, rejects the label (as he does virtually all labels), because it is used to undermine those who speak out against the powers that be: "We don't call critical discussion of the Soviet Union 'muckraking.' The term, with its connotations of gossip and unseriousness, serves as one of the many devices used by Western power to protect itself from scrutiny, in my opinion" (30 May 1994). Distancing himself even further, he writes: "There is another activity—political analysis, diplomatic history, social and intellectual history, etc.—which is sometimes called 'muckraking' if it departs from the doctrine and the style that is used by professionals to make simple things look obscure and profound. But it's not a terminology I favor.... and [I] do virtually nothing of that sort" (8 Aug. 1994). And Edward S. Herman responds to the suggestion that Chomsky's work has a muckraking element with words of caution:

[I]n dealing with Noam Chomsky as a muckraker, I would urge giving weight to the scholarly component, intellectual power, and originality of much of his political writing. Time and again he has taken up a subject like the Cold War, Haiti, the Central American peace process, East Timor, and even western colonialism (chapter 1 of *Year 501*) and produced original materials, laid out with remarkable exhaustiveness, in a compelling frame that is very convincing. His dredging up the 1954 and 1965 documents on U.S. policy in Central America (see his *Managua Lectures*) is a case in point; his sections in *Necessary Illusions* on "Demolishing the Accords," and "On Critical Balance," are devastating. He has to be ignored because he can't be handled by honest debate. (2 Aug. 1994)

But what concerns Chomsky first and foremost is the danger of losing sight of what is truly important in a given situation. If, for example, one criticizes the individual decisions of a particular government administration, one implies that some decisions are better than others within the existing framework of that administration, and therefore tacitly endorses it. The goal should be to test the ideological soundness of the framework, to free oneself from its limitations and constraints. There is an echo here of the hard-science-versus-social-science debate: political analysis is situated in the realm of the obvious; virtually anybody who stops watching television, paying attention to sporting events, or playing the stock market, and concentrates, instead, on the society in which he or she lives, could, in Chomsky's view, effect an appropriate political critique. He writes: "Intellectuals try to make it look difficult; postmodernism carries this to extremes, in my opinion. But outside the hard sciences and mathematics, there really isn't a lot that is beyond the reach of people without special training" (8 Aug. 1994).

Chomsky's disdain for those who practice this type of obfuscation, who divert public attention from what is essential, is often palpable:

[Theodore] Draper's work on Iran-contra [*A Very Thin Line: The Iran-Contra Affairs* (1991)] is, to answer your question, a good example of "muckraking," highly respected although it scrupulously ignores everything important—such as the fact that the sale of U.S. arms to Iran via Israel with Saudi Arabian funding began in the early 1980s, when there were no hostages, and the reasons were clearly and explicitly explained by high Israeli officials and fit precisely within standard operating procedure for overthrowing civilian governments; and that the illegal funding of the contras was well known as well, but suppressed until the shooting down of the Hasenfus plane made suppression impossible.... [Such an approach is] standard, and entirely understandable in a corrupt intellectual culture. (31 Mar. 1995)

To go beyond political critique, to go beyond muckraking, one must have an understanding of the mechanisms—economic, psychological, legal, sociological—that limit our ability to comprehend, or act in favor of, a left-libertarian society. From the standpoint of adherents to radical critique, these mechanisms are extremely complex and require a general analysis of the conditions (sociopolitical, for example) that promote certain kinds of behavior, rather than the details of particular events. Chomsky, however, does not pretend that such deeper analysis is, at present, possible. He applies himself to exposing the events that he considers to be not very well understood, or else distorted by (for example) the media. As Abramovitch has remarked:

I always enjoy reading stuff by these muckrakers; one of the best recent examples is I. F. Stone, and the things that he discovered about the Vietnam War are really mind-boggling. Not that anybody should be surprised that governments are capable of doing these things; it is always interesting to read about them and to have these events exposed. That is something that Chomsky does very well in terms of American society. But that is only one aspect. The other aspect is trying to understand more fully, if one can, how society functions; more specifically, what kinds of crises will society undergo? Will society be able to circumvent complete breakdowns of their structures? Until now they have been able to survive; many radicals predicted for so long that "the end has arrived," and tomorrow morning a new society will emerge. That does not seem to happen. This suggests that society has a way of temporarily resolving some of its problems so that it can maintain its momentum or its existence or its structure. It would be interesting to try to discover whether this is a nonending type of process. (12 Feb. 1991)

In Chomsky's opinion, there are no theories that can address such issues: "I'm not aware of the existence of any theories, in any serious sense of the term, that yield insight in the analysis case, including work on the nature of totalitarianism, internal filtering, and all the rest." This, of course, separates him from theoreticians with whom he would otherwise be sympathetic, in terms of their interests, such as Erich Fromm or Herbert Marcuse. In fact, he continues, this kind of work "seems to me pretty obvious, and frankly, I get irritated when intellectuals dress it up as something more than that. Furthermore, I think we can give an analysis of that as well: that's the way you become a respected public intellectual, who can preen before others of the same type. But if there is anything that can't be told to high school students in monosyllables, I haven't yet heard it" (18 May 1995).

This all raises a perhaps unresolvable distinction. One could claim that Chomsky's political efforts, initiated in the late 1960s and clearly on course by the early 1970s, are designed to alert the population to crucial

events about which they know very little because they have been successfully diverted by highly organized propaganda campaigns and numerous
other consciously, and sometimes unconsciously, employed tactics. Or,
alternatively, one could claim that Chomsky's political work is built upon
particular precepts that are explained with regard to individual issues
(Vietnam, Cambodia, the Middle East), but that it implicitly poses, without fully answering, questions such as: Why we are at this point in our
political history? How is change possible in the face of such powerful
impediments? What steps can we take to free ourselves from manifestly
oppressive structures?

Chomsky will not tell us how to act. We are faced with the problems of
determining what is appropriate action at a particular historical juncture
and deciding what kind of work should be undertaken in order to encourage the creative possibilities inherent in all human beings: these
problems may prove to have the same solution. Ken Coates suggests, in a
1973 pamphlet entitled "Socialists and the Labour Party," that neither
complex political philosophy nor accessible, straightforward prose is sufficient; what workers must do in order to take control of their lives is to
work in *both* areas. Beginning with the argument that workers can learn
from particular movements (the revolutions in China or Russia are good
examples, but his list does contain a few dubious choices) and that workers
require an international leadership and perspective, Coates goes on to
claim that workers also need both a philosophical and a practical point of
entry into debates concerning their own interests:

It is obviously implied in all this that we need to study Marx, Lenin, Luxemburg,
Lukács, Trotsky, Gramsci, Mao and many other great figures in the history of
socialist thought: but it is equally implied that we need to think for ourselves, and
that this is a most difficult task to perform in the manner required to help ordinary
workpeople in their struggles, if we remain artificially disengaged from all the
major problems which confront the working-class movement, as it is constituted
at present, in the organizations which it has evolved in the attempt to meet those
problems. (7)

Where the emphasis should lie, and what relation exists between "socialist
thought" and efforts to encourage workers to think for themselves is unclear, but Coates does offer a context in which to negotiate the seem-
ingly insurmountable distance between, say, Che Guevara and Theodor
Adorno.

Linguistic Wars

In the field of linguistics, and specifically in Chomsky's department at MIT, the late 1960s was a period of dissension and discord among faculty and students. A September 1972 *New York Times* article called "Former Chomsky Disciples Hurl Harsh Words at the Master" quotes Chomsky's colleague John Ross as saying that Chomsky was so committed to the framework he had elaborated that "he can't see where it's inadequate" (70). Ross and other "schismatics" insisted that "you can't do syntax without doing semantics as well," a premise that "transformational grammarians" such as Chomsky did not accept. The article also quotes George Lakoff, another MIT colleague: "Since Chomsky's syntax does not and cannot admit context, he can't even account for the word 'please.' . . . Nor can he handle hesitations like 'oh' and 'eh.' But it's virtually impossible to talk to Chomsky about these things. He's a genius, and he fights dirty when he argues. He uses every trick in the book, and he's the best debater I've ever met."

The linguistic wars took on such momentum that they broke out of academic circles and became known to the public. They were well rehearsed in the mainstream media—including the *New York Times*, roughly six years after the fact. A great number of persistent misconceptions arose from the schism these skirmishes created within the field of linguistics. Perhaps it is for these reasons that the public perception of linguistics is both frozen in time and based upon inaccuracies; knowledgable people working outside the field are likely to have heard of deep structure and generative grammar, but remain unaware of the substantial advances made by Chomsky and others since.

At first, those people who were working with Chomsky at MIT in the late 1960s on the work that was overturning Bloomfield-inspired linguistics rallied around him. He was calling into question a whole field as it had, until that point, been understood. Paul Postal recalls:

It was really a psychologically painful situation, because [Bloomfieldian linguistics] was itself a revolutionary linguistics that had gained its ascendancy by proclaiming that it was the scientific way to study language, and that traditional linguistics was unscientific. [The followers of Bloomfield] had, themselves, trampled on people rather forcefully, made a lot of enemies, did a lot of unpleasant things. Now, bang, not very long after they were really in place, *they* were suddenly being attacked, and in a way that was incomprehensible to them. They were being told that *they* weren't being scientific. That just had to be a nightmare for them. (qtd. in R. A. Harris 73)

Gradually, some of Chomsky's people came to the conclusion that his approach needed radical reworking, and they formulated what was considered by certain observers to be a more satisfactory one. Robin Lakoff describes it in rather dramatic terms:

As of 1965, and even later, we find in the bowels of Building 20 [the home of the MIT linguistics department] a group of dedicated co-conspirators, united by missionary zeal and shared purpose. A year or two later, the garment is unravelling, and by the end of the decade the mood is total warfare. The field was always closed off against the outside; no serpent was introduced from outside of Eden to seduce or corrupt. Any dissension had to be home-brewed. (qtd. in R. A. Harris 102)

Figure 16
Building 20 at MIT, immortalized as the center of Chomskian linguistic work.

Much has been made of this dissension; in fact, a recent book argues that the rift between the interpretivists (Chomsky) and the generative semantics program (George Lakoff, McCawley, Postal, and Ross) was not quite so clear. "The two programs were in fact quite complementary, and the tensions between them not only bound each to the other, but also steered them jointly on to a more productive path than either of them individually might otherwise have taken" (Huck and Goldsmith 3). But Chomsky downplays its importance and his own part in this "war." And he especially condemns R. A. Harris's view that "everything must be a power play, a religion.... The real world has no resemblance to these fantasies, a fact easily demonstrated by a look at the published literature" (31 Mar. 1995). Chomsky continues:

The "dissension" between, say, Jackendoff and others (many of them not my students: Lakoff, Postal, etc.) was from about 1966 or so. I was never really part of it.... my one participation in the debate was in 1969, at a conference in Texas, where I flew in and flew out immediately at the impassioned request of a former student there, Stanley Peters, who wanted me to make some public response to the by then rather hysterical tone of the generative semanticists, all pretty childish in my opinion, and in 1969 I had quite different things on my mind. (3 Apr. 1995)

What kind of things? While the battle raged at MIT, Chomsky reached "the peak" of his antiwar activity. Between fulfilling this commitment, conducting his linguistic research, and publishing the results, he "hardly would have had time for 'power struggles' even if I had been interested" (14 Aug. 1995). It is also notable that "every single appointment in my own area in those years in my own department was a generative semanticist (Postal, Ross, Perlmutter, Kiparsky—insofar as he worked on these topics) and not a single person who I was actually working with (Lasnik, Jackendoff, Emonds, Kayne, etc.) was appointed—facts always omitted by the 'postmodern historians' (i.e., R. A. Harris) of this period, though they know them perfectly well" (14 Aug. 1995).

The other issue that was generated by this conflict involved the left's perception of Chomsky's scientific work: many began to consider it rigid because it was founded upon principles of inherited genetic abilities and immutable categories, the anathema of left-wing thinking, which stresses the role that environment plays in individual development. Chomsky dismisses this point of view as "completely irrational" for the following reasons:

First, the denial of inherited genetic abilities is simply ridiculous. Looking beyond truisms, we find, as everywhere in the biological world, that the effects of inherited genetic abilities are enormous. Second, why the enormous prevalence and success of ideas that could not conceivably be correct, like the various "empty organism" theories? That question arises *after* one has shown these theories to be wrong, in this case, scarcely more than absurd. I also suggested an answer: empty organism theories are very useful to those who are engaged in manipulation and control, because they remove all moral barriers to such actions (for the good of the targets, of course!). I suggested that that is one likely reason for the appeal of these absurd notions to what is called "the left" ... and to the other advocates of engineering of consent and social management.... Third, not only is it very clear that there are highly significant genetic factors in the mental (as all other) domains, but we should be delighted to discover the fact, since without such initial constraints, there can be no significant development, creative acts, and so on. (13 Feb. 1996)

Another row erupted in 1972 that had a familiar echo to it. In December of 1971, Chomsky had reviewed, once again (in the *New York Review of Books*), the work of B. F. Skinner, this time his extremely popular *Beyond Freedom and Dignity*. The book advocated applying the techniques of behavioral science to mute antisocial tendencies in society with the objective of creating a more benign civilization. Skinner had been denounced by numerous libertarians and humanists as authoritarian, but it was Chomsky who, after a long and detailed analysis of the alleged substantive content of the work under review, described his envisioned society as akin to "a well-run concentration camp with inmates spying on one another and the gas ovens smoking in the distance." An article in the *London Times* in February of 1972, "America's Great Intellectual Prizefight," quoted Skinner: "I wonder how a man of such intelligence can do a thing like that," he said sullenly. "We are on opposite sides of the debate, and I'm very content with that. I can't take him seriously as a critic. He's a mentalist and refuses to accept that there is a science of behaviour. He's unaware of what's going on in the field of behaviour modification, and he's having trouble with his linguistics."

A Modern-Day Soothsayer

Chomsky was by now a famous, but marginalized (by the mainstream press) critic of American policy. As always, he challenged mainstream organs to justify their methods of presenting facts, but with limited success: scarcely any of his letters to the editor, for example, were ever published. The exceptions were often those missives authored by others that he cosigned, such as one to the editor of the *New York Times*, dated 16 February 1972, in which he, along with Mark Sacharoff, Robert Jay Lifton, and Fred Branfman expressed the following opinion: "No doubt, the destruction of Indochina by the U.S. passed [the point of atrocity] long ago. Nevertheless, another intense and highly visible outbreak of deranged obliteration, concentrated into a few weeks and conducted brazenly before the eyes of the world, would add a new dimension of repellent conduct to our shameful record in Southeast Asia." So Chomsky continued to write, march, and collaborate with a range of groups and individuals in pursuit of well-established goals. In 1973, for example, Chomsky, Dellinger, Hentoff, Spock, Boyle, Ginsberg, Macdonald, and Day headed a committee to commemorate the fiftieth anniversary of the War Resisters' League.

From the hundreds of articles and rebuttals that he wrote during this period concerning Vietnam, Cambodia, and Laos, emerges an image of Chomsky as a kind of modern-day soothsayer. Unlike many leftists of his generation, Chomsky never flirted with movements or organizations that were later revealed to be totalitarian, oppressive, exclusionary, anti-revolutionary, or elitist. Leninism, Stalinism, Trotskyism, and Maoism offered to many of Chomsky's disillusioned contemporaries an alternative to what they saw as blatantly exclusionary American-style capitalism. When reports about what had actually occurred in the former Soviet Union and China began to filter through, many felt betrayed. We now hear a lot about how the left has been discredited, the hopelessness of utopian thinking, the futility of activist struggle, but little about the libertarian options that Chomsky and others have so consistently presented.

The type of dismay that has permeated contemporary intellectual circles has not touched Chomsky. He has very little to regret. His work, in fact, contains some of the most accurate analyses of this century. And yet, most of his criticisms of American policy, past and present, are seldom mentioned in the mainstream press or by the instructors and professors who teach history or politics. Political science departments rarely use his material on Vietnam, the Cold War, Central America, or Israel. Commenting on this with regard to Vietnam, Chomsky says: "I think you'll find virtually no one anywhere near the mainstream who is even familiar with, let alone admits, any aspect of my criticism of the war. That extends to the left. Thus on the left, who described, or now describes, the war as a U.S. war against South Vietnam, which the U.S. had largely won by the early 1970s?" (31 Mar. 1995). The prevailing critical viewpoint on the bombardment and destruction of Vietnam Chomsky summarizes this way: "At the critical end of the mainstream spectrum, the war began with 'blundering efforts to do good' and ended as a 'disaster' because the costs were too high. *Dissent*, which supported the U.S. attack in 1964 (calling it 'defense') concluded after the war that its position had been right all along. On the left, the standard view is that the Vietnamese won and the U.S. lost." And again he stresses his exclusion: "My own view, shared with Edward Herman, is virtually non-existent in the debate, and our (together and separately) detailed documentation of what in fact happened in crucial periods, from the beginning through the 1973 peace accords, is unknown" (31 Mar. 1995).

Of course, in the first days of opposition to American policies on Vietnam, Chomsky and those sympathetic to his views were even more severely marginalized. He foresaw the government ensuring that Indochinese-style invasions launched to protect domestic interests would become the norm (think of El Salvador, Nicaragua, Tripoli, the Gulf War). Most of the re-evaluation of the Vietnam War concerns the mistakes, generally tactical mistakes, that the American government made. These assessments are often considered radical; their acceptance by policy makers is also taken to be an indication that the American political system is working—after all, it has the capacity to admit its own errors. But this is a long way from Chomsky's view:

I never criticized United States planners for mistakes in Vietnam. True, they made some mistakes, but my criticism was always aimed at what they aimed to do and largely achieved. The Russians doubtless made mistakes in Afghanistan, but my condemnation of their aggression and atrocities never mentioned those mistakes, which are irrelevant to the matter—though not for the commissars. Within our ideological system, it is impossible to perceive that anyone might criticize anything but "mistakes" (I suspect that totalitarian Russia was more open in that regard). (31 Mar. 1995)

Even when opponents of Chomsky's position came around to questioning American involvement in Vietnam (still a long way from questioning the fundamentally immoral objectives that the United States had for Indochina), they found ways to overlook the underlying message of his work in favor of tangentially related matters. For example, the author of a generally positive review of *For Reasons of State* and *The Backroom Boys*, published in the 21 December 1973 edition of the *Times Literary Supplement*, objects to the fact that the material was written some time before it was published (even though it was based on documentation that appeared just as the book did—notably the Pentagon Papers); that it was brought out as two books rather than one (the publisher's decision); and that Chomsky did not revise the text more completely. In another review of *The Backroom Boys*, this time in the 5 April 1974 edition of the *Times Higher Education Supplement*, Nigel Young also takes on Chomsky's style; though it resembles scholarship, he maintains, Chomsky's book is polemical. And, much later, in a *Times Literary Supplement* review of *The Chomsky Reader*, Charles Townshend indulges in a long tirade on Chomsky's style; he condemns the fevered pace, the overabundance of reference and detail, and the way that the reader is hit over the head at the beginning of a piece, before the argument is brought to a climax.

This obsession with issues of style or genre seems to serve as a means of avoiding the essential arguments in Chomsky's work, and may therefore lend, further credibility to his claim that the intelligentsia cannot resist conforming to official doctrine. The author of the 21 December 1973 TLS review does recall, near the end of the piece, that Chomsky lays bare America's real interests in Indochina and reveals the ways in which consecutive American administrations have played God in Asia. The reviewer also condones Chomsky's decision to expose the deliberateness and the ferocity of those administrations' attacks against Asia's rural communities. But this review does not accurately reflect its subject, because it seems to suggest that there are less arrogant and more imaginative ways to slaughter people; it also ignores Chomsky's (and Herman's) view that the price America has paid is negligible in light of the fact that it largely achieved its goals in Indochina (just as it did in the long Cold War; although the exercise may have appeared pointless, it ultimately allowed

America to divide up the world according to its interests and to subsidize its industries for defense purposes).

What distinguishes Chomsky's work (and these books are good examples) from the work of the muckrakers who might have said similar things is the degree to which he has consistently described the kind of thinking that brought on the Vietnam War as endemic to the system. No official is likely to have learned anything that could prevent future regimes from committing such atrocities; humanistic approaches and lessons have been banned from playing a part in imperialist power struggles. All these officials have proven themselves capable of learning is how to make fewer tactical errors and, therefore, how to be more murderous. Chomsky's reviewers have, almost universally, failed to mention this. The 1973 TLS reviewer was no exception, and actually ended by suggesting that the end of imperialism was nigh.

Plato's Problem, Orwell's Problem, and Life in the Spotlight

In the mid-to-late 1970s, Chomsky's *Reflections on Language* and *Essays on Form and Interpretation* appeared, as did *Logical Structure of Linguistic Theory* (although it had been written between 1955 and 1956). Studies that Chomsky had been working on for years entered the public domain. He was also lecturing widely: he delivered the Whidden Lectures at McMaster University in Hamilton, Ontario; the Huizinga Memorial Lectures at Leiden; the Woodbridge Lectures at Columbia University; and the Kant Lectures at Stanford University. He was named Corresponding Fellow of the British Academy in 1974. But it was *Reflections on Language* that sparked the greatest amount of discussion within the field, partly because of John Searle's review article "The Rules of the Language Game," which appeared in the 10 September 1976 edition of the *Times Literary Supplement*. In Searle's opinion, *Reflections* confirmed that Chomsky was retreating from his previous positions, in particular the idea that a sentence's meaning is determined by its syntactical deep structure. Searle argued that Chomsky was now seeking to determine meaning through an altered notion of surface structure. Chomsky merely remarked that the review proved Searle had lost interest after *Aspects* came out.

Reflections—comprised in part of the Whidden Lectures—addresses the first of three problems that Chomsky has explored in a number of contexts. He has called it "Plato's problem," and Bertrand Russell, in his later works, poses it like this: "[H]ow comes it that human beings, whose contacts with the world are brief and personal and limited, are able to know as much as they do know?" (qtd. in Chomsky, *Language in a Psychological Setting* 3–4). The second problem, more often addressed in the course of political rather than linguistic discussions, is what Chomsky (in *Knowledge of Language*) has called "Orwell's problem": How is it that human beings know so little given the amount of information to which they have access? The third problem, which was examined in the previous chapter, is what Chomsky refers to as "Descartes's problem": How can we account for the many "mysteries for humans," or even determine what lies beyond epistemic bounds?

The first problem is taken up in *Reflections on Language* as a means of gaining insight into universal grammar. Searle differs with Chomsky not over the problem itself, but over Chomsky's approach to it, particularly what Searle calls Chomsky's "thesis of the autonomy of syntax." But, Chomsky writes, "It's a logical impossibility for Searle, or anyone, to differ with my 'thesis of the "autonomy of syntax," ' because I've never held any such thesis. There is a very large 'debate' about it, with many people attacking the thesis (but without telling us what it is) and no one defending it, surely not me, because I have no idea what it is" (31 Mar. 1995). According to Searle, Chomsky's argument in support of this "thesis" is that "the rules of syntax of natural languages, that is the rules of sentence construction, can be stated using only syntactical notions: the rules, for him, make no reference to meaning or function or any other non-syntactical notions: all the rules of syntax of all natural languages are in this sense formal." Searle counters this argument that he attributes to Chomsky by stating: "if, as seems probable, language evolved in human prehistory to serve certain needs of communication, it is likely both that there will be some rules that make reference to the communicative functions of language and to the meanings of syntactical elements, and that many of the purely syntactical rules of language will have a deeper explanation in terms of the functions that the syntactical forms serve...." This review, which contains fundamental misreadings of Chomsky's work, prompted further discussion, which, in Chomsky's view, concerned nothing more than "what might be shown if such proposals [about the role of functions] could be formulated" (31 Mar. 1995). At least part of the fallout from the review took the form of letters to the editor of the *Times Literary Supplement*. The issue of "the unargued assumptions about the nature of language" (Searle, letter), and the question of how meaning and function are related to the rules for the distribution of syntactical features of sentences, continued to fuel linguists and other language theoreticians for years.

In the mid-1970s, Chomsky was approaching the age of fifty. His children were teenagers, and Carol was teaching half-time at the Harvard Graduate School of Education. The children, all excellent students, undoubtedly benefitted from the rich conversation and the intense cultural environment of their home. But they also lived in the shadow of the Chomsky name. Family life was also somewhat difficult, at times, because the spotlight, frequently shining on Noam, also sought out his wife and children. Carol and Noam held fast to their decision to allow their children the freedom to choose their own career paths and to shield them from the controversies surrounding Noam's political work. And so very little information concerning the Chomsky family has been circulated over the years, and even colleagues of the Chomskys were routinely kept at an arm's length from their domestic life.

But whatever trepidation he might have felt about the dangers that he faced as an individual and the difficulties that his family might encounter as a result of the intensifying spotlight, Chomsky did not relinquish his beliefs or soften his stance. In his political work of the mid-to-late 1970s, he maintained his focus on issues that he had talked about since the late 1950s: the Middle East, the Spanish Civil War, the background to World War II, the framework of American global planning, global order, Indochina, and so on. But he was also becoming more and more absorbed by Orwell's problem, paying special attention to the question of why, after almost a century of destruction and invasion that had been heavily reported as a result of the new technologies (television images of the Vietnam War were beamed into living rooms across America), and after events that should have shaken American confidence in their institutions (the social unrest of the 1960s, the war, the oil crisis), the population did not rise up. Nevertheless, "the movements of the 1960s really expanded in the 1970s, and even more in the 1980s. They also became much more deeply rooted in the mainstream society" (13 Feb. 1996).

At this point, in the early 1970s, Chomsky began to collaborate with Edward S. Herman, who shared his interests and who had also published books on the Vietnam War in 1966 and 1971. This marked the beginning of a new phase in Chomsky's work, one in which he would complement his previous political analysis with closer scrutiny of the institutions that manufacture consent.

Chomsky and Edward S. Herman

Herman, who was working on media analysis, wrote to his friend David Peterson:

My collaborations with Chomsky arose out of shared interests and views, and a perceived synergy in working together—we could meld together our individual ideas and ways of saying things, benefit from mutual editing, and get things done faster and better working collectively. From the beginning we rarely saw one another, but had an active correspondence, exchanging papers and ideas and comments on the passing scene. (12 Aug. 1992)

In summarizing the advantages of working with Chomsky, Herman validates Chomsky's belief in the value of collective endeavors: "There is also a psychological benefit in occasional joint work, knowing that your ideas are appreciated and that you are not alone in your otherwise marginalized thoughts." In his 1992 talk "Creation and Culture," Chomsky makes a similar point in a typically droll and ironic manner: "People are just too dangerous when they get together" because then "they can have thoughts, and ideas, and put them forth in the public arena, and they begin to enter that area where they don't belong, namely influencing public affairs." He then goes on to discuss various aspects of thought control, a subject that also held fascination for Herman. "Separating people, and isolating people, is a technique of control.... Television is inherently an isolating device. You are alone watching the tube. That is very advantageous for control of people. As long as you can keep people isolated ... as long as each person thinks thoughts individually and nobody else knows that they have this crazy idea, it is not a problem...."

The Chomsky-Herman collaboration ultimately netted several articles and books, including *Counter-Revolutionary Violence: Bloodbaths in Fact and Propaganda* (1973), *The Political Economy of Human Rights* (1979), and *Manufacturing Consent: The Political Economy of the Mass Media* (1988).

Censorship

Counter-Revolutionary Violence describes in intimate detail the bloodbath that the United States was perpetrating in Vietnam. Chomsky had long been suspicious that certain elite groups were combining their efforts to suppress anti-status-quo versions of events, but he was about to learn that, if anything, he had underestimated the lengths that these powers would go to quell their opposition.

Counter-Revolutionary Violence was suppressed by Warner Communications, the giant parent company of the publisher Warner Modular. This, in itself, sounds implausible: an American megacorporation decides to destroy a book it has already published. Furthermore, because Warner Modular refused to stop distributing the book after Warner Communications issued the order to kill it, the parent company actually put the publisher out of business. It gets worse. The book appeared in French translation (*Bains de sang*) the following year (1974), but, Chomsky insists, it was "mistranslated to satisfy the ideological needs of the French left at that time" (31 Mar. 1995).

The idea that a corporation would be willing to forgo profits in the name of ideology, or that a work would be tampered with in translation because it doesn't conform to specific ideological needs, invariably raises the eyebrows of those who have come to believe in the sanctity of the free market and such concepts as freedom of expression. It also raises nagging questions. Why did Warner feel that in order to suppress a single book (a book, moreover, by two established intellectuals employed by leading American universities) it was worth it to cripple one of its own subsidiaries? Ben Bagdikian's book *The Media Monopoly* (published by Beacon Press in 1983) confirms Chomsky's account of the incident and is an important source in the canon of references that Chomsky cites in his later condemnation of, among other things, media collusion with powerful elites.

Warner Communications had acquired Warner Modular in order to capitalize on the surge in university enrollment and the concomitant growth in interest in the country's institutions. Located in Andover, Massachusetts, and therefore close to the large intellectual community in and around Boston, Warner Modular published books, pamphlets, and monographs that could be used to supplement required-reading lists for university courses. Its publisher was Claude McCaleb, who "was developing a list to meet the growing request for fresh analyses of national and world events" (Bagdikian 33). The Chomsky-Herman book was a part of this list. It upheld the thesis that "the United States, in attempting to suppress revolutionary movements in underdeveloped countries, had become the leading source of violence against native people" (Bagdikian 33). When the president of Warner Communications, William Sarnoff, saw the ads for the book in August of 1973, he phoned Warner Modular to find out if "this was another Pentagon Papers case that would embarrass the parent firm"; the answer was no, it was a book written by two respected intellectuals.

Later on in the day, Sarnoff called again, asking that McCaleb bring a copy of *Counter-Revolutionary Violence* to him in New York City that night. This was not possible, as the book was just being printed because advance copies were scheduled to be delivered to the New York meeting of the American Sociological Association in a few days. So the next morning, someone from McCaleb's office delivered the manuscript to Sarnoff. Shortly thereafter, McCaleb was summoned to Sarnoff's office. An incensed Sarnoff attacked McCaleb for having published the book. In McCaleb's words, Sarnoff claimed that *Counter-Revolutionary Violence* was "a pack of lies, a scurrilous attack on respected Americans, undocumented, a publication unworthy of a serious publisher." He then announced that the book was not to be released, cancelled the ads for it, and "ordered the destruction of the Warner catalogue listing the Chomsky-Herman book and its replacement by a new catalogue with the book omitted" (Bagdikian 34).

McCaleb, not surprisingly, was stunned by the news. He reminded Sarnoff about previous agreements between Warner Communication and

Warner Modular concerning who would be responsible for making publication decisions, and cautioned him about the impact that this decision would have on the academic community. According to McCaleb, "Sarnoff answered that 'he didn't give a damn what I, my staff, the authors, or the academic community thought and ended by saying we should destroy the entire inventory of [*Counter-Revolutionary Violence*]'" (qtd. in Bagdikian 34). Warner Modular was subsequently sold to another firm, only to disappear shortly thereafter.

But the censorship wasn't over yet. Efforts continued that year to seal off the the few small access routes that Chomsky had to the mainstream press. Herman explains:

During the Vietnam war era, a period of a sizable and active anti-war movement, roughly from 1965 to 1972, Chomsky wrote and spoke extensively, but even then his access was confined to radical publications like *Ramparts* and *Liberation*, plus the *New York Review of Books*, the mainstream exception through 1972. Chomsky has never had an Op Ed column in the *Washington Post*, and his lone opinion piece in the *New York Times* was not an original contribution but rather excerpts from testimony before the Senate Foreign Relations Committee. The *New York Review of Books* exception closed down in 1973, not as a result of any change in Chomsky but following a sharp move to the right by the editors of the journal, who thereafter excluded a number of left critics. ("Pol Pot" 599)

That one of America's most well-known intellectuals and dissidents would be thus ignored and even ostracized by the mainstream press seems quite remarkable. But, according to Chomsky, this kind of thing had been going on since he first became publicly involved in political issues:

When wasn't I ostracized? In the '60s and early '70s, I was indeed virtually ignored, with the sole exception of the *New York Review of Books*, which, from about 1968–1972, allowed an opening for dissident opinion, reacting to currents among young intellectuals and academics that they couldn't ignore; when these subsided, the window closed. During that period, they also ran articles by Paul Lauter, Peter Dale Scott, and many other dissidents. Since then, they've kept almost entirely to exactly the types who were criticized by the dissidents they formerly allowed (they were always open to mainstream liberals and the right, of course). (31 Mar. 1995)

This seems to suggest that the late 1960s and early 1970s were periods during which diversity, debate, and dissent were permitted to flourish. Certainly, such a view would coincide with official accounts of the period. Chomsky disagrees: "In the '80s, as popular movements became more vigorous ... the press opened up too, to some extent. So, I've had far more media opportunities since the early '80s than ever before, though the national media in the U.S. (*New York Times, Washington Post*, national public TV-radio) remain as closed as ever" (31 Mar. 1995).

In sharp contrast to the increasingly enthusiastic interest in Chomsky's political work demonstrated by a growing segment of the population, the intellectual elite seems to have been broadly influenced by easily digested generalizations: he's anti-Zionist, he's a Communist, and so on. Those who have not actually read his political works express total disbelief that Chomsky has been ostracized on the basis of his dissident opinions. The standard line is that such opinions are the very backbone of the mainstream press, and that people with various perspectives are regularly given the opportunity to attack the government. Those who are more familiar with Chomsky and his work, and who have a better understanding of his relationship with mainstream media organs, have a different view. Chomsky's own assessment of all this is characteristically insightful, acerbic, and humorous:

There are many illusions ... concocted for obvious reasons ("we used to allow him to appear all over, but then he went crazy, so what can we do ... " etc.). And much of this is actually believed by people who don't know the facts, which can easily be ascertained. In the late '70s, for example, after the collapse of *Ramparts* and *Liberation*, just about the only journal in which I could publish regularly was *Inquiry*, the journal of the ultra-right Cato Institute. Remember: that was before my alleged crimes. Again, easily checked, but not known. ... (31 Mar. 1995)

5

The Intellectual as Commissar

The Function of the Academic

Chomsky has, over the years, pursued his early interest in the academic's role and the university's function in contemporary society. He is quick to note the degree of collusion between intellectuals and state policies, even when these policies are clearly oppressive, violent, or illegal. The reasons academics often assume this managerial role in relation to society, Chomsky feels, are related to their quest for power, their belief (carefully cultivated by those institutions closest to the centers of power) in the fundamentally benign nature of Western institutions, and the high level of indoctrination to which they have been submitted as members of the ruling elite. Chomsky's views on these matters are often similar to those of the thinkers who had a formative influence on his outlook, notably Bakunin and Pannekoek. Typically, these views are based on values such as social responsibility, academic integrity, and commitment to a truthful and undistorted representation of facts. They lead Chomsky to confrontations with groups and individuals who are concerned only with serving the interests of power, who promote the cause of one group while turning a blind eye to the larger principles at stake.

By the mid- to late 1970s, Chomsky had already experienced such clashes on numerous fronts. He had faced pro-Israeli groups, anti-Communist groups, pro–Cold War groups, just as, during the Second World War, people such as Dwight Macdonald had faced anti-Nazi groups who denounced the refusal of Macdonald and the others to support the Allied side. Chomsky adamantly rejected the assumption that a given group might have an intrinsic right to act aggressively simply

Figure 17
Chomsky listening attentively to a talk given in Nanaimo, British Columbia, 1989.

because of its history: Israelis do not have the right to employ brutal
tactics against the Palestinians because they themselves have been perse-
cuted, the American government should not get away with terrorist activities because it allows for more debate than the Bolsheviks did, and
the fundamental rights of individuals should not be expunged because
their views don't correspond with those of the ruling elites. Though they
may seem to be truisms, these basic tenets led Chomsky to engage in a
number of high-pitched debates that began in the early 1960s and still
continue. In the case of Israel, the earliest public confrontation occurred
in 1969, during a public talk at MIT. Chomsky recalls: "I was embar-
rassingly mild, and elicited a huge furor, including very sharp criticism
from what was considered the dovish left, even delegations coming to my
house to talk me out of my evil ways (namely, suggesting that maybe
Palestinians were human, and recalling the actual history of Zionism)"
(13 Feb. 1996). Beginning in the early 1970s, Chomsky's university talks
on this subject began to elicit violent reactions. As a consequence, he
has had to take precautions, "including undercover police protection
(when I refuse uniformed police protection) at universities, if I am giving
a talk on the Middle East" (13 Feb. 1996).

There is a rhetorical side to these issues. Much of the debate they spark
exploits a similar kind of language: words such as "subtleties," "complexities," and "niceties" keep the uninitiated at arm's length from the
decision-making process. The American people, the line goes, cannot
be directly involved in foreign affairs because they don't understand the
"subtleties" of the international situation. Individuals should not have a
voice in government finance because they don't comprehend the stakes—
the "complexities" are beyond their grasp. Citizens should not have direct
access to the institutions that control their lives, notably corporations and
governments, because they don't have the highly technical knowledge
required to appreciate the "niceties" of domestic and foreign trade.
Chomsky naturally abhors these views; there is, he assures us, a deliberate attempt on the part of intellectuals and government representatives (and journalists, but in different ways) to shroud simple facts in
obtuse language in order to keep the "rabble" out. This deliberate obscuring of facts is, in his view, typical of the so-called postmodern period,

and symptomatic of a much larger problem concerning social control. Another striking feature of postmodernism is, he writes, its "extreme character and the fact that it absorbs elements that consider themselves 'on the left'—the kind of people who years earlier would have been organizing and teaching in worker schools" (31 Mar. 1995).

Chomsky's disparaging descriptions of the ivory-tower mentality—which dictates not only that academics will be allowed intellectual freedom, but that they will also be worshiped, given special privileges, and encouraged to speak only to other full-fledged members of the elite—are probably best understood within the kind of framework envisioned by Bakunin. He maintained that intellectuals in a good society should be workers whose primary tools happen to be their intellects. By extension, laborers in the same society would also employ the necessary tools, but, like the intellectuals, would be called upon to do tasks traditionally executed by managers; they would organize, plan, and control the products of their own work. The prestige normally associated with select kinds of work would evaporate in the same way as it had in the Deweyite school that Chomsky had attended until the age of twelve.

This is not to say that the advantages of one kind of work as opposed to another would disappear. Intellectuals, by the very nature of their job, would continue to have access to certain kinds of information. But, just as the product of the miners' work is shared for the collective (and individual) good, so, too, would the product of the intellectuals' work. And the miners, now more accustomed to perceiving themselves as people capable of analyzing and planning, would be in a better position to make use of the knowledge that would help to improve their own lives (this is the kind of argument proposed by, for example, Ken Coates).

Consistent with Chomsky's overriding approach is a rejection, as well (for virtually the same reasons), of authoritarian socialism, of enlightened rulers, and of other organs, benign or not, that attempt to dictate to people what they should consider to be in their own best interests. Chomsky utilizes this approach on several occasions during this period—such as in the paper "Equality: Language Development, Human Intelligence, and Social Organization," delivered at the Conference on the Promise and Problems of Human Equality held at the University of Illinois in 1976;

and an interview with Chomsky that was published in a 1978 edition of *Working Papers in Linguistics*. It can also be found, however, in many of his linguistic texts.

In fact, because of the interest manifested by a growing segment of academia in Chomsky's linguistic work, and due to the increasing recognition among activists of his political work, many of the talks that he gave from this point onward included discussions of both linguistic and political issues. Sometimes both would be included in the same talk, and sometimes they would be covered in back-to-back talks: Chomsky often speaks to both linguistic and political issues wherever he goes. But he is careful never to set up these talks like academic conferences:

> What are called "conferences"—gatherings of intellectuals—I almost never attend. I do give endless talks and take part in many forums, but not the kind that would be called conferences. I almost always turn down invitations to these. Thus I almost never go to the Socialist Scholars Conference (though I have a lot of personal friends there), or to academic and professional conferences, etc. Virtually all of my talks are for popular and activist groups, though typically, they are combined with talks at universities, sometimes seminars, but more often for mass audiences interested in the general area. (31 Mar. 1995)

In the kind of talks that he is referring to here are represented an astonishing diversity of concerns: "To mention some current and typical examples, I've been on several forums with local organizers trying to react to the Gingrich assault (welfare mothers, etc.), a panel organized by the Decatur Illinois strikers seeking broader understanding of the very fundamental issues involved in that attempt to destroy the last functioning industrial union, local community groups, etc." (31 Mar. 1995).

The texts Chomsky published during this period, particularly *Language and Responsibility* (1979) and *Radical Priorities* (1981), contain wide-ranging discussions of the many disciplines that have interested him since his youth; they also, quite separately, demonstrate the development of his ideas on politics and linguistics. He continued to discourage his audience's tendency to identify overlaps between the two realms. But he did employ his own method of prioritizing the two subject areas: "I have a rule of thumb to determine how serious a place it is: relative audience size. In a sane community, most would come to the political talks. Often it's the other way around" (18 Feb. 1993).

Provoking Ire

Chomsky's political talks during this time stirred up considerable controversy in different sectors. In some instances, this was exacerbated by
"experts" who seemed to be suffering from amnesia. Alan Dershowitz, for
example, claims in his best-selling book *Chutzpah* (1991) that he had had
a public discussion with Chomsky immediately following the Yom Kip-
pur War in 1973, during which Chomsky had proposed a "hare-brained
scheme" that involved abolishing the state of Israel and replacing it with
"a secular, binational state." Calling Chomsky a "false prophet of the
left," "who would willingly sacrifice Jewish values and the Jewish state to
some Marxist view of the world," Dershowitz declared that neither his
"children, friends, [n]or students" could accept such a vision (199). There
are two points here. First, Chomsky's alleged position is a restatement of
that put forward by the Zionist organizations Avukah and Hashomer
Hatzair in the 1930s and 1940s, and this "hare-brained scheme" had
been elaborated and discussed by Zionist Jews prior to the creation of
Israel. In a properly historical context, in other words, Dershowitz is
no more Zionist than Chomsky. Second, Chomsky's opinions concerning Israel and the Israeli-Arab situation are not accurately reflected in
Dershowitz's book; this is evident to those who have read and retained
Chomsky's *Peace in the Middle East? Reflections on Justice and Nationhood* (1974) and *Towards a New Cold War: Essays on the Current Crisis
and How We Got There* (1982). Chomsky remarks: "the fact that he cites
an alleged statement that is uncheckable (his 20-year old memory of
something he claims he heard) rather than the easily checkable articles I
was writing about the topic at just that time tells any sane person all they
need to know" (27 June 1995).

The views Chomsky upheld were consistent with the traditional left
binationalist program, and were directed towards resolving the Israeli
question in the long term:

In the short term, everyone's interests (including Israeli Jews) would be best served
by steps towards some kind of federalism in cis-Jordan, leading eventually to
closer integration and cooperation as the two communities involved determined
through choices that are as free and uncoerced as possible. Interestingly, that was
the position that Shimon Peres and others also reached many years later, when it

was far too late, after they saw the consequences of their extreme rejectionism. All that is readily checked; it's been in print for 25 years. (27 June 1995)

Chomsky recalls that at the time to which Dershowitz refers in his book, Israel's leading civil libertarian, Israel Shahak, then chairman of the Israeli League for Civil and Human Rights, was interviewed by the *Boston Globe* during a visit to that city. Dershowitz wrote to the *Globe* to denounce him, claiming that he had been thrown out of his position in the league, when, in fact, it had been demonstrated in court that during its annual meeting, the league, a small group, had been overwhelmed by a large mob of people who wanted to oust Shahak. As they had paid the registration fee, these people were able to claim the right to vote against Shahak. Chomsky elaborates:

The mob was organized by the governing Labor Party, who offered (in a secret document that was quickly leaked) to pay the registration fees for the people who stormed the meeting. It's rather as though the Communist Party in Russia had secretly organized people to break into the annual meeting of some tiny Amnesty International group and vote out the leadership, then pass a resolution denouncing the United States, the Communist Party paying their membership fees. That's what Dershowitz—the great civil libertarian—was endorsing, putting aside the shocking lies about Shahak and the Israeli Courts. One can see why he doesn't want the truth exposed. (27 June 1995)

As he already knew the details of the Shahak affair, Chomsky wasted no time in replying to Dershowitz's letter to the *Globe*, which, in turn, incited Dershowitz to denounce Chomsky and ask for proof in the form of court records. Chomsky happened to be in possession of these:

I ... wrote a letter quoting them, which showed that he was a complete liar, as well as a Stalinist-style thug (that was implicit; I didn't bother saying it). He continued to try to brazen his way out, and was finally told by the *Globe* ombudsman that they would publish no more of his lies on the matter (that was after I'd sent the original Court records and a translation to English to the *Globe*, who had requested documentation so they could assess Dershowitz's increasingly hysterical charges). Ever since then, Dershowitz has been on a crazed jihad, dedicating much of his life to trying to destroy my reputation. (31 Mar. 1995)

So Chomsky became the lightning rod for the pro-Israel lobby: he was seen as the anti-Zionist, the pro-Arab, the anti-Semite. This, of course, was not all. His criticism of American policies in Vietnam and Cambodia had alienated him from establishment intellectuals and politicians; his condemnation of Cold War policies had led to his ostracization by the proponents of America's "free-world" vision. Those bent on questioning or ignoring him persisted in their efforts. Edward Herman claims that, as a consequence of his refusal to toe the line, Chomsky's work was "subjected to an ongoing and intense scrutiny for any literal errors or bases of vulnerability, a scrutiny from which establishment experts are entirely free. This search was perhaps more intense in the United States and among its allies in the late 1970s and early 1980s, with a growing body of hard-liners anxious to overcome the Vietnam syndrome, revitalize the arms race, strengthen support for Israel's rejectionism and policy of force and involve the United States in more aggressive actions towards the Soviet bloc and Third World" ("Pol Pot" 596).

It became obvious that Chomsky was a threat and a source of embarrassment to many: he was a Jew arguing for a democratic state in Israel (rather than "the sovereign State of the Jewish people"); he was a Zionist arguing for a gradual move towards binationalism; he was an intellectual exposing collusion between governments and intellectual elites; he was a linguist taking aim at the cherished assumptions of respectable fellow linguists, philosophers, psychologists, and historians; he was a scientist conducting political analysis and denigrating as fraud most of the work done by political scientists; and, moreover, he was a privileged American calling into question what were taken to be fundamental American values while noting that basic rights, even those entrenched in the American constitution, were consciously being squelched by those elected to propagate them because they were not in the best interests of the ruling elites.

Chomsky was not the only person making these observations. Zinn and Dellinger had a similar orientation, and, of course, Chomsky had inherited a tradition from a series of earlier left-intellectuals—those who populated the milieu from which he had emerged. Yet, he was marginalized, as many others who had preceded him had been. Unlike some previous and still-active dissenters, though, Chomsky was recognized as being the most important thinker in his field, and this both allowed him some latitude and increased his responsibilities: to his students, to his peers, to his community, and, perhaps most of all, to himself.

Respect within one's own field of expertise is not, and never really has been, a guarantee of safe haven within the university. In 1919, Harold

Laski wrote to Bertrand Russell. His words take on particular poignancy in light of Chomsky's position:

There is a more private thing about which I would like you to know in case you think there is a chance that you can help. I know from your *Introduction to Mathematical Logic* that you think well of Sheffer who is at present in the Philosophy Department here [at Harvard]. I don't know if you have any personal acquaintance with him. He is a jew and he has married someone of whom the University does not approve; moreover he hasn't the social qualities that Harvard so highly prizes. The result is that most of his department is engaged on a determined effort to bring his career here to an end.... Myself I think that the whole thing is a combination of anti-semitism and that curious university worship of social prestige which plays so large a part over here. (qtd. in Russell, *Autobiography* 2: 112)

Russell Jacoby recounts similar incidents that involved Paul Starr, David Abraham, Henry Giroux, and, perhaps most remarkably, the editor of *Telos*, respected historian Paul Piccone. He concludes:

The ordinary realities comprise the usual pressures and threats; the final danger in a liberal society is unemployment: denial of tenure or unrenewed contract. In a tight market this might spell the end of an academic career. The years of academic plenty were long enough to attract droves of would-be professors; they were brief enough to ensure that all saw the "No Vacancy" sign. Professionalization proceeded under the threat of unemployment. The lessons of the near and far past, from McCarthyism to the first stone thrown at the first outsider, were clear to anyone: blend in; use the time allotted to establish scholarly credentials; hide in the mainstream. (135)

Chomsky would not adopt these tactics for academic survival, and, as a consequence, he was denigrated by the organs of mainstream propaganda, ostracized or ignored, and scrutinized on all fronts.

Language Acquisition in the Animal World

In the mid- to late 1970s, linguists seemed, at least publicly, fascinated by language acquisition. Chomsky was no exception, and applied himself to distinguishing between animals and humans by means of his theory of innate language ability. A 25 September 1975 *New York Times* article, "Experts Labor to Communicate on Animal Talk," outlined the basic issues involved and brought them into the public domain. It also cited experts from various fields commenting on the possibility that chimpanzees, baboons, and even laughing gulls communicate in unexpectedly complex ways (but, as Chomsky notes, "don't all living beings?").

Efforts to teach animals to speak captured the scientific and public imaginations (perhaps because of the central role that cute and fuzzy animals play in children's stories, fables, and myths). The work referred to in the article, however, like much heavily hyped scientific research, was considered, in Chomsky's words, "an absurdity by every serious biologist I know of" (31 Mar. 1995). Indeed a 7 July 1980 London Times article by Michael Leaman, called "Diary of the Clever Me Phenomenon," addressed the hype surrounding the talking-animals issue; Leaman remarked that "experiments in teaching chimpanzees and gorillas to communicate using sign language or coloured bits of plastic to denote words, have become some of the most publicized in modern science."

Chomsky was quoted in the 1975 *New York Times* article as saying, "chimpanzee communication differed fundamentally from human speech, particularly in mode of use, structural properties and mode of acquisition. 'Human language is acquired by exposure, not training . . . just as breathing is.'" His opinion did not change in the ensuing years, although the 1980 London *Times* reports his observations on the public's concern with the issue: "for reasons that are unclear to me . . . this topic has aroused considerable emotion, at least in popular discussion." More recently, he has added, "this work has not the remotest relation to science, though people in white coats and with equipment sometimes do it" (31 Mar. 1995).

The London *Times* also reported, in an article entitled "Chomsky Debate Absorbs the Royal Society," that during a 1981 Royal Society conference on human acquisition of language, the question of innate abilities and universal grammar was linked to a variety of practical projects for researchers "seeking to perfect machines for automatic language translation, to develop computer systems with artificial intelligence, or simply to make vending machines that will dispense tickets at a spoken command." Chomsky, who in fact only attended the conference briefly, preferring to spend his time engaged in the subject in the context of "talks to popular audiences," insists that the *Times* misrepresented what had occurred at the meetings: "There was scientific interest, but it had nothing whatsoever to do with language translation (MT) and artificial intelligence

(AI). MT is a very low level engineering project, and so-called classic strong AI is largely vacuous, dismissed by most serious scientists and lacking any results, as its leading exponents concede" (31 Mar. 1995).

Entire research projects, on language acquisition and other topics, were now being conducted with the aim of either establishing or disproving Chomsky's theories. Chomsky himself fuelled these enterprises by maintaining a high level of productivity: he published *Reflections on Language* (1975), *Essays on Form and Interpretation* (1977), *Rules and Representations* (1980), and *Modular Approaches to the Study of the Mind* (1984). These works include essays and lectures that expand and clarify previous work, address issues raised by his critics, and update grammatical theory based upon his own recent work and that of others. All the while, he was developing a thesis that he had articulated some years earlier: "language (and other mental abilities) should be seen as 'growing' in the individual's mind, under genetic control, rather than as 'learned' by organisms lacking any initial predisposition to develop the particular kinds of mental faculty which are eventually acquired" (Sampson 14).

Chomsky's remarkable output reflected his constant interaction with professional milieus, such as the GLOW circle in Europe and their counterparts in the United States. The acronym GLOW stands for Generative Linguistics in the Old World(s). The organization's aim is to ensure that the intellectual and social issues that are of concern to transformationalists are communicated to other. Participants include Hans Bennis, Anneke Groos, Henk van Riemsdijk, and Jean-Yves Pollock, and they produce a GLOW newsletter in Amsterdam that is circulated worldwide. The GLOW manifesto includes this passage: "In our opinion, generative linguistics acquired a new momentum in Europe after Chomsky's 'Conditions on Transformations' (1973). This epoch-making paper shifted the interest of linguists from rather arbitrary rules to simple well-constrained rules operating under general conditions. A significant number of members of GLOW have found their common ground in the research programme that grew out of 'Conditions'" (qtd. in Otero, ed. 1: 345).

This kind of collaboration has led to significant advances in the field of linguistics, in particular the principles-and-parameters approach, described in *Lectures on Government and Binding*, the printed text that emerged from conferences Chomsky gave at Pisa's Scuola Normale in

1979. "The lectures in Pisa began," he says, "by considering some work of a fine young Norwegian linguist, and then went on to very significant work done mainly under Richie Kayne's influence in Europe, including [that of] the people who invited me to Pisa, some of the most outstanding scholars in the field (at that time not yet with faculty appointments)" (14 Aug. 1995).

Chomsky's description of the Pisa lectures and the GLOW conference that was held there afterwards gives us some sense of how advances are made in the field of linguistics: "I gave a workshop [in Pisa] with some of the most outstanding (mostly young) people in the field taking part, running through this material, which later turned into *Lectures on Government and Binding*. Very much a collective effort, as always, including a remarkably good group of students at MIT in those years. That's a real 'milieu'" (14 Aug. 1995).

Slinging the Mud: An "Elementary Moral Principle"

This period was also marked by the appearance of many contentious reviews, which questioned (among other things) the scientific status of Chomsky's linguistic work. Christine Carling and Terence Moore, for example, argued in the 10 December 1982 issue of the *Times Higher Education Supplement* that Chomsky's theories had encouraged linguists to move "not closer to but further away from the fundamental issues in language acquisition, understanding and production they initially appeared to be confronting"; they cited "Chomsky's own attempts to turn linguistics into a 'hard' science" (13). Chomsky, these critics asserted, wanted to "introduce into linguistics a scientific method that was novel in the human sciences." His competence/performance distinction drew linguistics away from concerns with language and nudged them towards a "methodology of science." Carling and Moore concluded that Chomsky was on the wrong track, and should instead adopt a "problem based approach," which would make explanation in the field of linguistics "teleological" rather than "reductive" (14). Otero states that the review betrays its authors' "total inability to understand Chomsky's work—and much else" (5 Apr. 1995). Reading through journals such as the THES, one is struck by the number of rebuttals that Chomsky has made to those who quarrel with his approach. Is there a cut-off point? Chomsky has suggested in correspondence that the decision to respond depends not only upon time constraints but also upon the seriousness of the criticism and the competence of the reviewer. In this case, Otero's comments suggest one reason why Chomsky never rose to the challenge.

In the political domain, Chomsky added substantially to his growing body of writing during this period, publishing *Human Rights and American Foreign Policy* (1978), *Language and Responsibility* (1979), and, with Edward S. Herman, *The Political Economy of Human Rights* (1979). There was—partly because his position was anathema to members of certain elites, who recognized that his popularity as a speaker among some segments of the disillusioned public was on the rise—an effort to find fault with Chomsky's work in the form of factual errors. But, aside from some trivial slips, Chomsky stood up to the test. Sometimes, however, support for fundamental principles can lead to conflict. And people who search for errors in order to discredit Chomsky's viewpoint play up these conflicts to their own advantage.

Freedom of expression is extremely precious to Chomsky, and he upholds his commitment to preserving it, even in the face of provocation from the critics who seem bent on misrepresenting him. It is also an issue that has a complex aspect. Chomsky does not, of course, believe in despots, enlightened or otherwise, either for government or institutions. Ideas and possibilities should be uttered, and their net worth determined in the public domain or in the field to which they belong. Muffling arguments or gagging people simply because they say things somebody doesn't want to hear, or playing down certain kinds of knowledge due to their negative implications, is not an acceptable way of proceeding. At the same time, however, it is not merely a question of *allowing* people to speak their minds, though at first glance this appears to be a suitably benevolent approach. Chomsky explains:

[N]o one should have the authority to "allow" anything, and—crucially—I don't at all argue that the reason for "allowing" free expression of thought is that things that work (or are valuable) might be suppressed otherwise. The right of freedom of thought is far more fundamental than that, and the right of free expression of what one thinks (however crazy) is also far beyond these pragmatic considerations. I simply do not agree that the state, or any other system of organized power and violence, should have the authority to determine what people think or say. If the state is granted the power to shut me up, my counterargument is not that what I am saying might be valuable. That would be a contemptible position, in my view (though I recognize that it is the standard one of the people called "libertarians," back very far). (31 Mar. 1995)

This is the overriding principle. It does not, however, preclude moral judgments of human concerns; knowledge is value-ridden in this regard, and each individual must be responsible for identifying a focal point: "True, individuals have to make their own decisions about what to 'play down' and what to 'play up.' The marginal fringe of intellectuals who are more or less honest [will make] moral judgments as to human consequences" (15 Dec. 1992). Regrettably, this is seldom the case for what Chomsky calls "the general run of commissars." They make their decisions "on the basis of career and power interests":

Thus in every society that I know of, surely Stalinist Russia and the West, intellectuals feign great indignation over (often real) crimes of official enemies and are silent, dismissive, or apologetic about those of their own states, those for which they bear some responsibility and those they could help mitigate or overcome if they were honest (leading, as they know, to loss of respectability and privilege). The most elementary moral principles would lead to "playing up" the crimes of domestic origin in comparison to those of official enemies, that is, "playing up" the crimes that one can do something about. But that elementary moral principle is so utterly foreign to commissar culture that anyone who expresses it simply calls upon him/herself instant denunciation as an apologist for the enemy's crimes. That is a reflex of the commissar culture, in Stalinist Russia, in the United States and England, etc. For good, institutional reasons. (15 Dec. 1992)

A great deal of the mudslinging that Chomsky has endured was prompted by the failure, in some quarters, of this "elementary moral principle." For taking issue with the American government, he has been accused of being pro-Soviet; for taking issue with Bolshevism and the Soviet government, he has been accused of being anti-Soviet; for taking issue with the Jews, he has been accused of being pro-Arab, and for applying similar principles to Arab actions, he has been accused of being anti-Arab; for taking issue with the Israelis, he has been accused of being anti-Semitic; for taking issue with the propaganda campaign in the West concerning Cambodia, he has been accused of being pro–Khmer Rouge; and for taking issue with those who would enforce censorship (against those, for example, who assert that the Holocaust never happened, rather than allowing the absurdity of their arguments to become self-evident), he has been accused of conspiring with the enemy (in this case the Nazis). The controveries that rage around him are invariably more complex than they are portrayed to be, and the facts are often difficult to procure. The Israeli situation is a good example:

A personal friend, Edward Said, has also criticized me for not paying attention to Arab sources and looking at things always from the Jewish-Israeli-Western point of view, and there's a lot more. Last time I was in Israel, I gave a lot of political talks, very critical of Israel (in Tel Aviv) and including some criticism of the PLO (for Bir Zeit, in the West Bank—the talk was in East Jerusalem because the college was closed). The only serious hassle developed with Palestinian intellectuals, because of my criticism of the PLO. That was accurately reported by the Israeli press, which is much more honest that anything I know of in the West. (31 Mar. 1995)

Chomsky was also attacked, at this time, for his views on the Faurisson affair and Cambodia's Pol Pot regime; on both occasions his detractors failed to come to terms with his message in their zeal to silence him.

The Faurisson Affair

Robert Faurisson, a professor of French literature at the University of Lyon, France, was relieved of his duties "on the grounds that he could not

Figure 18
Robert Faurisson.

be protected from attacks carried out against him as a result of his views, and he was sued in court for writings denying the existence of gas chambers in Nazi Germany and calling into question the Holocaust itself" (Herman, "Pol Pot" 600). He was successfully convicted for falsification of history by a judgment that, according to Chomsky, "reeks of Stalinism and fascism, and was naturally applauded by the French intellectuals, who proceeded to lie outrageously about it, as do Dershowitz and others—the truth being too embarrassing to allow" (31 Mar. 1995).

In the fall of 1979, Serge Thion, a friend of Chomsky's, asked him and roughly five hundred others to sign a petition in favor of the freedom to express opinions without persecution. It read:

> Dr. Faurisson has served as a respected professor of twentieth-century French literature and document criticism for over four years at the University of Lyon 2 in France. Since 1974 he has been conducting extensive independent historical research into the "Holocaust" question. Since he began making his findings public, Professor Faurisson has been subject to a vicious campaign of harassment, intimidation, slander, and physical violence in a crude attempt to silence him. Fearful officials have even tried to stop him from further research by denying him access to public libraries and archives. (qtd. in Vidal-Naquet 69)

The French press dubbed it "Chomsky's petition," and although Faurisson's specific views were not mentioned in the document he signed, Chomsky was accused of holding similar ones. Chomsky then wrote a "short memoir on the civil liberties aspects of the case ... to clarify the distinction between supporting somebody's beliefs and their right to express them" (Herman, "Pol Pot" 601), which he gave to Thion with his tacit authorization to use it as Thion thought best. It appeared as the preface to Faurisson's book *Mémoire en défense contre ceux qui m'accusent de falsifier l'histoire: La question des chambres à gaz* (1980) under the title "Quelques commentaires élémentaires sur le droit à la liberté d'expression." The following lines especially inflamed Chomsky's critics: "I have nothing to say here about the work of Robert Faurisson or his critics, of which I know very little, or about the topics they address, concerning which I have no special knowledge," as did his characterizing Faurisson as "a relatively apolitical liberal of some sort" (xiv–xv). A widely read French author, Pierre Vidal-Naquet, described Faurisson's *Mémoire* in his *Assassins of Memory: Essays on the Denial of the Holocaust*: "this work is neither more nor less mendacious and dishonest

Figure 19
The Faurisson affair.

than the preceding ones.... [H]is interpretation is a deliberate falsehood, in the full sense of the term" (65).

The Holocaust occurred. It was one of the most unspeakable acts of horror ever committed. Chomsky knows these statements to be true and points out that he has declared as much "in terms far stronger than Vidal-Naquet or Dershowitz have since used in my very earliest political writings: the introduction to *American Power*, the article in *Liberation* on the Middle East ... and endlessly since, quite independently of this silly affair" (13 Feb. 1996). But, somehow, for stubbornly upholding the principle of free speech and defending his own actions in the Faurisson affair, he was made responsible for the "mendacious and dishonest" content of Faurisson's works. Once again, the "elementary moral principle" had broken down, and Chomsky suffered for it.

The other issue that this affair raised was the question of reasonable evidence. Chomsky notes that Faurisson had been charged with being an anti-Semite and a Nazi, and that these were "serious charges that require evidence." He claims that he knew very little about Faurisson's writings and had no interest in them. After all, he had "felt no need to read *Satanic Verses* before signing endless petitions made for Rushdie." In formulating his position on the Faurisson case, Chomsky relied "mainly on charges conveyed to me by his harshest critics, which I then cited in full, pointing out, correctly, that they were utterly meaningless" (14 Aug. 1995). One of these critics was Vidal-Naquet, whom Chomsky did not name.

[B]ut Vidal-Naquet later identified himself (correctly) as the person who had con-veyed those charges to me as his strongest evidence, then charging that I had betrayed a confidence by identifying him (a lie, as he knows, one of many, which he also knows he can get away with). Since Vidal-Naquet, Faurisson's harshest and most knowledgeable critic, could come up with no evidence suggesting that he was an anti-Semite or had any political views at all, that charge seemed rather weak. (14 Aug. 1995)

What Chomsky did know about Faurisson "was that he had written letters to the press (which they refused to publish, apparently) praising the hero-ism of the Warsaw ghetto fighters and in general, praising those who fought the 'good fight' against the Nazis; and that he had privately pub-lished pamphlets denying the existence of gas chambers" (14 Aug. 1995).

In the United States, the charge has been led by Dershowitz and Werner Cohn. In his version of the Faurisson affair, Dershowitz describes Chom-sky as an "anti-Zionist zealot" who "welcomed the opportunity" to pro-test Faurisson's suspension "because Faurisson's writings and speeches are stridently anti-Zionist as well as anti-Semitic. Indeed, Professor Chom-sky has himself made statements about Zionist exploitation of the tragedy of World War II that are not, in my view, so different from some of those of Faurisson" (174). And Cohn's book, *Partners in Hate: Noam Chom-sky and the Holocaust Deniers*, was issued with the following release, written by Nathan Glazer:

When Noam Chomsky came to the defense of the French Holocaust-denier Robert Faurisson, he astonished friends and enemies alike. Chomsky has vigorously de-fended his action as being nothing more than the protection of an individual's civil liberties, quite unconnected with that individual's views and writings. Werner Cohn, in this meticulously documented study, shows that Chomsky's defense of Faurisson is much more than that, and indeed that it is connected to some of Chomsky's deepest political orientations, in particular his unwavering animus toward the United States and Israel. In doing so, he sheds surprising light on Chomsky's politics.

I attended a lecture Cohn gave on this matter in which he was, in my opinion, at best confused and at worst incoherent. His talk was riddled with errors concerning Chomsky's work (for example, he claimed that it had never been published by a major publishing house), Avukah (that it was the same as Hashomer Hatzair), Thion (that Chomsky and Thion had cowritten a book on Vietnam), and linguistics (that Chomsky's work in the field was wholly unfounded). Furthermore, during the question period he seemed unable to recall many details of his own "meticulously documented study," which suggested to me that perhaps somebody else had written the book.

Cohn has claimed elsewhere, specifically in *The Hidden Alliances of Noam Chomsky* (1988), that Chomsky's affiliation with Faurisson is rooted in Chomsky's own sympathy for anti-Semitism and anti-Zionism. Attempting to demonstrate this, Cohn sketches a series of tenuous connections between Chomsky and Faurisson, placing special emphasis on a number of comments that the former has made in defense of the latter's actions.

When all the facts are set forth, the Faurisson affair does tend to throw some of Chomsky's character flaws into relief, most clearly his unwillingness to practice simple appeasement when it comes to resolving his differences with those who attack him. Another remarkable aspect of the affair is the fact that it is used by Chomsky's detractors to divert attention away from his actual statements. Much energy has been expended quibbling over his use of certain words or particular argumentative strategies. Some of Chomsky's critics are more balanced and restrained: Vidal-Naquet, while he claims that "Chomsky is scarcely sensitive to the wounds he inflicts, but extremely attentive to whatever scratches he is forced to put up with" (68), is honest enough to recognize the obvious: "To be sure, it is not the case that Chomsky's thesis in any way approximates those of the neo-Nazis" (73). But others are somehow able to overlook the dozens of books and hundreds of articles Chomsky has written—as well as countless discussions and letters—which always take the side of the oppressed and the downtrodden. Such critics accuse him of alliances with neo-Nazis or with the German National Socialist Party, the very mandate of which was totalitarian oppression and genocide. Chomsky's tactics may not always be the most appropriate in light of the causes that he supports, but the values transmitted by his work are, according to virtually any reasonable measure, consistent with those of the libertarians.

The French reaction to Chomsky's participation in the Faurisson affair was equally forceful, and, particularly in the case of the media, propagandistic. In 1981, an interviewer for *Nouvel Observateur* modified the replies to questions he had sent Chomsky in order, as Chomsky himself put it, "to accord with [the newspaper's] ideological needs" (31 Mar. 1995). Attempts to publish the questions with Chomsky's original replies failed; Chomsky's responses to articles implicating him in the affair that appeared in *Matin de Paris* (1979), *Le Monde* (1981), and *Nouvelles littéraires* (1982) were not published; and *Libération*, according to Chomsky, "demanded that I cut out criticisms of France and Marxism, and when I refused, they wouldn't print" his rebuttal (31 Mar. 1995). Overall, Chomsky remarks, "It is striking that in France, alone in Europe, the press has regularly refused to grant me the right of response to lies and slander, though I read about a 'debate' that is supposedly in progress" (*Language and Politics* 316). In short, his experience with the French press and intelligentsia was a memorable one, but his treatment at their hands did not surprise him. He points out, in a December 1982 *Boston Magazine* article, that "for one thing, France does not have a civil-libertarian tradition of the Anglo-Saxon variety. For another thing, there simply is a totalitarian strain among large segments of the French intelligentsia. Marxism-Leninism and Stalinism, for example, were much more viable and significant doctrines among the French than in England or the United States. What's called the left, especially in France, has a large segment that is deeply authoritarian" (*Language and Politics* 309). This critique appears reductive and perhaps sounds like sour grapes, but a review of Chomsky's *Towards a New Cold War: Essays on the Current Crisis and How We Got There*, written by C. M. Woodhouse for the *Times Literary Supplement* in July of 1982, makes a similar point:

The Americans have a talent for self-criticism which they no doubt inherited from the British. Noam Chomsky's new book is a striking example. In any other country such a forthright and sustained diatribe against a national policy by a prominent academic would be nearly unthinkable. A French professor would not have written such a book about his government's foreign policy; a Russian could not

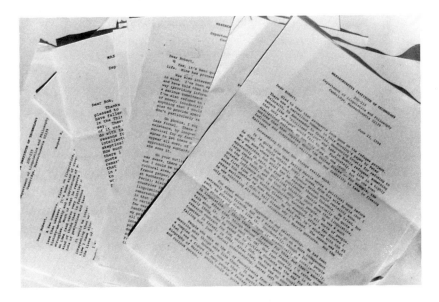

Figure 20
Chomsky spends twenty hours per week writing letters.

have done so except at the price of enforced exile or committal to a psychiatric hospital.

The Faurisson affair has had a harmful and lasting effect on Chomsky. Many people only know about him through his connection to this controversy. Chomsky's remark that, as far as he knew, Faurisson was some sort of "apolitical liberal" still haunts him. Critics have taken it to be an indication that he was sympathetic to Faurisson's work. After years of reiterating his anti-Nazi stance in dozens of new books, hundreds of public addresses, and thousands of letters, Chomsky remains tainted: when organizations or institutions consider inviting him to speak, to receive an honorary degree, or to participate in a high-profile function, there is often some discussion of the Faurisson affair (and/or reference to his position on Israel or the Pol Pot regime). Rather typically, Chomsky has refused to back down on the issue, even refusing to admit a momentary lack of judgment. As Jay Parini notes: "Given the opportunity to calm the debate, however, he elects to heighten it. He maintains to this day that he has never read anything by Faurisson that suggests that the man was pro-Nazi. 'If anything,' says Chomsky, 'he's anti-Nazi'" (41). Chomsky insists that even to engage in a discussion of this nature is to give an unacceptable legitimacy to the position of his opponents. Furthermore:

[M]y statement about the disgust one must feel at even entering into debate with apologists for the Nazis and Holocaust deniers has been widely quoted.... But it's been quoted to show that I oppose freedom of speech! (By refusing to debate you, I deny your freedom of speech!) And of course they systematically and without exception delete the fact that I was talking about Nazis and Holocaust deniers. That's quite something. You'd have to explore rather deep into the Stalinist archives to find something similar, and recall that all of these people know all of this perfectly well. (14 Aug. 1995)

Was signing the petition on behalf of Faurisson therefore a mistake? In light of the principle involved, Chomsky would say that it was not. What does it mean to sign a petition? Chomsky notes that included in many petitions for Salman Rushdie was praise for his banned book, *The Satanic Verses*: "irrelevent on a freedom of speech statement, and improper, since many of the signers (I'm one) hadn't even looked at [the book]." So why sign?

Because if one were to sign only statements that are formulated the way one thinks proper, no one would sign anything, except the author. It's understood that a signature means support for the general gist of the statement, not the specific formulations. I have no doubt that Mullas in Qom and Stalinist extremists fumed about the other petitions, analyzing every word for a possible connotation, much in the way that Vidal-Naquet, Dershowitz, and other clones of the commissars and Mullahs do in this case. (14 Aug. 1995)

In 1969, Chomsky described the Holocaust as "the most fantastic outburst of collective insanity in human history" (*Peace* 57–58). He also noted that the moment we enter into "a technical debate with the Nazi intelligentsia," the moment we consider such questions as, "[I]s it true that the Jews are a cancer eating away at the vitality of the German people?" "What is the evidence that the Slavs are inferior beings?" we are plunged into "this morass of insane rationality." He then voiced his most impassioned and powerful plea of all: "By entering into the arena of argument and counterargument, of technical feasibility and tactics, of footnotes and citations, by accepting the presumption of legitimacy of debate on certain issues, one has already lost one's humanity" (*American Power* 9). Yet it is a petition, not the sum total of his writings, that is taken as the measure of Chomsky's commitment.

The Pol Pot Affair

Collaborators once more, Chomsky and Edward Herman published *The Political Economy of Human Rights* in 1979. In the second volume of this two-volume work, *After the Cataclysm: Postwar Indochina and the Reconstruction of Imperial Ideology*, they compared two sites of atrocity—Cambodia and Timor—and evaluated the diverse media responses to each. It embroiled Chomsky in an entirely new controversy.

In a 7 November 1980 *Times Higher Education Supplement* article called "Chomsky's Betrayal of Truths," Steven Lukes accused Chomsky of intellectual irresponsibility. He was contributing to the "deceit and distortion surrounding Pol Pot's regime in Cambodia," Lukes charged, because, "obsessed by his opposition to the United States' role in Indochina," he had "lost all sense of perspective" (31). Lukes concluded that there was "only one possible thing to think": Chomsky had betrayed his own anarchist-libertarian principles. "It is sad to see Chomsky writing these things. It is ironic, given the United States' government's present pursuit of its global role in supporting the seating of Pol Pot at the [United Nations]. And it is bizarre, given Chomsky's previous stand for anarchist-libertarian principles. In writing as he does about the Pol Pot regime in Cambodia, Chomsky betrays not only the responsibilities of intellectuals, but himself" (31).

Lukes makes no mention here of the subject of the book, which is clearly stated in the introduction to volume 1, which is entitled "Cambodia: Why the Media Find It More Newsworthy than Indonesia and East Timor." It is an explicit comparison between Cambodia and Timor—the latter being the scene of the worst slaughter, relative to population size, since the Holocaust. Now if the atrocities perpetrated in Timor were comparable to those perpetrated by Pol Pot in Cambodia (and Chomsky claims that they were), then a comparison of Pol Pot's actions to those committed in Timor could not possibly constitute an apology for Pol Pot. Yet somehow Lukes suggested that it did. If such comparisons cannot be made without the intellectual community rising up in protest, then the entire issue of state-instigated murder can become lost inside the polemics of determining which team of slaughterers represents a lesser evil.

That Lukes could ignore the fact that Chomsky and Herman were comparing Pol Pot to East Timor "says a lot about him," in Chomsky's opinion:

By making no mention of the clear, unambiguous, and explicit comparison [of Pol Pot and East Timor], he is demonstrating himself to be an apologist for the crimes in Timor. That is elementary logic: if a comparison of Pol Pot to Timor is apologetics for Pol Pot, as Lukes claims (by omission of the relevant context, which he could not fail to know), then it must be that the crimes in Timor were insignificant. Lukes, then, is an apologist for the worst slaughter relative to population since the Holocaust. Worse, that is a crime for which he, Lukes, bears responsibility; UK support has been crucial. And it is a crime that he, Lukes, could have always helped to terminate, if he did not support huge atrocities; in contrast, neither he nor anyone else had a suggestion as to what to do about Pol Pot. (13 Feb. 1996)

The vigor of Chomsky's remarks reflects the contempt that he feels for this kind of by-now-familiar tactic. Decorum must not take precedence over decrying slaughter and falsity, and Chomsky is compelled to demonstrate this: "Let us say that someone in the US or UK ... did deny Pol Pot atrocities. That person would be a positive saint as compared to Lukes, who denies comparable atrocities for which he himself shares responsibility and knows how to bring to an end, if he chose. That's elementary. Try to find some intellectual who can understand it. That tells us a lot ... about the intellectual culture" (13 Feb. 1996). The point of course goes beyond Lukes, and extends into a general discussion concerning the intellectual community, which itself, in Chomsky's opinion, "cannot comprehend this kind of trivial, simple, reasoning and what it implies. That really is interesting. It reveals a level of indoctrination vastly beyond what one finds in totalitarian states, which rarely were able to indoctrinate intellectuals so profoundly that they are unable to understand real trivialities" (14 Aug. 1995).

Within weeks, two long and lucid replies to Lukes's piece were sent in to the *Times Higher Education Supplement*, accusing him of selective reading, of missing the entire point of *both* volumes of *Political Economy*, of ignoring the first volume, of trivializing the moral potency of Chomsky's thesis, of cold-bloodedly manipulating the truth, of misrepresenting Chomsky and Herman's work, and of disrespect. Neither reply came from Chomsky; one was from Laura J. Summers, the other from Robin Woodsworth Carlsen.

Figure 21
Chomsky at his summer cottage in Wellfleet, Massachusetts, 1986.

Though bolstered by the support of those sympathetic to his position and his larger aims, Chomsky knew that a smear campaign could be much more effective and have a much wider dissemination than rational argumentation. In Herman's opinion,

the Cambodia and Faurisson disputes imposed a serious personal cost on Chomsky. He put up a diligent defence against the attacks and charges against him, answering virtually every letter and written criticism that came to his attention. He wrote many hundreds of letters to correspondents and editors on these topics, along with numerous articles, and answered many phone enquiries and queries in interviews. The intellectual and moral drain was severe. It is an astonishing fact, however, that he was able to weather these storms with his energies, morale, sense of humour and vigour and integrity of his political writings virtually intact. ("Pol Pot" 609)

As ever, Chomsky is quick to point out that being the subject of such treatment did not make him unique. But the ferocity of the attack on him does reveal something about the power of popular media, the lengths to which endangered elites will go to eliminate dissent, and the nature of what passes for appropriate professional behavior. In a letter he wrote to the *Times Literary Supplement* in January of 1982—a reply to an article by Paul Johnson in that same publication in which he, like Lukes, accused Chomsky and Herman of sympathizing with the Khmer Rouge—Chomsky examined one of the tactics used against him: "[A] standard device by which the conformist intellectuals of East or West deal with irritating dissident opinion is to try to overwhelm it with a flood of lies. Paul Johnson illustrates the technique with his reference to my 'prodigies of apologetics ... for the Khmer Rouge' (December 25). I have stated the facts before in this journal, and will do so again, not under any illusion that they will be relevant to the guardians of the faith." Chomsky asserted that the smear campaign was a side issue; the larger concern was, of course, the intellectual apologists' ability to forgo reasonable analysis when their own government was at fault:

The context was extensive documentation of how the mainstream intelligentsia suppressed or justified the crimes of their own states during the same period. This naturally outraged those who feel that they should be free to lie at will concerning the crimes of an official enemy while concealing or justifying those of their own states—a phenomenon that is, incidentally, far more significant and widespread than the delusions about so-called "socialist" states that Johnson discusses, and correspondingly quite generally evaded. Hence the resort to the familiar technique that Johnson, and others, adopts. ("Political Pilgrims")

Otero even goes so far as to describe (in a note he added to *Language and Politics*) the reaction to Chomsky's positions on Faurisson and Pol Pot as a coordinated attempt to undermine his credibility and thereby sabotage his powerful critique of policies on Indochina:

The major international campaign orchestrated against Chomsky on completely false pretexts was only part—though perhaps a crucial part—of the ambitious campaign launched in the late 70s with the hope of reconstructing the ideology of power and domination which had been partially exposed during the Indochina war. The magnitude of the insane attack against Chomsky, which aimed at silencing him and robbing him of his moral stature and his prestige and influence, is of course one more tribute to the impact of his writings and his actions—not for nothing he was the only one singled out. (310)

Such commentary assigns to the ruling elite a uniformity that is based on the values shared by its members. Evidence for this may be found in the heavy media coverage given to the Lukes camp and the general reluctance to allow Chomsky space for rebuttal (particularly in France).

Chomsky as Teacher

As he tackled the enormous job of fending off his attackers, Chomsky refused to put aside any of his scientific, political, and libertarian projects: he gave conferences, wrote letters, completed his books, and taught his classes. He was, and is, for generations of dissenters a figure of enlightenment and inspiration; for students of linguistics he was, and is, a leader in the field. Chomsky has spoken about the role of the teacher, and his remarks offer insight into the style he has developed over the years—a style grounded in his own experience as a student:

Most problems of teaching are not problems of growth but helping cultivate growth. As far as I know, and this is only from personal experience in teaching, I think about ninety percent of the problem in teaching, or maybe ninety-eight percent, is just to help the students get interested. Or what it usually amounts to is to not prevent them from being interested. Typically they come in interested, and the process of education is a way of driving that defect out of their minds. But if children['s] ... normal interest is maintained or even aroused, they can do all kinds of things in ways we don't understand. ("Creation")

There is a wide range of opinion about Chomsky's abilities as a teacher, but certain observations do recur in the recollections of students he has taught in the course of his long career. Many, for example, report that Chomsky answers all questions carefully and thoughtfully, no matter what the intellectual level of his interrogator. His classes are sometimes attended by upwards of one hundred people, and within any given audience one is likely to find leading scholars—from the fields of linguistics, philosophy, psychology, or mathematics—sitting arm-to-arm with interested individuals from all walks of life. There are people who have not missed more than a handful of Chomsky's lectures in twenty years; some travel great distances to hear what he has to say. As one might imagine, this makes for a classroom atmosphere that can be intimidating for his own graduate students. Following his open seminars, he spends an hour alone with his graduate students and offers prolific and penetrating comments on each student submission. Former Chomsky student Lisa Travis, now a professor of linguistics at McGill University, says, "Though it's hard to describe, he generates an atmosphere of intense rationality, a sense of discovery. Whatever he's thinking about is the leading edge of his discipline" (qtd. in Parini 39). Others claim, however, that towards those who pursue research that doesn't interest him Chomsky displays little enthusiasm. Robin Lakoff, a linguistics professor at the University of California, remarks that "he thinks he's in possession of the Truth, and that everybody should listen when he speaks. But not everyone goes along with him nowadays" (qtd. in Parini 39).

There have, as well, been complaints of traditionalism in the MIT linguistics department, and these led to strife in 1983. A student who was present in the department at that time says, "Chomsky thinks he is a feminist, but—at heart—he's an old-fashioned patriarch. Of course, he's a very good person. He just has never really understood what the feminist movement is about" (qtd. in Parini 39). Chomsky disagrees:

The students have been pressuring for years for more women faculty. They are pushing an open door, however. It's long been a faculty initiative, along with efforts to bring in minority faculty. When push comes to shove, [these students] make the same recommendations faculty has. In the early '80s, the one woman faculty member (Joan Bresnan, who was brought in at my personal initiative, over lots of objections from younger faculty members who didn't agree), decided to leave for Stanford. Not long after, Donna Steriade was hired, and then left because we weren't able to find a job in the area for her husband. But there have been no faculty-student disagreements to speak of about the issue, either at the general level or on specifics. There have been periodic student initiatives over the years, some even pretty heated, but on other matters; how to run the general exams, course requirements, etc. (25 July 1995)

The sheer volume of graduate students with whom Chomsky has had contact over the years, and, by extension, the number of Chomsky-trained linguists teaching in universities around the world, is quite incredible. Otero calculates that by 1991 Chomsky had had a hand in supervising more than sixty-seven Ph.D. theses and two M.S. theses ("Background" 819). He has also participated in the supervision of other theses, both at MIT and other universities (as of 1996, over eighty at MIT).

The Postmodern Era

Between the late 1970s and the early 1980s, French-theory-driven postmodernism took the milieu of American social sciences and humanities by storm. Chomsky formed strong opinions on this school of thought, and these were directly related to his ideas about what intellectuals *do* in the academy, and why much of what they do is trivial and/or self-serving. It may seem ironic, then, that his work has been an important resource for those interested in structural approaches to texts, and continues to be used by theorists, including postmodern theorists, who are grappling with issues emerging from the study of structuralism, poststructuralism, poetics, linguistic approaches to literature, and linguistic argumentation.

Language studies (excluding linguistics) in North America have been profoundly influenced by French theoreticians ever since Saussure, but by the early 1980s the canon of French theory had expanded considerably: the popularity of Baudrillard, Bourdieu, Derrida, Deuleuze, Foucault, Guattari, Lacan, and Lyotard was on the rise (although Barthes, Todorov, and Kristeva remained contenders in the battle of the bibliographies). These were the new stars on the theory scene, and although other thinkers were allowed into the canon of literary and language studies, it was the postmodernists who shone brightest.

Theorists seldom agree on how to define postmodernism, and the problem is compounded when one moves from one discipline to another (from postmodern architecture to postmodern poetry, for example). Chomsky's own definition of the term does not accord with that used by many other academics, and has thus been a source of tension. One of the most useful references to postmodernism and its theorists as they are related to Chomsky is Christopher Norris. Norris's detailed criticism of the overall movement—and in particular works by Baudrillard, de Man, Derrida, Lyotard—is a careful and well-reasoned version of Chomsky's own rather dramatic assessment. Norris's critique of Jean Baudrillard's postmodernism, in particular, serves to contextualize Chomsky's stance. In his *Uncritical Theory: Postmodernism, Intellectuals and the Gulf War* (1992), Norris responds to Baudrillard's article "The Gulf War Has Not Taken Place" with a sustained polemic aimed at the excesses and errors of postmodernism. He begins by summarizing Baudrillard's position:

[I]t is Baudrillard's contention that we now inhabit a realm of purely fictive or illusory appearances; that truth has gone the way of enlightened reason and such-like obsolete ideas; that "reality" is nowadays defined through and through by the play of multiplied "simulacra" or reality-effects; that there is no point criticizing "false" appearances (whether on epistemological or socio-political grounds) since those appearances are all that we have, like it or not; and that henceforth we had better make peace with this so-called "postmodern condition" rather than cling to an outworn paradigm whose truth-claims no longer possess the least degree of operative (i.e. persuasive or rhetorical) force. (14–15)

It is easy to imagine what Chomsky would have to say about Baudrillard's postmodernism: think of his Cartesianism, his concern with social and individual responsibility, and his commitment to intervene on behalf of the oppressed (such as those natives of Baghdad upon whom the coalition dropped bombs during the so-called Gulf War).

While Norris condemns Baudrillard's ideas as "absurdities" based upon "ludicrous theses" (17), he also makes it clear that he feels Baudrillard does not represent postmodern thinking as a whole. Consigning Baudrillard to the category of extremist, he presents Derrida as an example of postmodern lucidity. Norris refutes the notion that Derrida is "falling into that facile strain of postmodernist rhetoric that cheerfully pronounces an end to the regime of reality, truth, and enlightenment critique," suggesting instead that his work "raises issues of ethical accountability (along with epistemological questions) which are rendered invisible by the straightforward appeal to reference, intentions, textual authority, right reading, authorial warrant and so forth." Derrida "carries the argument by sheer force of reasoning and meticulous attention to the blind-spots in his opponents' discourse, as well as through his quite extraordinary skill in turning their charges back against themselves in a *tour de force* of sustained *tu quoque* polemics." Nevertheless, Norris admits, postmodernism has been rejected "by many who lack the time or interest to examine the relevant texts at first hand, or to read them with anything like an adequate sense of their complex philosophical prehistory, their implicit axiomatics, specialized modes of argument, etc." He adds: "And a further source of misunderstanding is the fact that these texts have been taken up with enthusiasm by the members of a different 'interpretive community'—U.S. and British literary theorists—who approach them with quite a different set of motivating interests and priorities" (18).

Chomsky, however, has taken Baudrillard as a kind of touchstone for postmodernism, and therefore does not agree with Norris's contention that there is value to postmodern work, even though the two have often been in accord: Chomsky maintains that they are "on the same side," and that he knows of Baudrillard "from Chris Norris's critique" (31 Mar. 1995); Norris writes, in *Uncritical Theory*, "it seems to me that the superior cogency of Chomsky's arguments should be obvious to any reader whose mind remains open to persuasion on rational grounds" (110). It is true that Chomsky does not claim to be an expert on postmodernism; he could, in fact, have ignored the entire movement, as neither mainstream linguistics nor the domain of political dissension has been significantly touched by it the way, for instance, literary studies was. But postmodernism nonetheless says something, in its own obfuscated language, that is an affront to Chomsky's sensibilities. He does grant that "Derrida and Lacan at least should be read; in fact, I quoted early work of Lacan in essays based on talks for psychoanalysts, reprinted in *Rules and Representations*." However, "The others I don't mention because I don't regard them as even minimally serious (to the extent that I'm familiar with their work, which is very slight). Kristeva I met once. She came to my office to see me about 20 years ago, then some kind of raving Maoist, as I recall. I was never tempted to read further" (31 Mar. 1995).

One postmodern thinker with whom Chomsky has successfully engaged, however, is Michel Foucault. Since his death Foucault has emerged as one of the figureheads of postmodernism. Chomsky has met and discussed issues with him, and has also made congenial comments about some of his work. In 1971, Chomsky and Foucault appeared together on Dutch public television. Foucault has emerged relatively unscathed from his encounters with Chomsky, despite the scorn the latter has exhibited for what he sees as the historical relativism, self-indulgence, and self-serving language Ludditism of postmodern theory. In fact, except when the question of whether justice and human nature are historically contingent is concerned, Chomsky and Foucault are often on the same wavelength. Norris writes:

[T]here is a measure of agreement between Foucault's and Chomsky's positions. . . . Thus Chomsky goes some way toward conceding the point that our ideas of truth are very largely the product of "internalized preconceptions"; that subjects may indeed be conditioned to accept certain facts as "self-evident" merely by virtue of their fitting in with some established, consensual, or professionalized code of belief; that censorship often operates not so much "from above" as through forms of self-imposed discipline and restraint that don't involve the exercise of overt, coercive powers; that there may be "honest," "right-thinking" individuals (as Chomsky is willing to describe them) who are none the less involved in propagating falsehoods that service the "political economy of truth"; and moreover, that resistance to those falsehoods or abuses of power must always be *to some extent* reliant on the "discourses"—the available sources of information—that circulate at any given time. (113–14)

While emphasizing, again, the trivial and self-interested character of most political-science theory, Chomsky mentions Foucault's contribution to historical studies:

One can learn a lot from history, as from life, as long as it avoids the pretentious tomfoolery required by intellectuals for career and power reasons. Take Foucault, whom you mention. With enough effort, one can extract from his writings some interesting insights and observations, peeling away the framework of obfuscation that is required for respectability in the strange world of intellectuals, which takes on extreme forms in the weird culture of postwar Paris. Foucault is unusual among Paris intellectuals in that at least something is left when one peels this away. (15 Dec. 1992)

Chomsky on the French Intellectual Tradition

France has become the site of the kind of intellectual work that Chomsky most abhors. He observes: "almost no one in France has ever had any idea of what my political or academic work is about. Of course they write about it all the time, but that is the standard infantilism of French intellectual life." Although, he persists, they may boast "a few very fine linguists and other scientists, anarchist circles, and a handful of others," the French have "a highly parochial and remarkably illiterate culture." For this reason, "during the 60s and 70s, I almost never gave political talks in France.... the distorting effects of dogma were so extreme that it was a waste of time" (30 May 1994). Althusser, Bachelard, de Beauvoir, Camus, Levinas, Levi-Strauss, Sartre, or Serres, all highly respected in certain circles, Chomsky does not mention specifically, but his intention is to question the star status assigned to certain French theorists and the reverence bestowed upon the dogma that is generated by the schools of thought that they have established (in *Language and Politics*, for example, he mentions existentialism, structuralism, Lacanianism, and deconstruction [310–11]). Americans, incidentally, seem equally guilty of fomenting the type of cultishness that Chomsky decries. It is often the American academics that latch onto these trends, hire the leading lights at exorbitant salaries, and prolong the life spans of particular movements by recruiting their faithful followers.

Many French (or French-style) intellectuals believe that Chomsky's work employs outdated strategies that are unable to accommodate the subtleties of political movements. Chomsky's reply to this is that the French are unwilling to see what is set out clearly before them, and should learn "how to tell the truth, to pay attention to facts, and to reach standards of minimal rationality" (31 Mar. 1995). He also charges that the French intellectual scene has refused to interact with work undertaken outside of France—its elite is insular and backward. Numerous examples are proffered: Viennese positivism, studied around the world since the 1930s, is virtually unknown in France (the school's major works were only published in French translation in the 1980s); most French biologists were, in the 1970s, still pre-Darwinian; most German philosophy is still unknown in France. There is, in Chomsky's view, a parochialism and a level of suppression existing in France that is virtually unparalleled, and it extends through all domains. "When the truth about France under the Nazis began to appear in studies in the U.S., there was astonishment and turmoil in France because the facts had been almost completely suppressed—and still largely are" (31 Mar. 1995).

Chomsky's objections to French studies of language and interaction apply, in a more general way, to postmodernism. Many observations made by its practitioners are couched in vague terminology and then elevated to the status of "theory." Chomsky has made some devastating remarks about the kind of postmodern theory that passes for academic achievement in the present era. With reference to Bourdieu and Lyotard, he writes:

Doubtless there is a power structure in every speech situation; again, that is a truism that only an intellectual could find surprising and seek to dress up in appropriate polysyllables. As honest people, our effort should be to unmask it and diminish it, as far as we can, and to do so in association with others, whom we can help and who can help us in this necessary libratory task. Will it ever end? I presume not. As for Lyotard and the post-modern age, I await some indication that there is something here beyond trivialities or self-serving nonsense. I can perceive certain grains of truth hidden in the vast structure of verbiage, but those are simple indeed. Again, maybe I'm missing something, perhaps a lot. If so, I apologize for my simple-mindedness. Maybe I'm missing a gene. I seem to be able to understand other difficult things, but virtually nothing here. Furthermore, in other difficult areas (say, quantum physics), friends and colleagues can explain to me what I want to know (as do serious "popularizations") at a level that I can understand, and I know how to go on if I want to understand more (and have sometimes done so). In these [postmodernist] areas, no one can explain anything to me, and I have no idea how to proceed. It could be that some entirely new form of human intelligence has arisen, beyond those known before, and those who lack the appropriate genes (evidently, me) just can't see it. Perhaps. As I said, I'm open-minded. If there is another explanation, I'd like to hear it. (31 Mar. 1995)

Once one has assimilated Chomsky's objections and grasped his criteria for identifying what constitutes valid academic research, it becomes difficult to credit much of what is proposed as serious scholarship in the social sciences and the humanities. To evade cynicism—to avoid losing all faith in academic work that does not fall into the category of hard

Figure 22
David Barsamian and Chomsky.

science—one must nurture the intellectual skill of distinguishing between what is useful and what is simply self-serving, retrograde, or dangerous.

Armed with his dry, laconic wit Chomsky devotes himself to making this distinction. His use of such terms as "fascist," "lawless," "corrupt," and "fraudulent" when speaking of highly respected government or academic figures raises eyebrows; it also elicits nervous laughter from the audiences he goads into recognizing the absurdity of positions or actions that we have come to consider normal, and provokes the intense animosity of those who consider his sweeping generalizations inappropriate or ill informed. David Barsamian's alternative radio station in Colorado distributes tapes of conversations with Chomsky (as well as other marginalized thinkers such as Samir Amin, Alex Cockburn, Edward Herman, Christopher Hitchens, and Howard Zinn), which offer the listener the opportunity to experience the eloquence of Chomsky's speech. The vivacious humanity of Chomsky's prose is reinforced by powerful articulation, provocative rhetorical techniques, and a tangible enthusiasm for intellectual engagement. He has employed these strategies to force his readers to consider their own humanity through reference to the creative aspects of human beings and to the environments most suited to their development.

Conclusion

In the early 1980s, Chomsky made important progress in his linguistic work, which led him to embark upon what has been described as a "new program." The products of this are recorded in *Lectures on Government and Binding: The Pisa Lectures* (1981), *Knowledge of Language: Its Nature, Origin, and Use* (1986), *Barriers* (1986), and, finally, in a more accessible form, in *Language and Problems of Knowledge: The Managua Lectures* (1988), which also includes some political discussion arising out of questions posed by the Managua audience. *The Minimalist Program*, although not published until 1995, took shape around questions that came into focus in 1980 with the principles-and-parameters model.

These texts emerge from the postulate that languages have no language-particular rules or grammatical constructions of the traditional sort, but rather universal principles and a finite array of options for application. They represent significant advances in the field. In 1988, Chomsky stated that contemporary insights into "empty categories and the principles that govern them and that determine the nature of mental representations and computations in general," "the principles of phrase structure, binding theory, and other subsystems of universal grammar," are allowing us "to see into the hidden nature of the mind . . . really for the first time in history." These discoveries were, he insisted, comparable "with the discovery of waves, particles, genes and so on and the principles that hold of them, in the physical sciences"; furthermore, "we are approaching a situation that is comparable with the physical sciences in the seventeenth-century, when the great scientific revolution took place . . ." (*Language and Problems* 91–92). And, in the introduction to *The Minimalist Program*, he continued along this trajectory, claiming that "it is, I think, of considerable importance that we can at least formulate such questions today, and even approach them in some areas with a degree of success. If recent thinking along these lines is anywhere near accurate, a rich and exciting future lies ahead for the study of language and related disciplines" (9).

Chomsky's political work continued to evolve. While he consistently maintained the principles he had adopted so many years before, he now broadened his scope to address a larger number of issues. He delved deeper into media research (*Manufacturing Consent: The Political Economy of the Mass Media* [1988], with Edward S. Herman; *Necessary Illusions* [1989], and explored other areas, such as Cold War, post-Cold War, and terrorist-style politics (*Towards a New Cold War: Essays on the Current Crisis and How We Got There* [1982]; *Pirates and Emperors: International Terrorism and the Real World* [1986]; *The Culture of Terrorism* [1988]; *Terrorizing the Neighbourhood: American Foreign Policy in the Post-Cold War Era* [1991]; *World Orders, Old and New* [1994]; *Powers and Prospects* [1996]), Israel (*The Fateful Triangle: The United States, Israel and the Palestinians* [1983]), Latin America (*Turning the Tide: U.S. Intervention in Central America and the Struggle for Peace* [1985]), Vietnam (*Rethinking Camelot: JFK, the Vietnam War, and U.S. Political Culture* [1993]), and imperialism (*Deterring Democracy* [1991]; *Year 501: The Conquest Continues* [1993]). Two of the best anthologies of his work were also published during this period, *Language and Politics* (1988) and *The Chomsky Reader* (1987); two excellent introductions to his work were written by Carlos Otero (*Radical Priorities* [1981] and *Language and Politics* [1988]); and collections of interviews such as *Chronicles of Dissent* (1992) and *Keeping the Rabble in Line: Interviews with David Barsamian* (1994) gave the reader access to interviews on wide-ranging subjects.

Scanning this incomplete list of publications—produced during an era dominated by a virtual president named Ronald Reagan, an absurd arms race, the decline and dismantling of the Soviet Union, and superpower engagements with such world-menacing despots as Noriega, Hussein, Khaddafi, and Castro, as well as threats to the stability of the free world from Grenada, Nicaragua, and East Timor—it becomes evident that a synopsis of Chomsky's output over even a relatively short period would only amount to a scratch on the surface of an enormous body of work.

A better way to determine where Chomsky is standing at the present juncture, to communicate a sense of his current milieu, is to look at three issues in which he has become implicated. First, Chomsky has in recent times observed a growing cynicism in the American people, a conviction that the political system is manifestly biased against them and that real political power has eluded their grasp. Out of this cynicism they have, for example, voted against their own best interests (Chomsky cites a poll in which people were asked if they voted for Reagan; the majority responded "Yes," but when asked if they thought Reagan's policies would be beneficial to them they replied "No"). Second, Chomsky has noticed a related increase in the distance between the rulers and the ruled. This is the result of both the increased accumulation of power within a shrinking segment of the population, and the widely heralded "world market economy" (frequently described by Chomsky as a fraudulent label employed by the elite), which has been expanded thanks to the European Union, the North American Free Trade Agreement, and a new General Agreement on Tariffs and Trade treaty. Third, Chomsky has begun, in his political writings, to cite primary sources and media reports rather than the influential figures to whom he had once regularly turned. This phenomenon reflects the growth of popular movements and Chomsky's involvement in them. Also, Chomsky admits, "virtually no one shared my interest in anarchism (and Spanish anarchism) ... and the deepening of my own understanding of the (left) libertarian tradition back to the Enlightenment and before was completely isolated from anyone I knew or know of" (31 Mar. 1995).

Pushing the Limits of Understanding

Despite the fact that he has been so often mired in controversy, Chomsky continues to receive respect and admiration from his peers. They have rewarded him for his many accomplishments with such honors as: the Distinguished Scientific Contribution Award, American Psychological Association (1984); the Kyoto Prize in Basic Science, Inamori Foundation (1988); and the Orwell Award, National Council of Teachers of English

Figure 23
Kyoto Basic Sciences Awards ceremony, 1988. The award is the Japanese equivalent to the Nobel Prize.

(1987 and 1989). He was also made an honorary member, Ges. Für Sprachwissenschaft, Germany in 1990, and, in the same year, became a William James fellow, American Psychological Association.

Incredible advancements, beginning in the early 1980s, have transformed the field of linguistics. Chomsky has been at the forefront of this activity, but credit is also due to scholars outside the United States and to those linguists who have conducted empirical studies of a vast range of typologically different languages. In a very general sense, Chomsky's linguistic work to date falls into three areas of research. These take the form of questions:

1. What do we know when we are able to speak and understand a language?

2. How is this language acquired?
3. How do we use this knowledge? (*Language and Problems* 133)

To question one, the answer is descriptive, so to pursue it we must "attempt to construct a grammar, a theory of a particular language that describes how this language assigns specific mental representations to each linguistic expression, determine its form and meaning." Next, we have to explain it by constructing "a theory of universal grammar, a theory of the fixed and invariant principles that constitute the human language faculty and the parameters of variation associated with them" (*Language* and *Problems* 133). If we are able to construct a universal grammar, we can then approach the second question, because "language learning ... is the process of determining the values of the parameters left unspecified by universal grammar, of setting the switches that make the network function. ..." The third question involves the study of "how people who have acquired a language put their knowledge to use in understanding what they hear and in expressing their thoughts" (*Language and Problems* 134). What remains for the future is a fouth question: "What are the physical mechanisms involved in the representation, acquisition, and the use of this knowledge?" (*Language and Problems* 133).

This question concerns the limits of human understanding. Even as he is making breakthroughs in his field, Chomsky is also becoming more and more concerned with the biological limits of the human being as they pertain to the fundamental questions of existence. Although the physical sciences have afforded us great insight into the workings of matter, studies of the mind have not yielded anywhere near as much useful and scientifically proven information about the basics of human nature. Questions posed by the Greeks, and repeated with variations by generation upon generation of thinkers ever since, remain unanswered. Humankind will perhaps never be able to unravel these mysteries, but this does not mean that they cannot motivate research or generate other questions that might bring researchers closer to their goals.

In pursuit of answers to the overarching fourth question, Chomsky has asked, in the lectures he has given at MIT since the late 1980s:

(1) What are the general conditions that the human language faculty should be expected to satisfy? (2) to what extent is the language faculty determined by these conditions, without special structure that lies beyond them? The first question in

turn has two aspects: what conditions are imposed on the language faculty by virtue of (A) its place within the array of cognitive systems of the mind/brain, and (B) general considerations of conceptual naturalness that have some independent plausibility, namely: simplicity, economy, symmetry, non-redundancy, and the like? (*The Minimalist Program* 1).

He has proceeded along these lines with apparent success, but notes that "what looks reasonable today is likely to take a different form tomorrow" (*The Minimalist Program* 10). Though we have moved closer to uncovering some secrets that were previously thought to be impenetrable, there is, of course, no way of knowing where the limits to human knowledge lie.

Chomsky's own scientific work is dependent upon new empirical and theoretical ideas; the minimalist program, for example, owes its successes to the bold speculation that characterized the principles-and-parameters approach coupled with massive empirical data. This is not to say that Chomsky's most recent linguistic efforts represent a total break from his earlier work. Indeed, "the minimalist program shares several underlying factual assumptions with its predecessors back to the early 1950s, though these have taken somewhat different forms as inquiry has proceeded," and it borrows "from earlier work the assumption that the cognitive system interacts with the performance systems by means of levels of linguistic representation, in the technical sense of this notion" (*The Minimalist Program* 2).

Art and Literature: An Undefinable Influence

On occasion, Chomsky has suggested that the mysterious aspects of human existence and the limits of our knowledge are, in some ways, best explored in works of art. But he does not, like Adorno, Benjamin, Greenberg, or Hauser, seek within the domain of music, visual art, sculpture, or photography visions that offer, for example, alternatives to our present society:

I seem to have a tin ear for atonal music, I'm afraid: past some Berg I mostly listen out of a sense of duty (I have some friends who are well-known composers, and I go to their concerts, for example). As for abstract art, my tastes also tend to fade out after cubism, mainly. Do I find "motivation, inspiration or philosophical truths" in any of this? As for motivation and inspiration, who knows, maybe unconsciously. As for philosophical truths, not as I understand the term at least (in fact, I'm not convinced that the category exists—maybe my Wittgensteinian youth [is] showing). (8 Aug. 1994)

There are, however, frequent references to literature in Chomsky's writings, and several intersections exist between his work and literary texts. First, Chomsky-inspired linguistics has been employed by some critics in formulating their approaches to literary texts, particularly in areas such as semiotics, structuralism, and narratology. Second, Chomsky's philosophical work on creativity and performance has been used to enhance or critique theoretical treatments of literary texts. Third, the popularity of particular authors or literary texts, and the degree of ease or difficulty with which an author publishes a particular work in a particular place and time, are taken by Chomsky as gauges of the control exerted over public expression and the institutions that channel it. Chomsky's many remarks on Orwell bear upon this issue. For example:

> If Orwell, instead of writing *1984*—which was actually, in my opinion, his worst book, a kind of trivial caricature of the most totalitarian society in the world, which made him famous and everybody loved him, because it was the official enemy—if instead of doing that easy and relatively unimportant thing, he had done the hard and important thing, namely talk about Orwell's problem ... [how is it that we know so little given the amount of evidence we have], he would not be famous and honored: he would be hated and reviled and marginalized. ("Creation")

Finally, Chomsky has suggested that literature can offer a far deeper insight into the whole human person than any mode of scientific inquiry. This notion is an interesting anomaly, given his fundamental belief in the power and value of pure sciences over social sciences. He nevertheless remains reticent about drawing "tight connections" between literature and knowledge because he can't really say whether literature has ever "changed [his] attitudes and understanding in any striking or crucial way":

> [I]f I want to understand, let's say, the nature of China and its revolution, I ought to be cautious about literary renditions. Look, there's no question that as a child, when I read about China, this influenced my attitudes—Rickshaw Boy, for example. That had a powerful effect when I read it. It was so long ago I don't remember a thing about it, except the impact.... Literature can heighten your imagination and insight and understanding, but it surely doesn't provide the evidence that you need to draw conclusions and substantiate conclusions. (*Chomsky Reader* 4)

Literature from this standpoint is a means through which experiences can be reread and, potentially, reviewed. It would be difficult to determine whether certain attitudes precede someone's reading of literary texts (thus allowing certain ideas to resonate), or whether the literary texts themselves help form the attitudes (as Chomsky implies in his discussion of the role that these texts played for him as a child). But the actual relationship between literary knowledge and empirical fact is clearly problematic for Chomsky, to the point where he consciously blocks out any effects that literary texts might have for his analysis of particular situations. Nevertheless, Chomsky was, and continues to be, "powerfully influenced" by his broad readings of literary texts (8 Aug. 1994), although the nature of this influence is undefinable: "We learn from literature as we learn from life; no one knows how, but it surely happens. In fact, most of what we know about things that matter comes from such sources, surely not from considered rational inquiry (science), which sometimes reaches unparalleled depths of profundity, but has a rather narrow scope—a product, I assume, of special properties of human cognitive structure" (15 Dec. 1992). These "properties," like the physical mechanisms involved in the representation, acquisition, and the use of knowledge, are some of the areas of human nature that have always been virtually impenetrable. But, as his research and his remarks about literature imply, Chomsky considers that human nature may someday be describable, and aspects of it may even be understood—a possibility that many of his contemporaries don't admit, because they refuse to recognize that a human nature exists. To Chomsky, this kind of thinking is absurd: "Yes, I speak of human nature, but not for complicated reasons. I do so because I am not an imbecile, and do not believe that others should fall into culturally imposed imbecility. Thus, I do not want to cater to imbecility. Is my granddaughter different from a rock? From a bird? From a gorilla? If so, then there is such a thing as human nature. That's the end of the discussion: we then turn to asking what human nature is" (15 Dec. 1992). He goes on to speculate about the source of the denials of human nature:

For intellectuals—that is, social, cultural, economic and political managers—it is very convenient to believe that people have "no nature," that they are completely malleable. That eliminates any moral barrier to manipulation and control, an attractive idea for those who expect to conduct the manipulation, and to gain power, prestige and wealth thereby. The doctrine is so utterly foolish that one has to seek an explanation. This is the one that intellectual and social history seem to me to suggest. (15 Dec. 1992)

There is, in the attitude expressed here, some indication of Chomsky's linguistic theory (all people have a characteristic creative capacity and share particular innate abilities), his opinion of most intellectuals (he uses the term "managers" in the same sense that Bakunin and Pannekoek did), his thoughts concerning appropriate environments for human development (beyond control and manipulation), and his suspicions about a collusion between elite powers and those who promote certain doctrines. Also evident in his commentary is the characteristic goad—the quality that nudges his readers to evaluate and reevaluate their basic assumptions in the name of both common sense (the granddaughter-rock comparison) and social autonomy (preaching "no nature" paves the way for social control à la, for example, Skinner). Chomsky the worker never lets up— his long product list testifies to this—and Chomsky the thinker doesn't let things pass without scrutiny, because to do so would be to risk falling into some carefully designed trap, the type of pitfall that left libertarians have long been at pains to expose.

Fighting for Control

So what remains to be done? Struggle. Struggle in the face of biases that dog research of all types, of accepted dogma, of manipulation and propaganda; struggle to promote human freedom. Although the obstacles seem great, there are enough success stories from which to draw strength:

We don't live under slavery because of popular struggles. We have freedom of speech because of popular struggles. It is never a gift from above. James Madison, one of the founding fathers, put it very clearly. He said a parchment barrier will never protect against tyranny.... nor are you ever going to get any gifts from above. Protection against tyranny comes from struggle, and it doesn't matter what kind of tyranny it is. And if that is carried out, it can achieve many gains. There has been a considerable expansion of the sphere of freedom over the centuries, and it has a long way to go. ("Creation")

But while Chomsky has made progress in recent years on the linguistics front, he cannot rest on his political-activist laurels. He is compelled to point continuously to the ways in which oppressive structures such as fascism and totalitarianism (which we like to believe have been dismantled, at least within our own society), as well as concentration camps,

Figure 24
Chomsky speaking to an audience on political issues.

torture chambers, and "ethnic-cleansing" campaigns, still exist. Certainly anyone willing to take the time to examine the nature of governments, corporations—even leisure activities—knows this to be true: "Take professional sports.... It is hard to imagine anything that contributes more fundamentally to authoritarian attitudes. In professional sports you are a spectator, and there is a bunch of gladiators beating each other up, or something. And you are supposed to cheer for your gladiators. That is something you are taught from childhood" ("Creation").

Unfortunately, the task of publicly identifying such structures is arduous and time-consuming. Those who undertake it are also, in Chomsky's opinion, likely to be thwarted by a coerced and manipulative media, by government, and by corporate interests bent on obscuring pertinent information. While government may seem the most obvious culprit in such attempts at suppression, Chomsky stresses that the impression is purposefully constructed:

The problem isn't "governments," at least in the West. They are not much involved in doctrinal management (though there are exceptions, like Woodrow Wilson and the Reaganites, both of whom ran huge state propaganda systems—illegal in the latter case; there were no relevant laws in the Wilson era). Doctrinal management is overwhelmingly the task of corporate propaganda, which is extraordinary in scale and very significant in impact; and [it is also] the task of the general intellectual community, including the acceptable dissidents (Irving Howe, founder of *Dissent*, etc.) who perform a very important service by setting the bounds of discussion and thus entrenching the unspoken presuppositions of the doctrinal system, a matter again that I've discussed at length. Anyway, governments are marginal, outside of totalitarian states, though attention is always focused on them, to direct it away from what matters. (31 Mar. 1995)

Extra-governmental organizations—the IMF, the World Bank, the GATT council, and the G-7 executive—are also implicated in the campaign to exclude what Chomsky refers to as the "rabble" from the process of making the decisions and creating the policies that directly concern them:

[A] technique of control which is actually being sort of pioneered in the contemporary period, both in the United States and Europe, is raising the level of decisions to be so remote from people's knowledge and understanding that they don't even know what is going on. They can't find out what is happening, and certainly can't influence it even if they do. That is part of the meaning of the "*de facto* world government" [a citation from the *Financial Times* that refers to a new set of emerging institutions outside of the national state] that is developing. ("Creation")

This kind of argument has familiar echoes, at least in terms of the values that underwrite it. It is, in spirit, the argument that Chomsky has always put forward, and it exists, in embryonic form, in the work of those who populate the milieu from which he emerged.

There is a sense that Chomsky's political work is, in its stubborn reiteration of fact and its insistence upon the absolute relevance of particular events, somehow untheoretical. In light of his previous commentary on intellectual obfuscation, the trivial observations that pass for political science, and unnecessarily complex language, his reply to such a charge is perhaps predictable:

> If someone can come up with a nontrivial theory that has some bearing on matters of human concern, with conclusions of any credibility that would alter the ways in which I or others view these matters without access to the "theory," I'd be the first to immerse myself in it, with delight. What I find, however, is intellectuals posturing before one another. Maybe that's my inability to discern important things, but if so, it should be possible to explain this to me. Many people in the academic and intellectual left complain at length about my "non-theoretical" stance, as do those elsewhere. But so far, no one has even tried to respond to this very simple challenge that any sane person would make, as far as I can see. What am I to conclude from that? (31 Mar. 1995)

And so, Chomsky continues to publish political works that are as powerful and consistent as ever. In all of these, right up to the recent *World Orders, Old and New* (1994), may be found resonances of fundamentally left-libertarian values. As ever, though, there are those who object violently to Chomsky's offerings. Ken Jowitt, for example, who reviewed *World Orders* for the 10 February 1995 edition of the *Times Literary Supplement*, declared that the book is an expression of its author's "unrelenting anger"; it also communicates his belief in a transnational corporate conspiracy, his dismissal of ideology as anything more than a "disguise" to be "unmasked," his prophetlike scorn for intellectual pharisees, his ahistorical view of history, and his "one-dimensional conception of power as violence." But this work, like Chomsky's other recent political publications, is better understood as speaking to libertarian anarchist groups, popular organizations, inchoate movements, as well as concerned and even desperate people; indeed, writes Chomsky, "that's the milieu I want to be a part of." These groups, unlike the narrower one composed mainly of intellectuals to which he spoke earlier in his career, are less thoroughly indoctrinated by systems of power, including corpo-

Figure 25
Chomsky receiving a piece of Native art in British Columbia, 1989.

rations and institutions of higher learning, and more willing to think things through. To speak to these people is, for Chomsky, "an intellectual and emotional release, and I do, I'm sure, write and speak differently from 30 years ago, probably on all topics. But that's a step towards—not away from—the radical intellectual milieu that I've felt myself part of since adolescence" (31 Mar. 1995).

In electing to involve himself even more deeply in popular struggles, Chomsky has significantly accelerated his already hectic schedule. The range and pace of activities he records here (rather breathlessly) is typical:

I recently spent a week in Australia, at the invitation of East Timorese refugees who wanted to focus attention on Australia's (horrible) policies of support for the Indonesian invasion and rip-off of East Timor's petroleum resources (I also gave talks there at universities, and on every other imaginable topic, but the focus was this, including a nationally televised talk at the National Press Club critically analyzing Australia's foreign policy and the self-serving lies with which it is concealed—this is Australia, not the U.S., a far more ideological society, where nothing of this sort would ever be allowed). Before that I spent a week in California, at the invitation of the Berkeley philosophy department for several lectures and the Stanford University program on ethics and public policy, but with most of my time devoted to talks in Oakland organized by Catholic Worker (which works in the slums, mainly with illegal refugees), another organized by Timorese students, a third for the biggest and oldest peace and justice group around (Palo Alto), another for the Middle East Children's Alliance, etc. All of these were benefits—that's a major way for such groups to raise money and increase public outreach, since the audiences are usually huge, with people who are interested. (31 Mar. 1995)

This is where Chomsky chooses to be; in both word and action, he has embraced activism more closely than ever before, and has turned his back, for the most part, on discussions of social theory. But while his heart is with those who share in the struggle, he continues in his academic work. Yet another glimpse at his full-tilt itinerary serves to demonstrate the way Chomsky prioritizes the two worlds within which he operates and how he manages to strike an at times delicate balance between them:

The last time I was in Europe, a few months ago, was at the invitation of the U. of London for philosophy lectures, but that was combined with talks for popular audiences and activist groups at a town hall and downtown theatre, a visit to Portugal at the invitation of the Socialist Party, and a talk at Geneva organized by Women's International League for Peace and Freedom, mainly third world women and activist NGOS [non-governmental organizations]. (31 Mar. 1995)

Chomsky also gave the keynote address at a conference that he otherwise did not attend.

A Last Look

So, as he works on the minimalist program—conducting linguistic research that could lead us to a better understanding of the mind/brain— Chomsky is also participating in activist initiatives around the world that call into question the tyrannical and oppressive structures that limit individual freedom and creativity. All this is bolstered by fifty years of commitment to ideas that in both the linguistic and political domains have stood the test of time by remaining topical and applicable. Generations of scholars have been trained by Chomsky. The Chomskys' lives today are simple, comfortable, and filled with the rewards of passionate teaching and research, and of dedication to a consistent set of values.

Figure 26
The Chomsky family: Diane, Avi, Carol, Noam, and Harry.

I would like to leave the reader with one last picture of Noam Chomsky. It is 1990, and he sits in a pub in Govan (a suburb of Glasgow), surrounded by the participants of a Self-Determination and Power Event. These include social workers; literati ("Bohemian writers," Chomsky says, "mostly outcasts," the most famous of whom is Jim Kelman [31 Mar. 1995]); educationists ("radical critics of the educational system, like Derek Rodgers"); anarchists and libertarian socialists; and people variously describing themselves as "feminist therapist," "systems analyst," "anti-poll-tax activist," "mother/student," "prison governor," "retail manager," and "boatbuilder/writer." The event, accompanied by a wonderful pub photo, is covered by the *Times Higher Education Supplement* of 26 January 1990 under the headline: "Pubs, Power and the Scottish Psyche: Olga Wojtas Reports from Govan on a Conference on Self-Determination." The 330 participants of the event (many of whom [are] "unemployed working class, activists of one or another sort, those considered to be 'riff-raff' "—"the kind of people," Chomsky says, that "I like and take seriously" [31 Mar. 1995]), which has been organized by the

Figure 27
At the pub in Govan, Scotland, 1990.

magazines *Scottish Child* and *Edinburgh Review* and the Free University of Glasgow (not a university in the accepted sense of the term), are interested in self-determination and a guru named Noam Chomsky, self-described "scourge of United States policies and champion of the ordinary person." Chomsky gives keynote speeches on both days of the event. The fact that he has decided to attend at all mystifies both the press and the establishment.

> Thus when an announcement came that I was going to be in Glasgow, I got a letter on very fancy letterhead from something called "the Scottish Foundation" inviting me to give a talk for them on Nicaragua. I of course agreed. Shortly after, I got another letter saying they'd just learned that I'd also be giving a talk organized by the free university, Kelman, and other scum, and they insisted that I cancel that invitation because they wouldn't tolerate the guilt by association. I don't recall whether I even bothered answering. (31 Mar. 1995)

In his talks, Chomsky disparages nationalism, the exercise of political power by leaders who do not answer to citizens, instruments of social control and isolationism such as television, and the collusion of media in the process of oppression and the spreading of lies. There remains, at the end of the event, the problem of "how to take on the bastards," as well as "an imbalance in that people seemed to feel they had to stay on an intellectual plane." Said one participant, "If I sound a bit frustrated, it's because I'm a bit frustrated" (Wojtas). But Chomsky is not there to lead.

He's sitting in the Govan pub, and, as always, he's insisting that the participants consider their own situation as clearheadedly as possible, and that they make their own decisions. The *Times Higher Education Supplement* has reported: "Professor Chomsky continued to duck the role of oracle, denying the need for oracles at all. There had been a sense, he recognized, that there was something deeply unsatisfying about general and abstract discussion which did not direct itself to concrete discussion of oppression and justice." Somebody recalls Vaclav Havel's dictum that "truth and love will triumph over hatred and lies." Chomsky's response? "It's a nice thought." Yes, but is it true or false? "Neither. It could become true, to the extent that people struggle to make it come true." Noam Chomsky, sixty-eight years old, Institute Professor, linguist, philosopher, grandfather, champion of ordinary people.

Notes

1. Since 1991, I have corresponded with Noam Chomsky on a wide range of subjects. I quote these letters throughout this biography; each quote is followed by the date (in parentheses) of the letter from which it is taken. Accordingly, the quoted letters written to me by others and the personal interviews I conducted in preparing to write this book will be documented with the date in parentheses, rather than a reference to the works-consulted section.

2. The first ten entries on the list are, in order: Marx, Lenin, Shakespeare, Aristotle, the Bible, Plato, Freud, Chomsky, Hegel, and Cicero.

3. For information on the two-part video version of *Manufacturing Consent: Noam Chomsky and the Media* write to: Necessary Illusions, 24 Mount Royal Blvd. W., Ste. 1008, Montreal, QC, Canada, H2S 2P2. The company may also be contacted by phone: (514) 287-7337; fax: (514) 287-7620; or email: mail@NecessaryIllusions.ca[.]

Works Consulted

Abramovitch, Sam. Interviews with the author. 1 Aug. 1990–12 Apr. 1993.

———. Letter to the author. 4 Apr. 1995.

"America's Great Intellectual Prizefight." *Times* [London] 5 Feb. 1972: 14.

Anderson, Stephen R., Sandra Chung, James McCloskey, and Frederick J. Newmeyer. "Chomsky's 1962 Programme for Linguistics: A Retrospective." In Otero, *Noam Chomsky* 1: 691–707.

Avrich, Paul. *Anarchist Portraits.* Princeton: Princeton University Press, 1988.

Avukah. *An Approach to Action: Facing the Social Insecurities Affecting the Jewish Position.* Avukah Pamphlet Service. New York: Avukah, 1943.

———. *Program for American Jews.* Avukah Pamphlet Service. New York: Avukah, 1938.

Bagdikian, Ben H. *The Media Monopoly.* 3rd ed. Boston: Beacon, 1990.

Barsky, Robert. "Arguing the Choice of Host Country: Jewish Refugees from Israel and the Multicultural Society." *Multiculturalism, Jews and the Canadian Identity.* Ed. Howard Adelman and John Simpson. Jerusalem: Magnus, 1996.

Bruggers, H. "Stages of Totalitarian Economy." *Living Marxism* 6.1 (1941): 15–24.

Carling, Christine, and Terence Moore. "After Chomsky's Revolution." *Times Higher Education Supplement* 10 Dec. 1982: 13–14.

Carlsen, Robin Woodsworth. Letter. *Times Higher Education Supplement* 26 Dec. 1980: 18.

"Chomsky Debate Absorbs the Royal Society." *Times* [London] 12 Mar. 1981: 3.

Chomsky, Noam. *American Power and the New Mandarins.* New York: Pantheon, 1969.

———. *Aspects of the Theory of Syntax.* Cambridge: MIT Press, 1965.

———. *At War with Asia.* New York: Pantheon, 1970.

———. *Barriers.* Cambridge: MIT Press, 1986.

———. *Cartesian Linguistics: A Chapter in the History of Rationalist Thought.* New York: Harper, 1966.

———. *The Chomsky Reader.* Ed. James Peck. New York: Pantheon, 1987.

———. *Chronicles of Dissent.* Monroe, ME: Common Courage; Stirling, Scotland: AK, 1992.

———. "Creation and Culture." Audiotape. Alternative Radio. Rec. 25 Nov. 1992.

———. "The Creative Experience." *The Creative Experience.* Eds. Stanley Rosner and Lawrence E. Abt. New York: Grossman, 1970. 71–87.

———. *The Culture of Terrorism.* Boston: South End; Montreal: Black Rose, 1988.

———. *Current Issues in Linguistic Theory.* The Hague: Mouton, 1964.

———. *Deterring Democracy.* New York: Verso, 1991.

———. *Écrits politiques, 1977–1983.* Peyrehorade: Acratie, 1984.

———. *Essays on Form and Interpretation.* New York: North-Holland, 1977.

———. *The Fateful Triangle: The United States, Israel and the Palestinians.* Boston: South End, 1983; Montreal: Black Rose, 1984.

———. *For Reasons of State.* New York: Pantheon, 1973.

———. *Generative Grammar: Its Basis, Development and Prospects.* Kyoto: Kyoto University of Foreign Studies, 1987.

———. *Human Rights and American Foreign Policy.* Nottingham: Spokesman, 1978.

———. *Keeping the Rabble in Line: Interviews with David Barsamian.* Monroe, ME: Common Courage, 1994.

———. *Knowledge of Language: Its Nature, Origin, and Use.* New York: Praeger, 1986.

———. *Language and Information: Selected Essays on the Theory and Application.* Reading, MA: Addison-Wesley; Jerusalem: Jerusalem Academic Press, 1964.

———. *Language and Mind.* New York: Pantheon, 1968. Enl. ed. New York: Harcourt, 1972.

———. *Language and Politics.* Ed. C. P. Otero. Montreal: Black Rose, 1988.

———. *Language and Problems of Knowledge: The Managua Lectures.* Cambridge: MIT Press, 1988.

———. *Language and Responsibility.* Trans. John Viertel [*Dialogues avec Mitsou Ronat.* Paris: Flammarion, 1977]. New York: Pantheon, 1979.

———. *Language in a Psychological Setting.* Tokyo: Sophia University, 1987.

———. *Lectures on Government and Binding: The Pisa Lectures.* Dordrecht: Foris, 1981. Corrected ed., 1982.

———. *Letters from Lexington: Reflections on Propaganda.* Monroe, ME: Common Courage, 1993.

———. *Letters to the author.* 22 July 1992–13 Feb. 1996.

————. "Linguistics and Politics." *New Left Review* 57 (1969): 21–34.

————. *The Logical Structure of Linguistic Theory.* New York: Plenum, 1975 [1955–56].

————. *The Minimalist Program.* Cambridge: MIT Press, 1995.

————. *A Minimalist Program for Linguistic Theory.* Cambridge: MIT Department of Linguistics, 1992.

————. *Modular Approaches to the Study of the Mind.* Distinguished Graduate Research Lecture Series 1, 1980. Long Beach: California State University Press, 1984.

————. *Morphophonemics of Modern Hebrew.* New York: Garland, 1979.

————. *Necessary Illusions.* Boston: South End, 1989.

————. "Noam Chomsky Interviewed by Eleanor Wachtel." *Queen's Quarterly* 101.1 (1994): 63–72.

————. *On Power and Ideology: The Managua Lectures.* Boston: South End; Montreal: Black Rose, 1987.

————. *Peace in the Middle East? Reflections on Justice and Nationhood.* New York: Pantheon, 1974.

————. *Pirates and Emperors: International Terrorism and the Real World.* New York: Claremont, 1986; Montreal: Black Rose, 1987.

————. "Political Pilgrims." Letter. *Times Literary Supplement* 22 Jan. 1982: 81.

————. *Problems of Knowledge and Freedom: The Russell Lectures.* New York: Pantheon, 1971.

————. *The Prosperous Few and the Restless Many.* Berkeley: Odonian, 1993.

————. "Psychology and Ideology." *Cognition* 1 (1972): 11–46.

————. "Quelques commentaires élémentaires sur le droit à la liberté d'expression" [introduction]. *Mémoire en défense contre ceux qui m'accusent de falsifier l'histoire: La question des chambres à gaz.* By Robert Faurisson. Paris: Vieille Taupe, 1980. i–xxiii.

————. *Radical Priorities.* Ed. C. P. Otero. Montreal: Black Rose, 1981. Enl. ed. 1984.

————. *Reflections on Language.* New York: Pantheon, 1975.

————. *Rethinking Camelot: JFK, the Vietnam War, and U.S. Political Culture.* Boston: South End; Montreal: Black Rose, 1993.

————. Rev. of *Beyond Freedom and Dignity,* by B.F. Skinner. *New York Review of Books* 30 Dec. 1971: 18–24.

————. Rev. of *Verbal Behavior,* by B.F. Skinner. *Language* 35 (1959): 26–58.

————. *Rules and Representations.* New York: Columbia University Press, 1980.

————. *Secrets, Lies and Democracy.* Berkeley: Odonian, 1994.

———. *Studies on Semantics in Generative Grammar*. The Hague: Mouton, 1972.

———. *Syntactic Structures*. The Hague: Mouton, 1957.

———. "Systems of Syntactic Analysis." *Journal of Symbolic Logic* 18 (1953): 242–56.

———. *Terrorizing the Neighbourhood: American Foreign Policy in the Post-Cold War Era*. Stirling, Scotland: AK, 1991.

———. *Topics in the Theory of Generative Grammar*. The Hague: Mouton, 1966.

———. *Towards a New Cold War: Essays on the Current Crisis and How We Got There*. New York: Pantheon, 1982.

———. *Turning the Tide: U.S. Intervention in Central America and the Struggle for Peace*. Boston: South End, 1985. Enl. ed. [subtitled *The U.S. and Latin America*], 1987.

———. *What Uncle Sam Really Wants*. Berkeley: Odonian, 1992.

———. *World Orders, Old and New*. New York: Columbia University Press, 1994.

———. *Year 501: The Conquest Continues*. Boston: South End; Montreal: Black Rose, 1993.

———, and Morris Halle. *The Sound Pattern of English*. New York: Harper; Cambridge: MIT Press, 1968.

———, and Edward S. Herman. *After the Cataclysm: Postwar Indochina and the Reconstruction of Imperial Ideology*. Vol. 2 of Chomsky and Herman, *Political Economy*.

———, and Edward S. Herman. *Counter-Revolutionary Violence: Bloodbaths in Fact and Propaganda*. Andover, MA: Warner Modular, 1973.

———, and Edward S. Herman. *Manufacturing Consent: The Political Economy of the Mass Media*. New York: Pantheon, 1988.

———, and Edward S. Herman. *The Political Economy of Human Rights*. 2 vols. Boston: South End; Montreal: Black Rose, 1979.

———, and Edward S. Herman. *The Washington Connection and Third World Fascism*. Vol. 1 of Chomsky and Herman, *Political Economy*.

———, Riny Huybregts, and Henk van Riemsdijk. *The Generative Enterprise*. Dordrecht: Foris, 1982.

———, Mark Sacharoff, Robert Jay Lifton, and Fred Branfman. Letter. *New York Times* 16 Feb. 1972: 10.

Coates, Ken. *The Quality of Life and Workers' Control*. Nottingham: Spokesman, 1973.

———. *Socialists and the Labour Party*. Nottingham: Spokesman, 1975.

Coates, Ken, et al. "Bertrand Russell and Industrial Democracy." *Bertrand Russell and Industrial Democracy*. Nottingham: Institute for Workers' Control, 1970.

Cohn, Werner. *The Hidden Alliances of Noam Chomsky*. New York: Americans for a Safe Israel, 1988.

————. *Partners in Hate: Noam Chomsky and the Holocaust Deniers*. Cambridge: Avukah, 1995.

Dershowitz, Alan M. *Chutzpah*. Boston: Little, Brown, 1991.

Epstein, Norman. Letters to the author. 15 Dec. 1994–20 Apr. 1995.

"Experts Labor to Communicate on Animal Talk." *New York Times* 25 Sept. 1975: 74.

Falk, Richard. "Letters from Prison—American Style: The Political Vision and Practice of Noam Chomsky." In Otero, *Noam Chomsky* 3: 578–97.

"Former Chomsky Disciples Hurl Harsh Words at the Master." *New York Times* 10 Sept. 1972: 70.

George, Alexander. Introduction. *Reflections on Chomsky*. Ed. George. Oxford: Basil Blackwell, 1989. v–ix.

Goreing, Andrew. "Enduring Champion of Ordinary People." *Times Higher Education Supplement* 3 Feb. 1989: 15.

Haley, Michael C., and Ronald F. Lunsford. *Noam Chomsky*. New York: Twayne, 1994.

Harris, Randy Allen. *The Linguistics Wars*. New York: Oxford University Press, 1993.

Harris, Zellig S. *Methods in Structural Linguistics*. Chicago: University of Chicago Press, 1951.

Heny, Frank. Rev. *Logical Structure of Linguistics Theory*, by Noam Chomsky. In Otero, *Noam Chomsky* 1: 308–39.

Herman, Edward S. Letter to David Peterson. 12 Aug. 1992.

————. Letter to the author. 2 Aug. 1994.

————. "Pol Pot, Faurisson and the Process of Derogation." Otero, ed. 3: 598–615.

Huck, Geoffrey J., and John A. Goldsmith. *Ideology and Linguistic Theory: Noam Chomsky and the Deep Structure Debates*. London: Routledge, 1995.

Humboldt, Wilhelm von. *Humanist without Portfolio: An Anthology of the Writing of Wilhelm von Humboldt*. Trans. Marianne Cowan. Detroit: Wayne State University Press, 1963.

Jacoby, Russell. *The Last Intellectuals: American Culture in the Age of Academe*. New York: Basic Books, 1987.

J. B. and P. M. Introduction. In Pannekoek, *Workers' Councils* i–iv.

Jowitt, Ken. "Our Republic of Fear: Chomsky's Denunciation of America's Foreign and Economic Policy." *Times Literary Supplement* 10 Feb. 1995: 3–4.

Katz, Jerrold J., and Thomas Bever. "The Fall and Rise of Empiricism." In Otero, *Noam Chomsky* 1: 286–307.

Korsch Karl. "On Socialization." *Self-Governing Socialism*. Ed. Branko Horvat, Mihailo Markovic, and Rudi Supek. 2 vols. White Plains: International Arts and Sciences, 1975. 1: 201–07.

———. "War and Revolution." *Living Marxism* 6.1 (1941): 1–14.

Leaman, Michael. "Diary of the Clever Me Phenomenon." *Times* [London] 7 July 1980: 14.

Lees, Robert. Rev. *Syntactic Structures*, by Noam Chomsky. Otero, ed. 1: 39–80.

Lukes, Steven. "Chomsky's Betrayal of Truths." *Times Higher Education Supplement* 7 Nov. 1980: 31.

Lyons, John. *Chomsky*. 3rd expanded ed. London: Collins, 1991.

———. Rev. of *Syntactic Structures*, by Noam Chomsky. In Otero, *Noam Chomsky* 1: 81–87.

MacCorquodale, Kenneth. "On Chomsky's Review of Skinner's *Verbal Behavior*." *Journal of the Experimental Analysis of Behavior* 13 (1970): 183–199.

Macdonald, Dwight. *Memoirs of a Revolutionist: Essays in Political Criticism*. New York: Farrar, 1957.

Mailer, Norman. *The Armies of the Night: History as a Novel, The Novel as History*. New York: New American Library, 1968.

Matthews, P. H. *Grammatical Theory in the United States from Bloomfield to Chomsky*. Cambridge: Cambridge University Press, 1993.

———. "Saying Something Simple." Rev. of *Language and Information*, by Zellig Harris. *Times Literary Supplement* 23–29 Dec. 1988: 1430.

Mattick, Paul. "Two Men in a Boat—Not to Speak of the 8 Points." *Living Marxism* 6.1 (1941): 24–79.

Melman, Seymour. Interview with the author. 26 July 1994.

Noble, David. *Progress without People: New Technology, Unemployment, and the Message of Resistance*. Toronto: Between the Lines, 1995.

Norris, Christopher. *Uncritical Theory: Postmodernism, Intellectuals and the Gulf War*. London: Lawrence, 1992.

Orwell, George. *The Collected Essays, Journalism and Letters of George Orwell*. Eds. Sonia Orwell and Ian Angus. 5 vols. London: Secker, 1968.

———. *Homage to Catalonia*. San Diego: Harcourt, 1980.

Otero, Carlos P. "Background and Publication History of the Dissertations Written under the Supervision of Noam Chomsky, 1964–1991" [appendix]. In Otero, *Noam Chomsky* 1: 819–39.

———. "Chomsky and the Challenges Ahead: A Model for the Cognitive Sciences and a Beacon for the Humanities" [introduction]. In Otero, *Noam Chomsky* 4: 1–33.

————. "Chomsky and the Cognitive Revolution of the 1950s: The Emergence of Transformational Generative Grammar." In Otero, *Noam Chomsky* 1: 1–36.

————. "Chomsky and the Libertarian Tradition: A Renewed Egalitarian Vision, a Coherent Social Theory and Incisive, Up-to-Date Analysis" [introduction]. In Otero, *Noam Chomsky* 3: 1–26.

————. "Chomsky and the Rationalist Tradition: Support for Innateness, Metaphysics Vindicated and a Rare Kind of Intellectual History" [introduction]. In Otero, *Noam Chomsky* 2: 1–27.

————. "Introduction to Chomsky's Social Theory." Chomsky, *Radical Priorities* 11–58.

————. Letter to the author. 5 Apr. 1995.

————. "The Third Emancipatory Phase of History" [introduction]. In Chomsky, *Language and Politics*, 22–81.

Otero, Carlos P. ed. *Noam Chomsky: Critical Assessments.* 4 vols. London: Routledge, 1994.

Pannekoek, Anton. *Workers' Councils.* Cambridge: Root, 1970.

Parini, Jay. "Noam Is an Island." *Mother Jones* Oct. 1988: 36–41.

Putnam, Hilary. Preface. *The Form of Information in Science: Analysis of an Immunology Sublanguage.* By Zellig Harris, Michael Gottfried, Thomas Ryckman, Paul Mattick, Jr., Anne Daladier, T. N. Harris, and S. Harris. Dordrecht: Kluwer, 1989. i–xvii.

Rev. of *For Reasons of State* and *The Backroom Boys*, by Noam Chomsky. *Times Literary Supplement* 21 Dec. 1973: 1565–66.

Rocker, Rudolf. *The London Years.* Trans. Joseph Leftwich. London: Anscombe, 1956.

————. *The Tragedy of Spain.* New York: Freie Arbeiter Stimme, 1937.

Russell, Bertrand. *The Autobiography of Bertrand Russell.* 3 vols. London: Allen, 1968.

Salkie, Raphael. *The Chomsky Update: Linguistics and Politics.* London: Unwin-Hyman, 1990.

Sampson, Geoffrey. "Human Language Debates." Rev. of *Rules and Representations*, by Noam Chomsky. *Times Higher Education Supplement* 19 Sept. 1980: 14.

Searle, John R. Letter. *Times Literary Supplement* 22 Oct. 1976: 1330.

————. "The Rules of the Language Game." Rev. of *Reflections on Language*, by Noam Chomsky. *Times Literary Supplement* 10 Sept. 1976: 1118–20.

Segal, Willie. Letter to the author. 24 Apr. 1995.

Shenker, Israel. "Noam Chomsky." *Horizon* 13. 2 (1971): 104–09.

Skinner, B. F. "Verbal Behaviour." Letter. *Times Literary Supplement* 9–15 Mar. 1990: 253.

Sklar, Robert. "Chomsky's Revolution in Linguistics." In Otero, *Noam Chomsky* 3: 27–37.

Steffens, Lincoln. *The Autobiography of Lincoln Steffens.* New York: Harcourt, 1931.

Summers, Laura J. Letter. *Times Higher Education Supplement* 19 Dec. 1980: 22.

Townshend, Charles. "In the Name of Liberty." Rev. of *The Chomsky Reader*, by Noam Chomsky. *Times Literary Supplement* 15–21 July 1988: 777.

Tucker, Bea. Interviews with the author. Nov. 1995.

Vidal-Naquet, Pierre. *Assassins of Memory: Essays on the Denial of the Holocaust.* Trans. Jeffrey Mehlman. New York: Columbia University Press, 1992.

Whitfield, Stephen J. *A Critical American: The Politics of Dwight Macdonald.* Hamden, CT: Archon, 1984.

Wojtas, Olga. "Pubs, Power and the Scottish Psyche: Olga Wojtas Reports from Govan on a Conference on Self-Determination." *Times Higher Education Supplement* 26 Jan. 1990: 15.

Woodhouse, C. M. "The Anti-American Case." Rev. of *Towards a New Cold War*, by Noam Chomsky. *Times Literary Supplement* 23 July 1982: 784.

Yergin, Daniel. "The Chomskyan Revolution." In Otero, *Noam Chomsky* 3: 38–53.

Young, Nigel. Rev. of *The Backroom Boys*, by Noam Chomsky. *Times Higher Education Supplement* 5 Apr. 1974: 20.

Index

160, 177, 187, 188; *Powers and Prospects*, 200; *Radical Priorities*, 130, 169, 200; *Reflections on Language*, 156–157, 175; *Rethinking Camelot: JFK, the Vietnam War, and U.S. Political Culture*, 200; *Rules and Representations*, 175; *The Sound Pattern of English*, 91, 93; *Syntactic Structures*, 80, 87, 89–91; *Terrorizing the Neighborhood: American Foreign policy in the Post-Cold War Era*, 200; *Towards a New Cold War: Essays on the Current Crisis and How We Got There*, 170, 184, 200; *Turning the Tide: U.S. Intervention in Central America and the Struggle for Peace*, 200; *World Orders, Old and New*, 200, 211; *Year 501: The Conquest Continues*, 200
Chomsky, William [Dr. William (Zev) Chomsky], 9–13, 20
Churchill, Winston, 64
Churchill-Roosevelt Conference, 38
Churchman, C. West, 47
Classical liberalism, 24, 107, 113
CNT-FAI. *See* Confederación Nacional de Trabajadores-Federacion Anarquista Iberica
Coates, Ken, 132, 148
Cockburn, Alex, 199
Cognitive science, 87
Coffin, William Sloane (Dr.), 128, 130, 137
Cohn, Werner, 78, 182–183
Cold War, 31, 124, 155
Columbia University Press, 138
Columbia University strike, 131
Commentary, 135
Commissar, 154, 178. *See also* Intellectual
Common Courage Press, 138
Common sense, 209
Communism, 14, 29, 31, 39, 65
Communist Party, 14, 24
Cone, Edward, 104

Confederación Nacional de Trabajadores-Federacion Anarquista Iberica, 26, 30
Cordemoy, Géraud de, 113
Coser, Lewis, 34
Coughlinites, 69
Council for Arab-Jewish Cooperation, 73–74
Council Communism, 36–37, 40, 42–43, 65, 114
Creativity, 15–16, 21–22, 95, 97, 106, 108–110, 113, 152, 206
Crews, Fred, 122
Cuban Crisis, 124

Deconstruction, 196
Della Vida, Giorgio Levi, 47, 50
Deleuze, Gilles, 193
Dellinger, David, 127–128, 131, 136, 172
DeMan, Paul, 193
Deming, Barbara, 128
Democracy, 26
Depression, Great, 14–15
Derrida, Jacques, 193–195
Dershowitz, Alan, 170–171, 180–182, 186
Descartes, René, 106–108, 111
Descartes s problem, 157
Dewey, John, 15, 22, 168
Dickens, Charles, 19
Discourse analysis, 49, 85
Dissent, 135–136, 154
Dominion Textiles, 71
Dostoevsky, Fyodor, 19
Draper, Hal, 135
Draper Laboratory, 140
Dropsie College, 10, 44
Duff, Peggy, 136–137

East Timor, 187–188, 213–214
Edinburgh Review, 217
Einstein, Albert, 32–33, 63
Elias, Peter, 81
Eliot, George, 19
Ellsberg, Daniel, 129

U.S. military, 86–87, 139–140

Van Riemsdijk, Henk, 175
Van Schoonefeld, Cornelis, 88
Vanzetti, Bartolomeo, 124
Verso Press, 138
Vidal-Naquet, Pierre, 180, 181, 182, 183, 186
Viertel, John, 101, 104
Vietnam, 103, 124, 135–136, 143–144, 147, 153–156, 162
Vietnam International, 136
Viennese positivism, 197
Village Voice, 136
Volosinov, V. N., 50

Wachtel, Eleanor, 15
Warner Communications, 160–161
Warner Modular, 160–162
Warsaw Ghetto uprising, 76
Washington Post, 162–163
Waskow, Arthur, 128
Weil, Hannah, 63
Weinreich, Uriel, 91
White, Morton, 50
Whitehead, Alfred North, 54
Whitfield, Stephen, 35
Williams, Raymond, 132
Wilson, Dagmar, 128
Wilson, Woodrow, 211
Wintonick, Peter, 70
Wittgenstein, Ludwig Josef, 54
Women's International League for Peace and Freedom, 214
Women's liberation, 132–133
Woodcock, George, 35
World War I, 40, 42
World War II, 22–23, 27, 29–30, 35, 39, 44, 65, 67, 164
World Zionist Congress, 64

Yergin, Daniel, 111
Yishuv, 64
Yngve, Victor, 86, 90

Z Magazine, 70, 138–139
Zeitlin, Solomon, 44
Zinn, Howard, 136–137, 172, 199
Zionism, 11–13, 24, 48, 51, 58, 60–62, 64, 66, 76–78, 136, 167, 170, 172, 179
Zola, Émile, 19